W9-CSA-237

Bridges to Better Writing

English 121

Nazario | Borchers | Lewis

CENGAGE
Learning·

Australia • Brazil • Japan • Korea • Mexico • Singapore • Spain • United Kingdom • United States

Bridges to Better Writing English 121

Bridges to Better Writing
Nazario | Borchers | Lewis

© 2013 Cengage Learning. All rights reserved.

Senior Project Development Manager:
 Linda deStefano

Market Development Manager:
 Heather Kramer

Senior Production/
Manufacturing Manager:
 Donna M. Brown

Production Editorial Manager:
 Kim Fry

Sr. Rights Acquisition Account Manager:
 Todd Osborne

ALL RIGHTS RESERVED. No part of this work covered by the copyright herein may be reproduced, transmitted, stored or used in any form or by any means graphic, electronic, or mechanical, including but not limited to photocopying, recording, scanning, digitizing, taping, Web distribution, information networks, or information storage and retrieval systems, except as permitted under Section 107 or 108 of the 1976 United States Copyright Act, without the prior written permission of the publisher.

For product information and technology assistance, contact us at
Cengage Learning Customer & Sales Support, 1-800-354-9706
For permission to use material from this text or product,
submit all requests online at **cengage.com/permissions**
Further permissions questions can be emailed to
permissionrequest@cengage.com

This book contains select works from existing Cengage Learning resources and was produced by Cengage Learning Custom Solutions for collegiate use. As such, those adopting and/or contributing to this work are responsible for editorial content accuracy, continuity and completeness.

Compilation © 2013 Cengage Learning

ISBN-13: 978-1-285-89784-4

ISBN-10: 1-285-89784-6

Cengage Learning
5191 Natorp Boulevard
Mason, Ohio 45040
USA

Cengage Learning is a leading provider of customized learning solutions with office locations around the globe, including Singapore, the United Kingdom, Australia, Mexico, Brazil, and Japan. Locate your local office at:
international.cengage.com/region.
Cengage Learning products are represented in Canada by Nelson Education, Ltd.
For your lifelong learning solutions, visit **www.cengage.com /custom.**
Visit our corporate website at **www.cengage.com.**

Printed in the United States of America

Brief Contents

Writing Your Paper

© Gyro Photography/amanaimages/Corbis

Let's Talk About Writing

"Writing is an exploration. You start from nothing and learn as you go."

— E.L. Doctorow

YOUR GOALS

Understanding That Writing Is Thinking

1. Recognize the connection between writing and critical thinking.

2. Examine realities about writing.

3. Reconsider your own attitudes about writing.

4. Review and respond to writing myths.

Connecting Reading to Writing

1. Recognize the relationship between reading and writing.

2. Become an active reader by applying critical reading strategies.

Writing Your Papers

1. Preview prewriting techniques.

2. Discover the value of following a writing process.

3. Proofread for common grammar errors.

Access grammar exercises for this section in your English CourseMate, available through CengageBrain.com.

D o you feel dread and anxiety when you are asked to write a report, produce a research paper, or answer essay questions on a U.S. history test? Do you avoid the task as long as possible? And then, when you do sit down to write, do you find yourself blanking out or rambling on just to get something on the empty page?

How can you approach writing assignments in a more confident and systematic way? How can you develop a method for writing that works for a variety of situations, assignments, and readers?

We hope that this text, your writing class, and your writing instructor provide you with an approach and system that works for you and that applies to all three major writing occasions: college, professional, and personal.

In college, you will write some or all of the following: science and business reports, academic research papers, answers to essay questions on exams, summaries and critiques of professional articles, and reaction papers to specific theories and proposals.

In your professional career, you may have to produce monthly reports of your department's activities or progress on a long-term project, proposals for new marketing plans or patient treatment, summaries of customer satisfaction, or analyses of a patient's progress.

In your personal life, you may write to record a significant event or trip, explore your family history, sympathize with a family member over a traumatic event, or e-mail daily events to family members living far away.

If you think of writing as limited to the English classroom, you miss the opportunity to take the skills from your English class and apply them to your other classes, your profession, and your everyday life.

Let's Warm Up!

Each of us brings a special skill to our writing, whether it's our creativity, our ability to use words, our ideas, our style, our ability to spot errors, or our motivation. Reflect on yourself as a writer. What major strength do you bring to the writing process? Write a short paragraph explaining your strength.

Tetra Images/Jupiter Images RF

Understanding That Writing Is Thinking

Writing is a form of thinking. It certainly isn't the only form of thinking. Our brains process ideas in different ways: mathematically, musically, and visually. But our use of language allows us to share ideas, pass on knowledge, engage in debate, and advance our understanding of the world. In college, writing is the vehicle through which we learn new ideas and share them with one another.

During your college education, you will hear much about *critical thinking*. You may hear many definitions of this term, but basically, critical thinking means expressing your ideas in a logical way so that they *make sense*. Learning to write well is the best way to improve your ability to think critically. What are the components of critical thinking? According to the National Council for Excellence in Critical Thinking, the following components are key to the process:

- **Clarity.** When you express ideas clearly, your audience understands what you are trying to say without difficulty.
- **Accuracy.** Accurate thinking is true to reality as you understand it.
- **Precision.** Precise thinking isn't vague; it contains sufficient detail to be informative.
- **Consistency.** Consistent thinking "holds together"; it doesn't contradict itself.
- **Relevance.** Relevant writing sticks to the point; it doesn't digress into unrelated subject matter.
- **Sound evidence.** When you make a statement that needs to be supported, you provide solid evidence that proves your point.
- **Good reasons.** When you argue for or against an idea, you back up your argument with valid reasoning.
- **Depth.** Critical thinking is not superficial; it goes beyond the obvious.
- **Breadth.** Critical thinking incorporates a broad view of the subject matter, showing how it relates to other ideas.
- **Fairness.** Good writing is fair, both to the subject matter and to other people who may hold different viewpoints.

These components of critical thinking are also components of effective writing. As you work through this course, keep in mind the connection between the quality of your writing and the quality of your thinking. Having good writing skills can be your ticket to better grades in most of your courses in college.

Using and Understanding This Book

This book guides you through your writing experience, thus contributing to your growth as a professional. Here are some ways to get the most out of this text and this class:

1. **Read and mark your text.** Read actively by underlining useful ideas, writing brief summaries and reactions in the margins, and taking notes on main ideas. Remember that effective writing is closely linked to frequent and close reading.
2. **Do every assignment conscientiously.** Your instructor is helping you write a successful final paper by having you complete smaller steps to achieve the final product.
3. **Plan to keep your text for future reference.** You can refresh yourself on the principles of successful writing and use the writing skills in future assignments for school and work.
4. **Use the skills you learn in this course in your other courses.** Whenever you are assigned writing in another class or on the job, try to incorporate the techniques offered in this class.

Take five minutes and flip through this book. Each writing chapter, Chapters 2–12, starts with an activity called Previewing Your Task where you will read academic, professional, and everyday examples of the type of writing you will be drafting in that chapter. The rest of each writing chapter is divided into three main sections:

- **Understanding.** This section explains the writing task completely. In it, you will examine examples of key concepts and do activities to practice these concepts.
- **Connecting Reading to Writing.** This section provides a professional essay to help develop your critical reading skills and apply the writing concepts discussed in the chapter.
- **Writing.** This section guides you through the writing process: prewriting, drafting, revising, proofreading, and reflecting. In this section, you will follow a student's writing task from creation to the final draft as you go through the process yourself. This section also provides sufficient explanation and activities to help you understand specific tasks in the writing process.

Being Aware of Writing Realities

Another key to succeeding in your English course is to understand the realities of good writing. Effective writing requires hard work, patience, courage, thought, and honesty.

- **Hard work.** Few people can produce a polished report, essay, or business plan by just writing off the top of their heads. Instead, writers often must write several drafts, have others read and comment on them, and then carefully proofread and edit before submitting the final copy.
- **Patience.** Writers often run into dead ends, finding that a topic isn't working and needing to try a different topic, organization, or focus. Writers have to be patient and willing to experiment with ideas and ways to express them.

- **Courage.** It takes courage to write because fears of failure, errors, or lack of clarity are often lurking in our minds as we compose. We, the writers, fear that the reader may criticize our writing, which we view almost as an extension of ourselves.
- **Thought.** Writing can be perfect in grammar, punctuation, organization, and unity but still not succeed because it doesn't say anything of worth. Successful writing and critical thinking are inseparable, requiring us to be able to communicate our ideas.
- **Honesty.** As writers, we must present ideas honestly to the reader. If an idea comes from an article in a published source or from an interview, then we are obligated to give credit to the source. If we are communicating a personal observation or experience, then the information should be as accurate as possible unless the writing is fiction.

Writing is a social, communal activity, involving writers and readers joining together to exchange information, support each other, and work toward a transfer of ideas, experiences, and opinions.

Attitudes and Myths about Writing

PRACTICE 1-1

For the following statements, put a check mark by the ones you agree with and an X by those you do not.

_____ 1. Good writers have an inborn talent for writing, whereas weak writers are doomed to fail.

_____ 2. Good writers compose effortlessly because they need only to spill what is inside their minds onto the paper.

_____ 3. After someone has finished the English requirements for a college degree, writing is no longer important or useful.

_____ 4. Because professionals often have administrative assistants to edit their reports, the professionals can depend on their assistants to correct errors in grammar, punctuation, and wording.

_____ 5. Because essay writing is rarely required in most professions, writing essays applies only to English classes.

_____ 6. Writing is like riding a bike: After you learn how, it is an automatic skill.

_____ 7. Copying the writing of others without giving the original authors credit is acceptable because so much written material exists on the Internet that it is difficult to trace writing back to its originator.

_____ 8. Learning grammar and punctuation is unnecessary because most word processors provide a grammar-check and spell-check tool.

——— 9. Writing a research paper is just looking up information and pasting it into a larger document, somewhat like stitching together the pieces of a quilt.

——— 10. Writing is the mechanical process of typing words into a document, whereas reading and math require deep thinking and problem solving.

Reconsidering Your Attitude about Writing

Now that you've completed the preceding activity, you may realize that most of the statements in Practice 1-1 are false and that by adopting them you are undermining your ability to succeed as a writer. You can adjust your attitudes toward writing just as you would tune up a car engine or adjust the thermostat in your home.

- **Motivation.** There is nothing worse than studying a subject or taking a class and thinking that the material and skills won't be useful after the course is over. Nothing is further from the truth when it comes to writing. Most employers, when asked what skills are essential for their employees, say effective written and oral communication is vital. On-the-job training can familiarize employees with procedures and policies, but employers do not have the time to teach employees how to write.

- **Self-identity.** See yourself as a writer. Just calling yourself a writer can help give you the confidence to get the writing done.

- **Time and place.** Because writing takes time, work, and concentration, you need to set aside certain writing hours and specific places in which to write.

- **Reader or audience.** If you visualize your English instructor hovering over your paper with red pen in hand to highlight all your errors, then you may lose your desire to communicate. However, if you can imagine an "ignorant" and eager reader, enthusiastically soaking up your ideas, then you will be more committed to writing. By adopting a tone of voice in your writing that shows an understanding of and respect for your reader, you should produce an effective piece of writing.

- **Competition.** You might feel that you will never measure up to others in your English class. How do you deal with your sense of inadequacy when you read their successful essays and compare them to yours? In fact, you can benefit from their writing by analyzing their organization and details so that you can improve your own papers.

PRACTICE 1-2

In the spaces that follow, list your best times for writing and places that you feel give you the most peace and quiet (and resources) for the writing process.

Best times: _____

Possible places (for example, library, home, office, or coffee shop): _____

_____

Finally, view writing as thinking, as the process of examining ideas in depth and "toning" your mind as you tone your body in an exercise class. You have really learned and understood a concept, theory, philosophy, or process when you have written about it in such a clear and convincing way that your reader, who may not be familiar with the information, has learned it from you.

Connecting Reading To Writing

Stephen King states: "The real importance of reading is that it creates an ease and intimacy with the process of writing." However, few students realize the relationship between developing their reading skills and becoming better writers. *Bridges to Better Writing* helps you make this connection.

When many of us take up our biology or philosophy textbooks to complete a reading assignment, we plunge right in, reading the first sentence and then the next. Sometimes, because this approach forces us to create the context of the reading as we go along, we find our minds wandering to personal thoughts and daydreams. This approach is not the most effective use of your time; instead, try several of the strategies listed here to help you become a more efficient and more active reader:

- **Preview your reading.** Instead of starting with the first line, study the title, headings, and subheadings of the reading. Flip to the end to look for a summary, glossary of terms, and/or study questions that can help you focus on the most important information.
- **Ask questions.** Start reading with some questions in mind that you assume the reading answers; doing so keeps your mind focused on the material. Jot down your questions beforehand, and, as you read, record your answers to those questions.
- **Skim before reading in more depth.** Read the topic sentences of each paragraph to become familiar with the structure of the reading.
- **Mark your text (annotate).** Read actively by highlighting interesting and important information, and new vocabulary. Write in the margins to summarize key information and to note areas that are unclear or that you

want further information about. The more physically active you are when you read, the more you retain.

- **Take notes.** Have paper, note cards, or a computer handy so that you can write down significant information. Later you can use these notes to study from so that you rarely have to refer back to the text.
- **Review.** Carefully go over your questions, notes, and marginal notations to assess how much you have learned and what information you may need to reread. Quiz yourself to put the information in your long-term memory.

The reading selections and exercises provided in *Bridges to Better Writing* give you an opportunity to practice these critical reading strategies. They also represent professional models of the types of essays that you have been writing for this course. Each selection provides the following features to help you develop your reading-writing skills:

- A brief biography of the writer
- A warm-up question to ponder
- Vocabulary items that might be new to you
- Exercises in these three areas to help you connect your reading to the writing goals of the chapters:
  - Understanding the Reading
  - Understanding the Structure, Style, and Tone
  - Making a Personal Connection

Don't limit your definition of effective writing to grammar, mechanics, and paragraph development. Writing also involves how we think about and react to what we read.

Writing Your Papers

The *writing process* consists of the steps that effective writers follow, from the initial idea to the final paper that the intended audience reads. The chapters of *Bridges to Better Writing* guide you from one stage to another of the writing process—from prewriting to the final draft. This is not to say that the writing process is linear, where one stage must be completed before going on to the next one. Far from it—the writing process is recursive, meaning you repeat specific parts until you're satisfied with the results, as in Figure 1.1.

The Writing Process

The writing process used in *Bridges to Better Writing* consists of five stages: prewriting, drafting, revising, proofreading, and reflecting.

FIGURE 1.1 *Writing Process*

Prewriting

The prewriting stage of the writing process consists of six steps, as outlined in Figure 1.2.

In the first step, discovering and limiting your topic, you use various prewriting techniques to find topics and focuses for writing. The goal is to practice different strategies so that you don't limit yourself to those you are accustomed to. Prewriting techniques help you discover ideas during any stage of the writing process. Unfortunately, some students bypass prewriting or limit themselves to just one technique. To help you consider the possibilities of the various prewriting techniques, most writing chapters of *Bridges to Better Writing* ask you to experiment with different types of prewriting techniques. During this exploratory stage, remain open to all ideas that surface through prewriting.

Be sure to set aside time for prewriting. There are no strict rules for prewriting, and there is no such thing as one technique for a specific essay. Combine and use several techniques for any writing assignment and at any point during the writing process. If necessary, alter the techniques to suit your needs.

Also in the prewriting stage, *Bridges to Better Writing* helps you identify your audience, establish your purpose, set the tone of your essay, formulate your thesis, and outline your ideas. If this isn't enough to break your writer's block, each chapter offers topic ideas to help you start your prewriting activities.

Outlining your ideas

Discovering and limiting your topic

Formulating your thesis

PREWRITING

Identifying your audience

Setting your tone

Establishing your purpose

FIGURE 1.2 *Prewriting Stage*

Prewriting Technique	Technique Description	Technique Explanation
1. Branching	Branching, also referred as a tree diagram or map, is an effective way to sort items or see clearly the various components of a topic (see Figure 1.3). Although you can use branching in any writing assignment, you will find this technique especially helpful in division and classification. 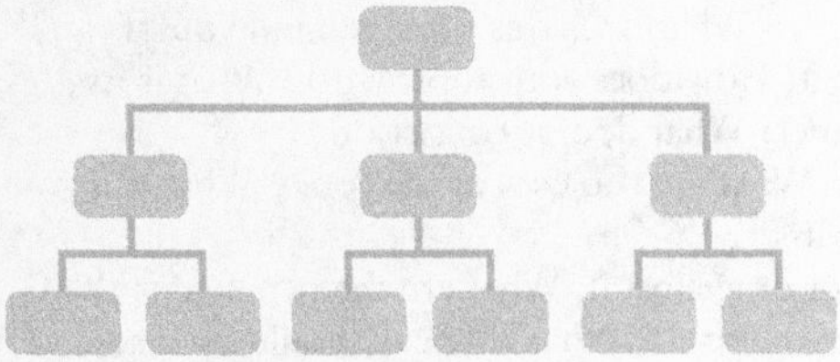	Chapter 9, page 290, explains and illustrates this technique.

FIGURE 1.3 *Branching Example*

Start this technique by writing your topic in the top box. For each branch, list the main components of your topic. Continue to branch, listing the qualities and other relevant information for each component that you have identified.

Prewriting Technique	Technique Description	Technique Explanation
2. Clustering	Clustering, also known as mapping or webbing, allows you to see and explore the relationships among ideas visually (see Figure 1.4). 1. Start with a circle in the center of your paper. 2. As you think of ideas related to the topic in the center circle, draw smaller circles, and link these ideas with lines. 3. As you think of new ideas related to the smaller circles, draw additional circles and lines to show their relationships. 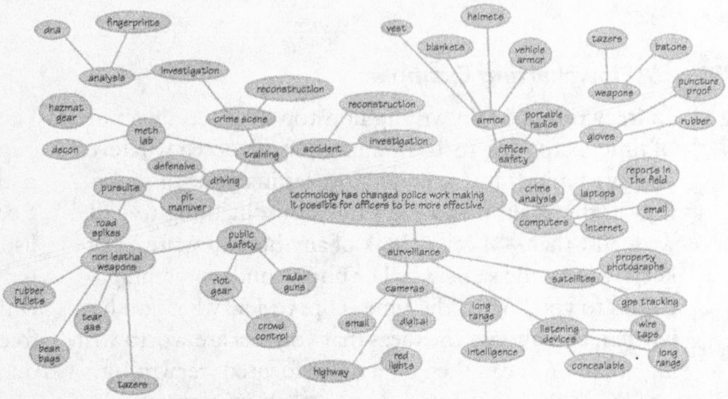	See Chapter 5, page 127, for a full explanation and illustration of clustering.

FIGURE 1.4 *Clustering Example*

3. Cubing

Cubing helps you look at your topic from the six different angles, thus permitting you to explore various approaches to your topic. Draw a six-sided cube with each side representing a way to examine your topic (see Figure 1.5). In cubing, you respond to the following six prompts, freewriting your answers:

1. Describe it: What does your topic look like?
2. Compare and contrast it: What is your topic similar to or different from?
3. Associate it: What does this topic remind you of?
4. Analyze it: How does your topic work? What is its significance? What does it consist of?
5. Apply it: What are the uses of the topic? What can you do with it?
6. Argue for or against it: What are the benefits or challenges of the topic? What changes should be made?

See Chapter 10, page 329, and examine how cubing was used by a student-writer to gather information for a definition essay.

FIGURE 1.5
Cubing Example

4. Flowcharting

Popular in analyzing a process, flowcharting is also a great way to show cause/effect relationships. You visually explore the causes that led to a specific event or result or the effects that resulted from a specific event (see Figure 1.6).

See Chapter 7, page 208, for an example of using flowcharting to gather ideas for cause/effect essays.

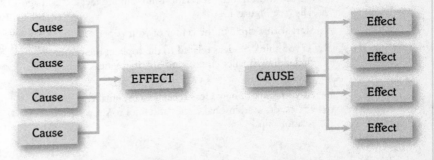

FIGURE 1.6 *Flowcharting Examples*

5. Freewriting

In freewriting, begin writing nonstop for a certain amount of time, perhaps 5 to 10 minutes, jotting down whatever comes to mind. Just keep writing, letting your thoughts flow as they will. If you can't think of something to write, write just that—"I can't think of anything to write"—or keep writing the same word or phrase until something comes to you. When the time is up, review what you have written, and choose the ideas that you feel are worth writing about. You can then do a more focused freewriting session on these ideas to generate relevant information on these possible topics.

Chapter 2, page 30, explains and illustrates freewriting and listing. Chapter 4, page 97, combines listing, freewriting, and questioning.

6. **Listing**	Listing, also known as brainstorming, is an effective way to get ideas down on paper quickly. Start with an idea—a word or a phrase—and jot down every idea you can think of related to that word or phrase. The goal is to free associate, so keep your pen, pencil, or word processor moving—writing down one thought after another, whether a word or a phrase. Do this for at least 10 minutes. After your time is up, review all your ideas. See what ideas are related, what ideas stand out in your list, and what ideas you want to explore further. You will end up listing not only good topics to consider for your essays but also details that you can use to support your topics.	Chapter 2, page 30; Chapter 4, page 98; and Chapter 5, page 127 demonstrate how listing, in conjunction with other prewriting techniques, helps you focus and gather information for your topics.
7. **Looping**	Looping is excellent for narrowing your topic. After 5 to 10 minutes of freewriting, pause to choose the best idea, and start your next freewriting loop on that idea for another 5- to 10-minute freewriting session. You take the best idea of that loop and again freewrite on that new idea, repeating the process and making each loop more specific than the previous one.	Chapter 6, page 164, explains and illustrates how a student used looping during the prewriting stage of her essay.
8. **Questioning**	The questioning technique asks you to take a journalist's approach in gathering information. Ask yourself the six important questions that most journalists rely on to compile information: Who? What? When? Where? Why? How? This technique is a quick way to gather a lot of information on a specific topic. However, focusing each of these questions so that it applies to your topic may take a little practice.	Chapter 3, page 62, and Chapter 4, page 98, illustrate how to use this technique.
9. **Venn diagram**	The Venn diagram analyzes similarities and differences on a specific topic. Start this technique by drawing two overlapping circles (see Figure 1.7). In the outer areas, list the differences between your topics, each topic in its own circle. In the area that overlaps, list the similarities that your topics share.	See Chapter 8, page 247, for a full explanation and illustration of a Venn diagram.

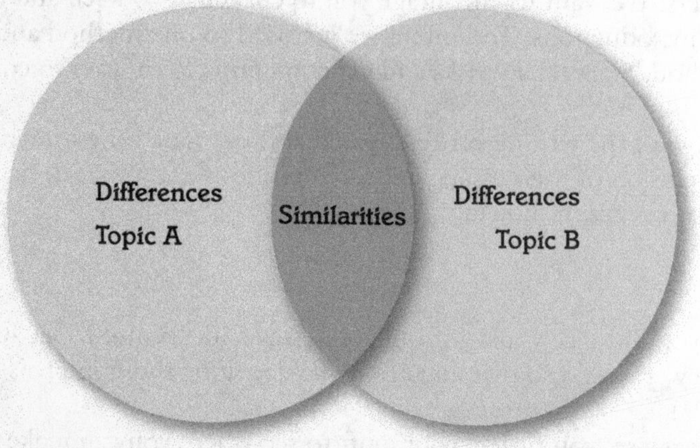

Differences
Topic A

Similarities

Differences
Topic B

FIGURE 1.7 *Venn Diagram Example*

As you leave the prewriting stage, always keep in mind that you can return to any step of this stage from any later stage of the writing process. In each chapter, we introduce a student's essay to serve as your model for the writing process. These student models are far from perfect, so if you're asked to critique any section, it's okay to be brutal. No writing is ever complete.

Drafting

In the drafting stage, you shape your essay. See Figure 1.8 for all the steps involved in drafting.

As we guide you through the introduction, body, and conclusion of the essay, we continue to point out that you don't need to follow this order. It probably makes more sense to write the body of the essay and then determine the most appropriate and effective introduction. However, for the purpose of discussion, we follow a linear approach. Each chapter explains and illustrates specific strategies you can use and combine to write your introduction. Rather than present in one chapter more than a dozen ways to write your introduction, we spread the various techniques throughout the chapters. We want to encourage you to challenge yourself and try new ways to write your introductions. Too often, we get used to one method and depend on only that method. Start taking risks and experimenting with ways to connect with your reader.

FIGURE 1.8 *Drafting Stage*

In this stage of the writing process, you'll also examine how students draft the body and conclusion of their essays and use transitions and other devices to keep their ideas and paragraphs flowing smoothly.

Revising

In this stage, you distance yourself from your essay and attempt to see it as an outsider or a reviewer would so that you can make decisions about improving your draft (see Figure 1.9).

When you revise, you review your draft to see where you can make your writing clearer, more exciting, more meaningful, more informative, or more convincing.

Also, you try to examine your paper from different perspectives to determine whether the organization is effective, the tone appropriate, and the information coherent. Each writing chapter includes a style tip to help you write more clearly and accurately, as well as a problem–solution section addressing basic student concerns.

This stage of the writing process concludes with a peer review activity, in which you share your revised draft with one or more classmates for their comments and suggestions. Your job as the writer is to consider the

Asking a peer for input

Checking your support

Revising

Troubleshooting problem areas

Considering a style update

FIGURE 1.9 *Revising Stage*

feedback and incorporate suggestions into your paper that you feel strengthen it. You may even choose to ignore some suggestions; the decision is yours.

Proofreading

In the proofreading stage, you examine your essay for punctuation, spelling, sentence structure, and word usage. Each chapter presents a common grammar error as a starting point for proofreading. To determine the grammatical rule to include in the chapter, we considered two factors: First, we chose grammatical concepts that are the most problematic to most students, and second, we included those concepts that seem to be the most appropriate to the specific writing tasks. Hold yourself accountable for previous errors by eliminating them in your next writing task. For your convenience, the proofreading sections for Chapters 3 through 12 end with an editing checklist that includes the common errors presented in previous chapters. Each error is cross-referenced to its handbook section, where the rule addressing that specific common error is fully explained and illustrated.

Reflecting

The final stage of the writing process is reflecting. To bring closure to the process, you start by reflecting on your writing experiences in that chapter. You should think of the challenges you encountered as you created your draft and consider how you might address these challenges in your next writing task. You should also comment on your success. What did you do that you initially thought you would be unable to do?

We also want you to consider the broader application of what you learned in the chapter. What connection does this material have to writing in college, for your profession, and in everyday life? Basically, we want you to see yourself as a writer, developing your skills as you grow to become an effective communicator—a crucial characteristic of a first-rate professional.

Collaborative Critical Thinking

In groups of three or four, discuss practical suggestions to resolve the following problems. Share your suggestions with other groups.

Problem

1. I can't meet the deadline for this assignment.
   _____
   _____

2. I have no clue as to what I'm going to write about.
   _____
   _____

3. I'll work on my essay the night before. I always work best under pressure.
   _____
   _____

4. I can never find my errors until somebody points them out. By then, who cares?
   _____
   _____

5. It's not fair that I received such a low grade. I worked on this essay for more than 12 hours.
   _____
   _____

6. I don't think my instructor likes me. My friend, who's an English major, told me my paper is great. But look at this grade!
   _____
   _____

7. I have questions, but I don't want my professor or my classmates to think I'm dumb.
   _____
   _____

8. Whenever I'm absent, I'm totally lost in class.
   _____
   _____

9. When I read the writing of other students, they seem to be getting it, and I feel left behind. Am I in the wrong course?
   _____
   _____

10. I don't like the idea of sharing my writing. Writing is very personal; I hate feeling exposed.
    _____
    _____

Developing Your Essay through Definition

"A definition is . . . enclosing a wilderness of an idea within a wall of words."

— Samuel Butler

YOUR GOALS

Understanding Definition

1. Distinguish between denotative and connotative meanings.

2. Generate two kinds of definition: formal and extended.

3. Use negation to supplement a definition.

4. Support and clarify definitions using a variety of methods.

Connecting Reading to Writing

1. Demonstrate an understanding of effective reading strategies.

2. Increase your vocabulary.

3. Analyze readings for comprehension, structure, tone, and style.

4. Show a personal connection to topics introduced by professional writers.

Writing Your Definition Essay

1. Use cubing to generate ideas.

2. Define concepts for specific audiences and purposes.

3. Integrate various writing techniques into the body of your essay.

4. Proofread for common grammar errors.

Access grammar exercises for this section in your English CourseMate, available through CengageBrain.com.

On a take-home essay exam, your biology instructor asks you to define *respiration*. Obviously, the goal is to test your knowledge of biological concepts, but you wonder what information to include beyond the one-sentence scientific definition from your textbook. Should you give examples of how different organisms breathe? Describe the process of respiration? Contrast respiration with other processes? You decide to use a combination of these techniques.

At work, you are required to attend workshops on sexual harassment every two years. As a supervisor, you need to know what sexual harassment is and how to prevent it. Recently, a male employee complained to you that a female employee had a calendar of pictures of men in skimpy bathing suits on the wall of her open cubicle. Having attended one of the sexual harassment workshops, you knew that the calendar must be removed to prevent a hostile atmosphere in the workplace. Now, as a supervisor, you need to educate your employees and write a policy defining sexual harassment so that all employees share a common definition.

While you are discussing a new love interest with a close friend, you comment that you think you might be in love for the first time in your life. Your friend counters with the question, "What do you mean by 'in love'?" You have to think carefully to respond honestly and accurately. How do you distinguish this emotion from others?

As professionals, students, and citizens, the meanings we attach to words form an important basis of our interactions with others. Therefore, we must learn to define the terms we use so that our meaning is fully understood.

Let's Warm Up!

Think of situations in which you had to work with other people as a team—on a work project, on a sports team, for a fundraiser, for a school project. How would you define *teamwork*? What qualities and beliefs must you have to work well with other people? What were some behaviors and attitudes that interfered with the progress of the team?

Comstock Images / Jupiter Images

Previewing Your Task

In college, definition is a major learning tool. In the workplace and everyday life, we are often asked to define or explain concepts to our coworkers, customers, friends, and family members. The following writing samples represent a range of writing that defines concepts to clarify and make a point.

Writing for College

In your college classes, you are required to develop definitions—on tests, in writing assignments, for oral presentations, and for in-class discussions—of specialized terms that are at the heart of all academic subjects. Read the following student essay by Lauren, written for a sociology class.

My Generation: "The Millennials"

Albert Einstein once said, "The most important human endeavor is striving for morality in our actions. Our inner balance and even our very existence depend on it. Only morality in action can give beauty and dignity to ourselves." This quotation accurately sums up the ethics of my generation. Young people today are striving to become more moral and to better themselves in unique ways. Many believe this is a peculiar characteristic of my generation—the "Millennial Generation." Born between 1980 and 2000, the Millennials have moved beyond the concerns of Generation X to establish our own claims to fame; we are seen as the most social, tech-savvy, and goal-oriented generation, and we hope to use these characteristics to improve the world we live in.

We Millennials are, first and foremost, social and open minded. Growing up in the diverse, rapidly evolving 1990s and 2000s has given us a chance to explore a variety of lifestyle choices. I once had a teacher who said, "You are the generation who most resembles that of the '60s." She may have held this opinion because we are more capable of understanding differences and change than our immediate predecessors could. For example, Millennials are more open to the practice of alternative lifestyles and religions than any previous generation. Just drop by the nearest Millennial hangout—the coffee shop on the corner—and you'll see the wildest mix of lifestyle choices, with everyone getting along beautifully.

Ironically—because many older people think technology interferes with social life—we Millennials are highly computer literate and savvy about technology. Today's modern technology ranges from jump drives that hold huge quantities of information to MP3 players that contain over 1,000 songs; these devices are specifically targeted to the tech-savvy Millennials. Most Millennials own their own computer and understand the technical aspects of how it works. By the click of a mouse, we are able to browse the Internet to gather information without leaving the house to search the library shelves. With the world at our fingertips, we are helping bring the world closer through our use of technology.

Finally, we Millennials are goal oriented, smart, and able to use a range of resources in our environment to get important jobs done. Unlike the baby boomers who feel that it is necessary to put in long hours at the office to get the job done right, Millennials prefer to work in informal groups to limit the time on the job while accomplishing the same tasks as those who work long hours at the office.

For example, in my work as an independent video producer, I was recently hired to create a promotional video for a statewide nonprofit agency, the Women's Bean Project. I chose to do most of the work on a laptop at my local coffee shop, where I could collaborate with friends, get input from passersby, and enjoy a conversation now and then.

In the movie *Bye, Bye Birdie,* an infuriated Mr. McAfee exclaims: "Kids! I don't know what's wrong with these kids today." Interestingly, this line applied to the kids of the 1960s, but I've heard it applied to us as well. The truth is that nothing is wrong that we can't help fix. My generation is growing into its own. We are no longer too young to understand world events; we are now the future leaders of America, and we have the social sensitivity, technology skills, and independence to move world events in more positive directions. You boomers can retire and relax. We'll take it from here.

PRACTICE 10-1

1. What is Lauren's purpose in defining Millennials? _____
   _____
   _____

2. List her three main points in your own words. _____
   _____
   _____

Writing in Your Profession

In your profession, you will often be called upon to clarify a term, reference, or idea by providing an in-depth definition. For instance, to implement a new concept or correct a problem in an organization, employees first need a clear definition of it. The following is a definition of sexual harassment from the U.S. Equal Employment Opportunity Commission (EEOC).

Sexual Harassment

Sexual harassment is a form of sex discrimination that violates Title VII of the Civil Rights Act of 1964. Title VII applies to employers with 15 or more employees, including state and local governments. It also applies to employment agencies and to labor organizations, as well as to the federal government.

Unwelcome sexual advances, requests for sexual favors, and other verbal or physical conduct of a sexual nature constitute sexual harassment when this conduct explicitly or implicitly affects an individual's employment, unreasonably interferes with an individual's work performance, or creates an intimidating, hostile, or offensive work environment.

Sexual harassment can occur in a variety of circumstances, including but not limited to the following:

- The victim, as well as the harasser, may be a woman or a man. The victim does not have to be of the opposite sex.
- The harasser can be the victim's supervisor, an agent of the employer, a supervisor in another area, a coworker, or a nonemployee.
- The victim does not have to be the person harassed but could be anyone affected by the offensive conduct.
- Unlawful sexual harassment may occur without economic injury to or discharge of the victim.
- The harasser's conduct must be unwelcome.

It is helpful for the victim to inform the harasser directly that the conduct is unwelcome and must stop. The victim should use any employer complaint mechanism or grievance system available.

When investigating allegations of sexual harassment, EEOC looks at the whole record: the circumstances, such as the nature of the sexual advances, and the context in which the alleged incidents occurred. A determination on the allegations is made from the facts on a case-by-case basis.

Prevention is the best tool to eliminate sexual harassment in the workplace. Employers are encouraged to take steps necessary to prevent sexual harassment from occurring. They should clearly communicate to employees that sexual harassment will not be tolerated. They can do so by providing sexual harassment training to their employees and by establishing an effective complaint or grievance process and taking immediate and appropriate action when an employee complains.

It is also unlawful to retaliate against an individual for opposing employment practices that discriminate based on sex or for filing a discrimination charge, testifying, or participating in any way in an investigation, proceeding, or litigation under Title VII.

PRACTICE 10-2

1. Who is the audience for this definition? _____

2. What else could be added to further clarify the definition? _____

_____

_____

Writing in Everyday Life

The following is an e-mail sent by a son who is caring for his elderly parents while his siblings live out of state. By defining his role as a caregiver, he urges his siblings to help out.

Greetings, Darla and Ron!

I would like to update you on Mom and Dad's situation and get some advice and assistance because I am becoming stressed and overwhelmed by my role as our parents' main caregiver.

First, I would like to describe a typical day for me. I'm up at about 5:30 a.m. so that I can check on Mom and Dad before going to work. I'm at their house by 6 a.m. I bring in their newspaper, brew the coffee, and set out their breakfast. When I'm sure that they are up and dressed, I rush off to work. After work I drop by their house to bring in their mail and check that Meals on Wheels has delivered their dinner. Once I'm assured that their evening routine has started, I head home, calling them once in the evening for a final check before they go to bed.

Not only must I be there for them physically, but I am also in charge of managing their finances and their medical needs. Once a month I pay their bills and balance their checkbook. I also make medical appointments for them that fit into my schedule and add these to my calendar.

I have to admit that because of these responsibilities, I'm beginning to lose sleep and suffer frequent headaches. I no longer have time to enjoy outings on the weekends with my friends to rock climb or mountain bike. Without exercise, I am becoming more stressed. Please know that I love helping our parents and repaying them for all of the years that they raised and loved us. However, I can no longer do it alone; I need help. I propose that since you both live so far away, we hire a part-time caregiver who could stay with Mom and Dad during the week to relieve me of the weekday duties. I would then take over on weekends. The three of us could share the cost so that it wouldn't be financially too onerous on any one of us. I hope to hear from you soon.

Love,
Leo

PRACTICE 10-3

1. List the methods of development that Leo uses to develop his definition of his role as a caregiver. _____

2. What is Leo's purpose in writing to his siblings? _____
_____

Understanding Definition

To define a term is to express its meaning. Sometimes, we can express the meaning of a term in a single phrase or sentence; at other times, we need to provide more information to flesh out a definition.

Denotative and Connotative Meanings of Words

The *denotative* meaning of a word is the literal, or primary, meaning: It is the type of definition we are most likely to find listed first in the dictionary. The *connotative* meanings of a word are the secondary, associated meanings that a word evokes. For example, the denotative meaning of *mother* is a female who has given birth to a child. But *mother* also connotes someone who is warm, caring, and generous. The denotative meaning of *girl* is a female child. Connotatively, *girl* could be used to describe someone who is immature. The connotations of words can have powerful uses; when used to refer to a middle-aged administrative assistant in the workplace, *girl* can be a form of disrespect and humiliation, indicating a subservient status. The use of *girl* to address a female employee may be considered sexual harassment. Notice the power of a word based on its context.

PRACTICE 10-4

For each of the following words or phrases, write down a dictionary definition (denotation) and then associated meanings (connotations).

Example: Telemarketer

Denotation: A salesperson who markets goods and/or services directly to customers, usually by phone.

Connotations: An annoying and invasive salesperson who interrupts family life and pesters people repeatedly by phone to buy unnecessary and high-priced goods and services

1. Patriotic

   Denotation: _____

   Connotations: _____

2. Liberal

   Denotation: _____

   Connotations: _____

3. Blogger

   Denotation: _____

   Connotations: _____

4. Creative

   Denotation: _____

   Connotations: _____

5. Homeland

   Denotation: _____

   Connotations: _____

The Formal Definition

When you need to define a term succinctly, you will likely give a *formal definition*. A formal definition has three parts: the *term* to be defined, a *general category* into which the term fits, and the *specific characteristics* that distinguish the term from other terms within the category.

For example, the term *appetite* might fit into the general category "strong urges or desires." However, other words fit into this category, too, such as *greed, passion,* or *anger.* To adequately define *appetite,* we need to list the specific characteristics that set *appetite* apart from the other terms. The way we might distinguish *appetite* from *greed* (the desire for greater wealth) is to include its objects—food, drink, activity, love, friendship. A formal definition can be expressed in a single sentence that contains all three elements.

Once your definition has all three elements, you must check that it makes logical sense. Just listing a few distinguishing characteristics is not enough.

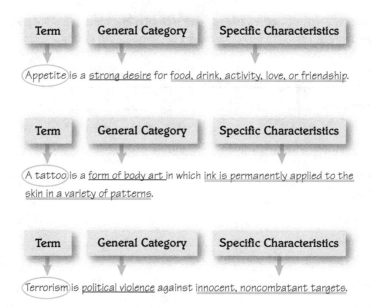

| Term | General Category | Specific Characteristics |

Appetite is a strong desire for food, drink, activity, love, or friendship.

| Term | General Category | Specific Characteristics |

A tattoo is a form of body art in which ink is permanently applied to the skin in a variety of patterns.

| Term | General Category | Specific Characteristics |

Terrorism is political violence against innocent, noncombatant targets.

Test your definition by applying it to what you know about the world.

A woman is a human who is able to reproduce.

At first, this definition may seem adequate, but you can test it by asking, "Does it distinguish *woman* from the other terms in the category *human?*" The answer is clearly no: Men are able to reproduce, too. Actually, because neither can reproduce alone, the definition has two problems. First, it is not specific enough to women, and second, it is incomplete. If not carefully thought out, definitions can be vague and inaccurate.

Collaborative Critical Thinking

In your group, read each definition and circle the term, underline the general category, and double underline the specific characteristic or characteristics. Explain what makes the definition inadequate. List other words or phrases that fit the same definition, and then rewrite the definition to improve its accuracy.

1.   A community college is an institution devoted to instructing students in the local community.
2.   A forest fire is nature's way of making room for new plant growth.
3.   A date is a formal meeting between a man and a woman for the purpose of getting to know each other better.
4.   Travel is a movement from place to place for the purpose of enjoying new locations.
5.   Anorexia nervosa is the medical condition of not eating enough.

Defining through Negation

Negation is a good way to get rid of any false notions your reader may have about your topic. In negation, you indicate what the term is *not* to separate it from other terms or concepts that might fit the definition. Negation is also a good way to introduce your thesis: First tell the reader what your topic is not, and then tell what it is. Notice how using negation in the following sentences helps focus the extended definition by simply mentioning what something or someone is not.

- Intelligence is not merely a score on an I.Q. test.
- Success is not necessarily material wealth.
- A biker is more than just a figure in leather riding a Harley.

The following example of negation focuses on the qualities of the deaf culture that the writer wants to discuss.

> Deaf culture is a community of people bound together not by race, religion, or ethnic background but by a shared history, shared experiences, and a shared means of visual communication.

PRACTICE **10-5**

Use negation with the following terms. Write a sentence stating what each term is not as well as what it is.

1. Apathy _____

_____

_____

2. Geek _____

_____

_____

3. Democracy _____

_____

_____

4. Fitness _____

_____

_____

The Extended Definition

Many concepts, theories, and philosophies are too complex for a one-sentence formal definition. Imagine trying to fully explain sexism in a sentence or two. Think of the various contexts and ways in which sexism can be defined.

To provide an in-depth understanding of the idea or your opinion, attitude, or judgment about a term, you need to write an *extended definition essay* so that your reader can gain a more complete grasp of the concept.

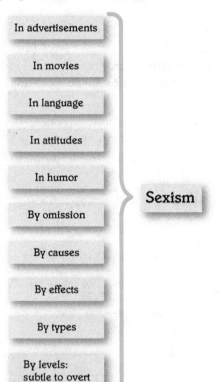

Developing an Extended Definition

The definition essay allows you to draw from the variety of techniques that you have mastered in previous chapters—description, narration, process, illustration, cause/effect, comparison or contrast, and classification or division. You probably won't use all of these modes in one essay—just the ones that are most appropriate for explaining your topic. In your prewriting process, you might try several of these methods of development to generate ideas and decide which are most useful for defining your topic.

For example, examine the topic *road rage*. Here are excerpts from a student essay using several patterns of development to explain this concept.

● Narration and description

The violent incident I witnessed when I was four is a prime example of motorists who fit in the category of violent offenders. My dad and I were in the turning lane, and two men in separate vehicles in front of us were arguing. Both men got out of their vehicles to confront each other. As soon as they reached one another, they started punching each other. The younger man was knocked down, his head slammed into the unyielding concrete. Remarkably, he started to slowly get up, but before he could get to his feet, the older man threw him into the busy street where traffic was quickly moving. My heart stopped when I saw him lying motionless and bleeding in the street. He was unconscious but alive, which is fortunate for incidents involving road rage.

● Process

Road rage begins with aggressive driving, which can be following too closely, speeding, and making rude comments or gestures to others on the road, and then escalates into a violent retaliation with intent to harm.

● Classification

It is important to know and recognize all types of aggressive drivers to better understand where road rage originates. I have categorized angry drivers into three groups: quiet steamers, outward aggressors, and violent offenders. The quiet steamers are the drivers who get irritated easily but keep their irritation inside their vehicles. Quiet steamers get aggravated but rarely let the source of their frustration know about it. The outward aggressors are another story. They will honk persistently, yell rude comments out their windows, display rude gestures, and tailgate. They are the type who will drive too close to others, honk needlessly, pass on the shoulder, flip people off, and yell at other drivers and pedestrians. While outward aggressors are seemingly precarious drivers, those who are violent offenders are the most dangerous and the epitome of road rage. They become overly enraged and try to physically harm others. They may start a physical confrontation or use a weapon to reprimand whoever is angering them. This type of driver has extreme road rage. These are the drivers who can cost lives and are consequently the most important type of driver to recognize and avoid.

● Illustration

Two women in our community were brutally murdered recently by a 23-year-old man in an episode of road rage. He felt he was wronged on the road while riding his bike, so he trailed the vehicle that almost harmed him. Even though the driver did not cause any actual damage to the man or his bike, the man decided to punish the driver for what she nearly did. He stopped the car by riding in front of it with his bike and then attacked them with his bare hands.

- Causes

Congestion, traffic jams, longer commutes, and road construction can all be possible causes for road rage. Delays are annoying to all of us but are not justification for violence. Many people are irritated and aggravated by others several times a day, but rarely do they respond by attempting to destroy the person responsible for their frustrations. So why do so many seemingly normal people react so viciously in their vehicles? I have noticed that many drivers feel their way of driving is the only correct way, and many are enraged easily when they feel someone is not following their "good driving rules." Our stressful lives can also contribute; stress can come from work, home, relationships, and other aspects of life and then be displayed by aggressive driving and road rage.

- Effects

The effects of road rage are numerous; they could be anything from mere annoyance or fear to serious injuries or even death.

The Informal Definition

One type of informal definition occurs when writers invent a definition using humor, extended metaphor, or other techniques—in conjunction with the various methods of development—to entertain and enlighten. For instance, you might define "reading" as "a convenient way to see the world" and then support your definition with illustration, narration, and contrast writing.

Another kind of informal definition occurs when writers make up their own words because they have an idea or concept that doesn't fit any current terms. This kind of creativity is the way many new words or phrases enter the language every year. Such words as *yuppie* or *Generation X* entered our language to describe specific types of social groups, whereas words such as *blog* and *googling* resulted from computer use. The growth in computer literacy has also given such common words as *crash, surfing, bug, virus, spam,* and *mouse* a whole new dimension of meaning. For example, what would you call a person who sits in front of a computer many hours a day? One website suggests *mouse potato* (similar to a *couch potato*). If you want to be creative and have a little fun, try inventing your own word that captures the gist of the concept you want to define.

Connecting Reading to Writing

What Is Poverty?
by Jo Goodwin Parker

ˈ Not much is known about Jo Goodwin Parker, the assumed author of this essay. George Henderson, a professor at the University of Oklahoma, received the essay from a person named Parker and included it in an anthology entitled *America's Other Children: Public Schools Outside Suburbia* published in 1971.

Preparing to Read
What comes to your mind when you envision poverty? What are its physical and emotional effects?

Increasing Your Vocabulary

- **stench:** stink, foul smell
- **privy:** outhouse
- **anemia:** low level of oxygen-carrying material, especially red blood cells, resulting in weakness
- **grits:** coarsely ground corn or other grains
- **antihistamines:** drugs to relieve allergy and cold symptoms
- **repossess:** take back possession
- **malnutrition:** poor nutrition due to a poor diet
- **commodities:** useful items
- **chisel:** a sharp-edged metal tool used for cutting wood, stone, or metal

1   You ask me what is poverty? Listen to me. Here I am, dirty, smelly, and with no "proper" underwear on and with the **stench** of my rotting teeth near you. I will tell you. Listen to me. Listen without pity. I cannot use your pity. Listen with understanding. Put yourself in my dirty, worn-out, ill-fitting shoes, and hear me.

Poverty is getting up every morning from a dirt- and illness-stained mattress. The sheets have long since been used for diapers. Poverty is living in a smell that never leaves. This is a smell of urine, sour milk, and spoiling food sometimes joined with the strong smell of long-cooked onions. Onions are cheap. If you have smelled this smell, you did not know how it came. It is the smell of the outdoor **privy**. It is the smell of young children who cannot walk the long dark way in the night. It is the smell of the mattresses where years of "accidents" have happened. It is the smell of the milk that has gone sour because the refrigerator long has not worked, and it costs money to get it fixed. It is the smell of rotting garbage. I could bury it, but where is the shovel? Shovels cost money.

Poverty is being tired. I have always been tired. They told me at the hospital when the last baby came that I had chronic **anemia** caused from

CONNECTING
Reading to Writing

poor diet, a bad case of worms, and that I needed a corrective operation. I listened politely—the poor are always polite. The poor always listen. They don't say that there is no money for iron pills, or better food, or worm medicine. The idea of an operation is frightening and costs so much that, if I had dared, I would have laughed. Who takes care of my children? Recovery from an operation takes a long time. I have three children. When I left them with "Granny" the last time I had a job, I came home to find the baby covered with fly specks, and a diaper that had not been changed since I left. When the dried diaper came off, bits of my baby's flesh came with it. My other child was playing with a sharp bit of broken glass, and my oldest was playing alone at the edge of a lake. I made twenty-two dollars a week, and a good nursery school costs twenty dollars a week for three children. I quit my job.

Poverty is dirt. You say in your clean clothes coming from your clean house, "Anybody can be clean." Let me explain about housekeeping with no money. For breakfast I give my children **grits** with no oleo or cornbread without eggs and oleo. This does not use up many dishes. What dishes there are, I wash in cold water and with no soap. Even the cheapest soap has to be saved for the baby's diapers. Look at my hands, so cracked and red. Once I saved for two months to buy a jar of Vaseline for my hands and the baby's diaper rash. When I had saved enough, I went to buy it and the price had gone up two cents. The baby and I suffered on. I have to decide every day if I can bear to put my cracked, sore hands into the cold water and strong soap. But you ask, why not hot water? Fuel costs money. If you have a wood fire, it costs money. If you burn electricity, it costs money. Hot water is a luxury. I do not have luxuries. I know you will be surprised when I tell you how young I am. I look so much older. My back has been bent over the washtubs for so long, I cannot remember when I ever did anything else. Every night I wash every stitch my school-age child has on and just hope her clothes will be dry by morning.

5   Poverty is staying up all night on cold nights to watch the fire, knowing one spark on the newspaper covering the walls means your sleeping children die in flames. In summer poverty is watching gnats and flies devour your baby's tears when he cries. The screens are torn and you pay so little rent you know they will never be fixed. Poverty means insects in your food, in your nose, in your eyes, and crawling over you when you sleep. Poverty is hoping it never rains because diapers won't dry when it rains and soon you are using newspapers. Poverty is seeing your children forever with runny noses. Paper handkerchiefs cost money and all your rags you need for other things. Even more costly are **antihistamines**. Poverty is cooking without food and cleaning without soap.

Poverty is asking for help. Have you ever had to ask for help, knowing your children will suffer unless you get it? Think about asking for a loan from a relative, if this is the only way you can imagine asking for help. I will tell you how it feels. You find out where the office is that you are supposed to visit. You circle that block four or five times. Thinking of your children, you go in. Everyone is very busy. Finally, someone comes out and you tell her that you need help. That never is the person you need to see. You go see another person, and after spilling the whole shame of your poverty all over the desk between you, you find that this isn't the right office after all—you must repeat the whole process, and it never is any easier at the next place.

You have asked for help, and after all it has a cost. You are again told to wait. You are told why, but you don't really hear because of the red cloud of shame and the rising black cloud of despair.

Poverty is remembering. It is remembering quitting school in junior high because "nice" children had been so cruel about my clothes and my smell. The attendance officer came. My mother told him I was pregnant. I wasn't but she thought that I could get a job and help out. I had jobs off and on, but never long enough to learn anything. Mostly I remember being married. I was so young then. I am still young. For a time, we had all the things you have. There was a little house in another town, with hot water and everything. Then my husband lost his job. There was unemployment insurance for a while and what few jobs I could get. Soon, all our nice things were **repossessed** and we moved back here. I was pregnant then. This house didn't look so bad when we first moved in. Every week it gets worse. Nothing is ever fixed. We now had no money. There were a few odd jobs for my husband, but everything went for food then, as it does now. I don't know how we lived through three years and three babies, but we did. I'll tell you something, after the last baby I destroyed my marriage. It had been a good one, but could you keep on bringing children in this dirt? Did you ever think how much it costs for any kind of birth control? I knew my husband was leaving the day he left, but there were no good-byes between us. I hope he has been able to climb out of this mess somewhere. He never could hope with us to drag him down.

That's when I asked for help. When I got it, you know how much it was? It was, and is, seventy-eight dollars a month for the four of us; that is all I ever can get. Now you know why there is no soap, no needles and thread, no hot water, no aspirin, no worm medicine, no hand cream, no shampoo. None of these things forever and ever and ever. So that you can see clearly, I pay twenty dollars a month rent, and most of the rest goes for food. For grits and cornmeal, and rice and milk and beans. I try my best to use only the minimum electricity. If I use more, there is that much less for food.

10   Poverty is looking into a black future. Your children won't play with my boys. They will turn to other boys who steal to get what they want. I can already see them behind the bars of their prison instead of behind the bars of my poverty. Or they will turn to the freedom of alcohol or drugs, and find themselves enslaved. And my daughter? At best, there is for her a life like mine.

But you say to me, there are schools. Yes, there are schools. My children have no extra books, no magazines, no extra pencils, or crayons, or paper and the most important of all, they do not have health. They have worms, they have infections, they have pinkeye all summer. They do not sleep well on the floor, or with me in my one bed. They do not suffer from hunger, my seventy-eight dollars keeps us alive, but they do suffer from **malnutrition**.Oh yes, I do remember what I was taught about health in school. It doesn't do much good. In some places there is a surplus **commodities** program. Not here. The county said it cost too much. There is a school lunch program. But I have two children who will already be damaged by the time they get to school.

But, you say to me, there are health clinics. Yes, there are health clinics and they are in the towns. I live out here eight miles from town. I can walk that far (even if it is sixteen miles both ways), but can my little children? My neighbor will take me when he goes; but he expects to get paid, *one way or another*. I bet you know my neighbor. He is that large man who spends his time at the gas station, the barbershop, and the corner store complaining about the government spending money on the immoral mothers of illegitimate children.

Poverty is an acid that drips on pride until all pride is worn away. Poverty is a **chisel** that chips on honor until honor is worn away. Some of you say that you would do *something* in my situation, and maybe you would, for the first week or the first month, but for year after year after year?

Even the poor can dream. A dream of a time when there is money. Money for the right kinds of food, for worm medicine, for iron pills, for toothbrushes, for hand cream, for a hammer and nails and a bit of screening, for a shovel, for a bit of paint, for some sheeting, for needles and thread. Money to pay *in money* for a trip to town. And, oh, money for hot water and money for soap. A dream of when asking for help does not eat away the last bit of pride. When the office you visit is as nice as the offices of other governmental agencies, when there are enough workers to help you quickly, when workers do not quit in defeat and despair. When you have to tell your story to only one person, and that person can send you for other help and you don't have to prove your poverty over and over and over again.

15   I have come out of my despair to tell you this. Remember I did not come from another place or another time. Others like me are all around you. Look at us with an angry heart, anger that will help you help me. Anger that will let you tell of me. The poor are always silent. Can you be silent too?*

---

*From "What is Poverty?" by Jo Goodwin Parker from America's Other Children: Public Schools Outside the Suburbs, by George Henderson. Copyright © 1971 by University of Oklahoma Press, Norman. Reprinted by permission of the author and the publisher. All rights reserved.

Reading Connection

Understanding the Reading

1. How does Parker establish her credibility and voice in the first paragraph? How does she immediately connect to the reader?
2. List some of Parker's sensory details—sound, sight, smell, touch, taste.
3. Who is the *you* in the essay?
4. What is Parker's goal or purpose in this essay?

Understanding the Structure, Style, and Tone

1. How does Parker organize her definition? Does it follow the traditional essay structure—an introduction, a thesis, topic sentences, and a conclusion?
2. How do the repetition of the word *poverty*; the short, simple sentences and fragments; and the use of *you* contribute to the overall impact of the essay?
3. How would a more formal, more academic essay on poverty written by a sociologist differ from Parker's essay?
4. How would you describe the style of writing—formal, informal, educated, emotional?
5. Who wrote this essay—a sociologist, a poor person, a person close to the poor?

Making a Personal Connection

1. Think of a time that you have struggled financially. Explain your experience to someone who hasn't had to struggle.
2. Describe a difficult situation that you have encountered in the same direct, vivid, and intimate way that Parker does.

Writing Your Definition Essay

To illustrate the writing process, we follow the definition essay of a student, Gabriel. Gabriel has not yet made a career choice. As a student, he's still exploring different areas, but he's sure that his final choice will involve music in some way. He's part of a rock band and feels that this passion provides an interesting topic for a definition essay.

Punk: Oddity or Oracle?

Punk rock is a loud, fast, and deliberately offensive style of rock music, perhaps best exemplified by the California punk band Guttermouth, adored by fans but derided by fans' parents. For decades, punk has been looked upon as the frightening underbelly of Western culture. With spiked hair and colored Mohawks, and clad in leather, chains, and safety pins, punk bands and their fans cut a wide path wherever they go. I remember walking down the street one afternoon with my Mohawk. I was wearing my studded black leather jacket and my 10-hole Doc Martens. A lady with a little girl was walking toward me. About a half a block away, she noticed me, immediately grabbed the girl's hand, and ran across the street to avoid coming closer. Despite my appearance, however, if people only got to know me, they would realize how friendly and unbiased I am. I am hard to the core when it comes to my music, but I am also a loving father and a productive member of society.

Back in the 1980s, the world just didn't get it—"What's wrong with these kids, grinding and pounding idiotically on their instruments, shouting against authority?" At a time when the Cold War was intensifying and shady political deals were being made, punk broke out of the United Kingdom and became a worldwide phenomenon. Few people, however, noticed the connection between the political developments and the ascendance of punk music. Then, along with its popularity, punk gained musical talent and legitimacy. Punk bands now shred leads and rip scales far beyond the simplistic three-chord format that the music evolved from. Yet punk has always been more than just a musical phenomenon; it's a way of life. Although some still associate it with violence and negativity, it actually promotes unity, equality, and world peace.

Punk promotes unity through mixed venues and all-ages shows. Bands from all over the world, with wide varieties of styles and ethnicities such as German thrash, Jamaican ska, Norwegian black metal, British punk, and American hardcore, get together to entertain and educate crowds of all ages and all walks of life. They bring forth a sense of social communion that is otherwise lacking in the world. Blacks, whites, Asians, and Hispanics, men, women, and children can be spotted at the shows, whether in the pit, surfing the crowd, at the merchandise booth, or at the skate ramps. The different styles of artists and entertainment attract many types of people with one common interest—music. In my days as a promoter, I rounded up local bands ranging from female pop music, to thrash, to punk and even grindcore. I also brought bands from Denver, Colorado Springs, and New Mexico, as well as my own, and we had our own outdoor fest at a friend's junkyard.

Racism is sometimes associated with punk because the shaved heads, flight jackets, and Doc Martens were also worn by neo-Nazi groups in the 1980s. However, because society started viewing punks as Nazis and white supremacists, many bands started writing anthems and sing-alongs opposing Hitler, white power, and any Nazi activity. NOFX released a record titled *White Trash, Two Heebs, and a Bean* to display the group's diverse ethnic backgrounds. Murphy's Law, a skinhead band with three black members, did a rendition of Stevie Wonder's "Ebony and Ivory" to pay tribute to equality. Agnostic Front is another band that championed equality with the lyrics, "united strong / blacks and whites, united strong / for everyone." My friends consist of metal heads, skaters, thrashers, jocks, and preps of all races and ages. One reason punk is now so popular is that it promotes the equality of all.

> Punk also promotes world peace. Food Not Bombs was started by a West coast punk band to feed the poor and promote world peace. Bands such as Anit'flag, Aus-Rotten, Cryptic Slaughter, Bad Religion, and others dedicate their lyrics to relinquishing arms, freeing humanity, eliminating violence and hatred, stopping political corruption, erasing racism, and emphasizing "No more war / No more."
>
> Punk has become more accepted these days. Everywhere I go, I see people with colored hair, spiked wristbands, and studded belts. I'm willing to bet that most of these people are not punk or don't know what punk is, but the prevalence of punk regalia demonstrates the deep impression the movement has made on society. It also indicates that along with the studs and leather, the positive values of punk are filtering down to every level of our culture, where they will help make the world a better place.

This extended definition of punk culture obviously goes far beyond a mere dictionary definition. The essay offers a nonstandard view of a subculture against which many people react in fear. Notice that an extended definition can be carefully crafted to educate a reader who, in the opinion of the writer, may have based judgments on misinformation.

Prewriting

Sometimes, particular prewriting techniques are well suited to certain methods of development. In the case of definition, however, you should rely on your own favorite techniques to get started. One technique in particular—cubing—can help you move toward a complete and satisfying development of your topic.

Discovering and Limiting Your Topic
Prewriting Strategy: Cubing

Cubing has the advantage of allowing you to look at your topic from different angles or perspectives. In this prewriting technique, you visualize (or draw) a cube and its six sides, each side representing a different dimension of your topic. Each side contains a prompt for you to respond to:

1. **Describe it.** Visualize your topic and list as many details, qualities, and characteristics as you can.

2. **Compare or contrast it.** What is your topic similar to? What is it different from? List as many comparisons as possible.
3. **Associate it.** What does your topic remind you of? What does it make you think of? What other ideas, events, or issues can you associate with your topic?
4. **Analyze it.** What does your topic consist of? What are its parts? How does it work? What types does it consist of? How is your topic meaningful and significant?
5. **Apply it.** What can you do with your topic? How is it meaningful? How is it useful?
6. **Argue for or against it.** What controversies surround your topic? What strengths or weaknesses does it have? What challenges does it face? How can it be improved?

Dedicate at least five minutes to each side. Don't worry if you have more on one side than another. Just keep your pen moving, writing ideas for each side. Continue repeating the prompt, either mentally or out loud, to keep yourself focused. Your cubing activity results in six ways of approaching your topic (see Figure 10.1).

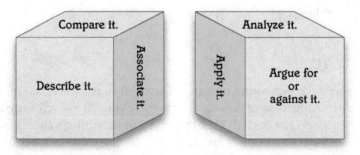

FIGURE 10.1 *Cubing Diagram*

Gabriel is taking a music appreciation course and has studied many styles and types of music. He decides to write a definition of punk rock because he listens to punk and wants to explore it in more formal terms to convince his middle-aged instructor that it is a respectable music genre. Choosing to list rather than freewrite, Gabriel spends a half hour jotting down ideas about punk rock, using the cubing method, and comes up with the following information.

Topic: Punk

Describe It	Compare It	Associate It	Analyze It	Apply It	Argue For or Against It
Fast	Hip-hop	My encounter	Stereotypes	Leads to peace	Against Nazis,
Harsh	Rap	with woman	Types: street	Diversity	white power
Mohawks	Heavy metal	on street and	punk, crust	Equality	For racial
Chains	Ska	her avoid-	punk, anar-	Unity	diversity,
Spikes	Nazi	ance of me	cho punk,	Being yourself	Food not
Blue hair	Skinheads	because of	Celtic punk	Standards =	Bombs
Ripping scales	Punk versus	the way I		rejection of	Freedom of
Swastikas	poser	looked		conformity	speech
Safety pins	Anarchist	Beginnings of			No censorship
Body	Goth	punk			Don't like
mutilation		People react			politics, don't
Leather		with disgust			like ideals,
Tattoos		and fear			don't want
Violence		NOFX			someone's
Freedom		Aus-Rotten			dream—just
					let me live my
					life; that's a
					controversy
					Antiestablish-
					ment

WRITING   10-1

Start generating ideas for each "side" of your cube. Dedicate at least five minutes of non-stop listing or writing to each dimension of your topic. Examine the relationship between ideas in different sides of the cube. Do you see any ideas developing? This activity demonstrates the true complexity of your topic. Review the information carefully, and determine the points you want to use to define your topic.

Topic: _____

Describe It	Compare It	Associate It	Analyze It	Apply It	Argue For or Against It

TOPICS TO CONSIDER

If you're still having problems finding a topic, here are some topics that might interest you. Use cubing with these topics to understand the complexity of these ideas. You can then determine how best to define your topic and organize your essay.

Writing for College		
▪ The definition of poverty in the United States ▪ The meaning of existentialism	▪ The definition of DNA ▪ The meaning of magical realism or minimalism as literary styles	▪ The definition of a polynomial ▪ The definition of media bias

Writing in Your Profession		
BUSINESS	▪ Ponzi scheme ▪ Bankruptcy	▪ Depreciation ▪ Embezzlement
CRIMINAL JUSTICE	▪ Probation ▪ Plea bargain	▪ Reasonable doubt ▪ Appeals process
EDUCATION	▪ Charter school ▪ Learning style ▪ Standardized tests	▪ Critical thinking ▪ Distance learning
HEALTH	▪ A disease ▪ Any health profession	▪ A health insurance plan ▪ Euthanasia
SOCIAL WORK/ PSYCHOLOGY	▪ Abnormal behavior ▪ Anger management	▪ Phobia ▪ Peer pressure ▪ Bullying
TECHNICAL	▪ Computer virus ▪ Arc welding	▪ Network ▪ A hybrid car
OTHERS	▪ Self-control ▪ Professionalism	▪ Cult ▪ Reggae music

Writing in Everyday Life		
▪ Procrastination ▪ Long-term goal	▪ Ideal career ▪ Soul mate	▪ Trust ▪ Faith

Identifying Your Audience and Establishing Your Purpose

Examine several definition topics in terms of their audience and purpose.

● Imagine that you just finished a unit in physics about Einstein's theory of relativity. You are confident that you understand the theory well and could explain it to another student in the class who is struggling with the concept. You decide that the best way to test your own comprehension of the theory and to prepare for the upcoming physics test is to write an essay defining the theory of relativity to a class of eighth graders. Your purpose, then, is twofold:

1. To establish and review your own knowledge of the topic
2. To ensure that eighth-grade students are helped by reading your definition, forcing yourself to be basic, concrete, and visual in your essay

- Imagine that you have a child or relative with attention deficit disorder. You have watched firsthand the symptoms, challenges, and treatment of this condition. Your purpose might be to educate someone else who is in a similar situation to make sure that this person understands the condition and has some ideas for dealing with it.
- If you have been poor at some time and want those who may never have experienced poverty to empathize with those who have, then your definition of poverty might be personal and powerful. You could use the senses so that your reader could feel the poverty—the cold, the hunger, the pain, the rawness.

Warning: If you choose a personal topic, be sure that it has an audience beyond yourself. For example, if you write a definition of your relationship with your girlfriend or boyfriend, be sure that you have something to say to others in a relationship, rather than just recounting your own and leaving the reader to wonder, "Who cares? So what?"

Setting Your Tone

Sensitivity to your audience requires that you pay attention to tone. In definition, you often find yourself arguing with others about the "true" meaning of particular words. Gabriel's essay about punk culture is a good example; it's easy to imagine the parents of teenagers disagreeing strongly with Gabriel, especially if their children have been harmed in any way as a result of involvement with punk culture. Similarly, words that carry political or philosophical "baggage" have to be handled with care. Be careful not to offend a reader who might potentially learn something from your definition by writing from a slanted, or biased, position. Be objective, reasonable, and informative when you are writing about controversial ideas.

WRITING 10-2

Use the following form to identify and analyze your audience, purpose, and tone.

Audience, Purpose, and Tone Analysis

Topic: _____

I. Audience

1. Who is your audience? _____

   Age(s): _____ Gender(s): _____ Education level(s): _____

2. Why would this audience be interested in your topic? _____

_____

3. What does your audience already know about your topic? _____

_____

4. What background information does your audience need to understand the topic?

_____

5. How do you expect your audience to read your essay—critically or for entertainment?

_____

II. Purpose

1. Why did you choose this topic? _____

_____

2. What is the controlling, or main, idea of your essay? _____

_____

3. What effect do you want your essay to have on your audience? _____

_____

4. What information must you provide to achieve the desired effect? _____

_____

III. Tone

1. What is your personal attitude about this topic? _____

_____

2. What tone do you want to establish for this essay? _____

_____

3. How does your tone help you relate to your audience and support your purpose?

_____

Formulating Your Thesis

One approach to creating a working thesis is to use the formal definition of your topic as the thesis of your essay. Another is to provide a formal definition just before the thesis; in this case, you might state the formal definition as a way of reminding the reader of the commonly accepted understanding of your topic and then present a thesis that introduces a new perspective on that definition. Yet another approach is to leave out the formal definition (for topics whose literal definitions are commonly known) and focus on other aspects of your topic to provide your reader a fuller understanding.

     General category   Specific Characteristics

[An effective manager] [motivates, inspires, and provides a sense of cohesiveness to employees.]

Especially for personal topics, you may be defining your own perspective on the topic, with which another reader may disagree. Your task is to clarify your outlook on the topic.

FORMAL DEFINITION:	Tattooing is the process of injecting ink into skin to create words or pictures.
THESIS:	Tattooing is body art meant to express feelings, beliefs, and/or personal history.

Gabriel comes up with the following tentative thesis:

> Punk is more than music; it's a way of life. It promotes unity, equality, and world peace, yet it is associated with violence and negativity.

WRITING 10-3

Write a tentative thesis for your definition essay. Remember, nothing is final—you can always come back to rephrase or refocus your thesis.

Tentative thesis: _____

Outlining Your Ideas

As you prepare to outline your essay, consider the most appropriate pattern for organizing your information. Also, consider the patterns that you might use within your paragraphs. As you explore all possibilities, keep your audience and purpose in mind. Review the following summary of the tools at your disposal for a topic on tattoos:

- Description (describe your favorite tattoos)
- Narration (tell a story that inspired you to get a tattoo)
- Process (explain how tattoos are done)
- Comparison or contrast (contrast tattoos to body piercings, or compare two types of tattoos)
- Classification (group tattoos—romantic, patriotic, group affiliations, and so on)
- Illustration or examples (describe different tattoo designs)
- Cause/effect (provide reasons people get tattoos and/or results or effects of showing off tattoos)
- Negation (explain that tattoos are not ugly, scarring disfigurements of the skin)

WRITING   10-4

After you have completed your outline, review it carefully. Is each point of the definition distinct from the others, without overlap? Do you plan to incorporate a variety of patterns to make your essay stronger and more interesting?

Essay Outline

Topic: _____

Audience: _____

Purpose: _____

Tentative thesis statement: _____

_____

I. Introduction

    A. Lead-in strategies

        1. _____

        2. _____

    B. Thesis and map _____

II. Body paragraphs

    A. Point #1: _____

        1. _____

        2. _____

        3. _____

        4. _____

    B. Point #2: _____

        1. _____

        2. _____

        3. _____

        4. _____

    C. Point #3: _____

        1. _____

        2. _____

   3. _____

   4. _____

D. Point #4: _____

   1. _____

   2. _____

   3. _____

   4. _____

E. Point #5: _____

   1. _____

   2. _____

   3. _____

   4. _____

III. Conclusion: Strategies you can use to wrap up your essay

   A. _____

   B. _____

   C. _____

Drafting

You may want to begin with the one-sentence dictionary definition of the term and then experiment with various methods of defining and explaining your topic, based on your audience and viewpoint. If you reach a dead end writing about causes, for instance, or process analysis doesn't apply to your topic, then try another method of development, such as examples or effects.

Writing Your Introduction

In previous chapters, you have been given a variety of strategies for beginning your essays, from vivid contrast, anecdote, humor, and rhetorical questions to historical detail and brief description. Especially with definition, you may want to start by exploring several meanings of a word or term before narrowing the topic to the focus of your essay. Be warned, however, to avoid the overused opening, "According to the dictionary. . . ." Also, avoid the phrases *is where* and *is when*, for example, "Patriotism is when. . . ."

Examine Gabriel's first attempt at his introduction.

Punk rock is a loud, fast, and offensive style of rock music. For decades, punk has been looked upon as a rebellious and delinquent influence on kids. With spiked hair and colored Mohawks, clad with leather, chains, and safety pins, punk rockers look intimidating. If people only got to know these rockers, they would see that Punk is more than music; it's a way of life. It promotes unity, equality, and world peace, yet it is associated with violence and negativity.

Gabriel begins with an unappealing definition of the music to deal with its stereotype before he moves on to his positive, inspiring definition, which sets up the body paragraphs. Through his use of vivid description, he gets his reader's attention. However, his introduction lacks development, and his thesis at the end fails to say anything definite or unique about his topic. His interesting start doesn't seem to connect with his thesis.

WRITING   10-5

Write a tentative introduction. Combine the different techniques you have practiced throughout the text. Don't forget to include your thesis. Without the thesis, your introduction goes nowhere.

Which techniques will you use? _____

Writing Your Body Paragraphs

As you compose your body paragraphs, keep the following points in mind:

1. **Try as many types of development as possible, even if some don't seem to apply to your topic.** For example, compare or contrast your topic to events, feelings, people, or ideas with which your reader may be familiar. Remember that you may use more than one type of pattern of development in a body paragraph if appropriate (comparison and narrative, for instance).

2. **Be sure that each topic sentence refers to a quality or characteristic of the topic.** Each topic sentence should further your definition, not discuss what your reader already knows or what you have already covered.

Every time **Computer** you stop work- **Tip!** ing on your paper, save it under a different file name, for example, "drafting #1, drafting #2" or "Revision #1, Revision #2." This way, you can keep track of your many changes and return to an earlier draft if necessary.

3. **Get rid of false notions by using negation.** You'll be surprised how much clearer your definition becomes when it is free of misunderstandings.
4. **Keep your purpose at the forefront of the essay.** Are you dispelling a misconception or introducing your reader to a new yet important concept? Are you providing your own personal definition of a commonly used word or phrase?

Examine a body paragraph from Gabriel's first draft.

> Punk spreads the message of unity through mixed venues and all-ages shows. Bands from all over the world with varieties of styles and ethnicities get together to entertain and educate crowds of all ages and all walks of life. They bring forth a sense of social communion that is otherwise lacking in the world. The different styles of artists and entertainment attract many types of people with one common interest—music. In my days as a promoter, I rounded up local bands ranging from female pop music, to thrash, to punk, and even grindcore. I also brought bands from Denver, Colorado Springs, and New Mexico as well as my own, and we had our own outdoor fest at a friend's junkyard.

Note that Gabriel has the main points that he wants to make in the paragraph—unity through geography, ethnicity, and age. However, as readers, we want examples of countries represented, ethnic groups, and diverse styles of music to convince us that punk rock is a unifying force. Gabriel also promises in the topic sentence that all ages are involved, yet in the examples, age groups are not mentioned. It's not uncommon that we are so familiar with and so connected to our topic that we forget our audience.

Coherence: Using Transitions

Transitions for definition essays are less obvious and mechanical than those for the directional process or comparison/contrast essays. You should use the transitions appropriate for the method of development that you choose to help you define your topic. See Chapter 4, page 106, for a list of transitions appropriate in different contexts.

WRITING 10-6

Start drafting your essay.
1. Start each body paragraph with a quality or type of development or statement of negation.
2. Develop each body paragraph as completely as possible, constantly checking the topic sentence to be sure that you are fulfilling its promise.
3. Add transitions so that the definition isn't jumping from one idea to the next.

Writing Your Conclusion

Your conclusion is your final impression on your audience, and it should bring closure to your definition. Look at Gabriel's conclusion.

> Punk has become more accepted these days. Everywhere I go, I see punk-looking people. I'm willing to bet that most of these people are not punk or don't know what punk is, but it shows the impression that it has left on society.

Does Gabriel's conclusion point out the main qualities of punk rock that make it a positive force in society? Does it leave the reader feeling as if understanding punk rock is worth the effort? Does it dispel some stereotypes of punk rock? Clearly, Gabriel has not yet addressed these important aspects of his conclusion.

WRITING   10-7

Write a tentative conclusion for your essay. Don't forget that you can use the same techniques in your conclusion that you used for your introduction. How do you want your reader to remember your definition?

Revising

As you approach the revising stage of the writing process, don't lose sight of two of the most important elements in writing: your audience and your purpose.

Style Tip: Use Parallel Constructions Correctly

Bridging Knowledge

See Handbook Chapter 7h for additional information and examples of parallelism.

In math, if two lines are parallel, they mirror each other visually. In the same way, in writing, if words, phrases, or sentences are connected in a list of two or more items, then they should be presented in the same structure.

> **INCORRECT:**   I enjoy a number of outdoor activities, including mountain biking, hiking, fishing, and I also like to rollerblade.

In this case, the writer inserts a clause into a list of nouns, creating a problem in parallelism.

> **CORRECT:**   I enjoy a number of outdoor activities, including mountain biking, hiking, fishing, and rollerblading.

Note that the list of activities is made up of all nouns. Problems occur when the writer lists items of different grammatical types.

PROBLEM	SOLUTION

WRITING
My essay seems too mechanical.

1. Did you vary the types of support? For example, did you use comparison, contrast, illustration, process, and so on?
2. If you did vary the types of support, are they appropriate and effective? Ask someone to read one or two paragraphs that you feel are weak. Ask your reviewer what is confusing or troublesome, and then revise these areas.

WRITING
My essay just doesn't seem engaging.

1. Did you choose a topic that you are interested in? If it's boring to you, it will be boring to your reader. Consider a new topic. If it's not the topic, then consider a new angle. Go back to your cubing exercise to see what other ideas you listed.
2. Review your writing style. Make sure you show variation in your sentence structure.
3. Examine your word choice. Use vivid verbs, an appropriate level of formality, and appropriate diction, especially nonoffensive language.

DEFINITION
My definition seems stale and predictable.

1. Did you choose the best points to define your topic? Review your points. Are they fresh, unique, and important? Tell your readers something they don't already know.
2. Don't get preachy or moralize to your reader. When defining such topics as faith, marriage, and family, it's easy to impose your values on your audience. What does your audience gain from your writing?
3. Avoid turning your essay into a self-help essay. You cannot solve a complex problem in a short essay, nor does your reader expect you to.

COHERENCE
The body of my essay seems to be in "chunks" of information that aren't connected smoothly.

1. When you move from one method of development to another within the body of your essay, make sure your transitions are strong enough to signal the switch from one method to another.
2. As you write your sentences, make sure that each sentence flows smoothly from one idea to the next. Use a combination of transitional words or phrases, repetition of key ideas, and pronouns to tie your sentences together.

WRITING
Your Definition Essay

WRITING 10-8

Start your revision. Don't leave any part of your essay untouched. As you revise, address the following questions:

- Does the essay have a strong purpose and a clear audience?
- Are the body paragraphs organized logically and effectively?
- Are there sufficient transitions so that the information is easy to follow?
- Does the conclusion sum up the definition and reinforce the essay's purpose?

Collaborative Critical Thinking

Asking Your Peers

When you have completed the writing process and have a polished final draft, exchange papers with a classmate for peer review, using these questions to guide your review.

1. Who is the writer? Who is the peer reviewer?

2. Read through the essay once, and then write a definition of the topic in your own words from what you gleaned from the essay.

3. What was the clearest, easiest-to-understand section of the essay?

4. What section of the essay is more challenging to read? Provide specific suggestions for improvement (add an example, reorder the information, add transitions, change wording in certain sentences, add a topic sentence, and so on).

5. Underline the thesis statement. Suggest any changes to make it fit the essay more effectively.

6. Evaluate the introduction. Does it provide interest, give necessary background information to the topic, and lead smoothly into the thesis?

7. What methods of development did the writer use to expand on the definition? What other methods could be used to clarify the definition?

8. Evaluate the conclusion. Does it sum up the topic well and give the reader a sense of the usefulness of the information in the essay?

9. Provide at least three specific suggestions for improving the essay.

Proofreading

Start the proofreading stage by looking for the major errors we list next. Also, learn to spot hard-to-miss errors in the use of punctuation. One of the most annoying errors, to your teachers if not to you, is the misuse of apostrophes.

Common Error # 11: Missing or Misplaced Apostrophes

The apostrophe has two uses:

1. To signal possession with nouns.

CORRECT:	This is John's notebook. [singular]
CORRECT:	The students' notebooks are on the bus. [plural]

    Note: Possessive pronouns do not use the apostrophe:

CORRECT:	The book is a beautiful example of the art of binding. Its cover is made of embossed leather.

2. To signal a contraction.

INCORRECT:	Its sitting on the desk, so it cant be in the closet
CORRECT:	It's sitting on the desk, so it can't be in the closet.
	[It's is a contraction of It is. Can't is a contraction of cannot.]

    Problems occur when the writer omits the apostrophe or puts it in the wrong place.

INCORRECT:	This is Johns notebook.
	OR
INCORRECT:	This is Johns' notebook.

Using "s" without the apostrophe indicates a plural noun, not possession. Placing the apostrophe after the "s" indicates plural possession.

> **Bridging Knowledge**
>
> See Handbook Chapter 13a for further information on apostrophes.

Applying Previous Knowledge

Be sure to check your essay for the most common errors presented in previous chapters.

Common Error #1	Sentence Fragments	
handbook **H-1b**	**fragment:** Because he was angry. **better:** I left early because he was angry.	☐

Common Error #2	Shifts in Verb Tense	
handbook **H-5c**	She got off the bus and then ~~walks~~ **walked** to the corner.	☐

Common Error #3	Fused Sentences

handbook
H-2a

fused: I left early they were angry.

better: I left early. They were angry.

☐

Common Error #4	Comma Splices

handbook
H-2b

comma splice: I left early, they were angry.

better: I left early. They were angry.

☐

Common Error #5	Commas after Introductory Clauses and Phrases

handbook
H-12a

■ When you start a sentence with a subordinate conjunction—*although, as, because, before, even though, if, since, unless, when, while,* and so on—use a comma **after the introductory clause**.
   Because I was late, they left me behind.   ☐
■ When you start with a long prepositional phrase or two or more prepositional phrases, use a comma.
   Near the park by the elementary school, the officer found the stolen car.   ☐
■ When you start with a participial phrase (*-ing, -ed,* -irregular past participle), use a comma.   ☐
   • Throwing the glass against the wall, John left angrily.
   • Wanted by the FBI, the fugitive left the country.
   • Written in 1802, the novel was a success.

Common Error #6	Shift in Person

handbook
H-4d

shift from third to second person: A **student** should get a topic approved so **you** don't waste time.

better: **Students** should get a topic approved so **they** don't waste time.

☐

Common Error #7	Pronoun-Antecedent Agreement

handbook
H-4a

A **person** should know what ~~they are~~ **she or he is** doing. Be careful with indefinite pronouns (*everyone, everybody, somebody, something, each, every,* and so on); they take singular pronouns.
Everyone decided to go ~~their~~ **his or her** separate way.

☐

Common Error #8	Pronoun Reference
handbook **H-4d**	• Rita skis and plays tennis. **Her participation in these sports** shows her interest in sports. Rita skis and plays tennis. **~~This~~ Her participation in these sports** shows her interest in sports. ☐ • At the flea market, **~~they~~ the vendors** sold new and used merchandise.

Common Error #9	Pronoun Case
handbook **H-4c**	• The president, treasurer, and **~~me~~ I** examined the proposal. ☐

Common Error #10	Lack of Agreement between Subject and Verb
handbook **H-3**	Each of the candidates **~~have~~ has** addressed the issue. ☐

WRITING 10-9

Start proofreading your own essay. Check for and correct any grammatical errors. Look for other obvious errors in spelling and punctuation.

Final Checklist

1. Does your introduction have an appropriate and effective lead-in? ☐
2. Does the thesis statement provide a brief definition of the topic? ☐
3. Does each paragraph have an appropriate topic sentence that clearly identifies a characteristic or quality of the topic or illustrates what the topic is not? ☐
4. Do the supporting details make use of a range of types of development? ☐
5. Does the essay contain appropriate, varied, and smooth transitions between paragraphs and sentences? ☐
6. Does your essay have varied sentence structures, complete sentences (no fragments, comma splices, or fused sentences), and insignificant errors in spelling, usage, and punctuation? ☐

WRITING
Your Definition Essay

Reflecting

After you have received feedback from either your peers or your instructor, incorporate as many of your reviewers' suggestions as needed to help polish your final draft. As you prepare to hand in your paper, begin reflecting on your writing process.

WRITING 10-10

Self-Reflection

Before you hand in your paper, write a brief paragraph in which you reflect on your final draft. Include your feelings on the following questions:

1. What peer suggestions do you find most useful? What should you change to address the suggestions?
2. What are you most proud of in this essay?
3. What is the weakest aspect of the essay?
4. What types of comments or feedback on this essay do you think would be most helpful to your writing progress?
5. What should you do differently as you write the next essay?

After you have completed this self-reflection, carefully review your instructor's comments. How are they similar or different from your own answers to the self-reflection? Make a list of your grammar, punctuation, and spelling errors so that you can follow up on the ones that recur. Consider what strategies you will employ to address your challenges or weaknesses and to improve the quality of your essay.

How might you use definition outside of this English course? Look back at the writing samples in Previewing Your Task in this chapter.

- **College:** _____
- **Your profession:** _____
- **Everyday life:** _____

11

Developing Your Essay through Argumentation

"In science the credit goes to the man who convinces the world, not to the man to whom the idea first occurs."

— *Charles Darwin*

YOUR GOALS

Understanding Argument

1. Use effective organizational patterns to support your arguments.

2. Support your position with sufficient evidence.

3. Respond to opposing arguments effectively.

4. Use logic to argue convincingly.

5. Eliminate logical fallacies.

Connecting Reading to Writing

1. Demonstrate an understanding of effective reading strategies.

2. Increase your vocabulary.

3. Analyze readings for comprehension, structure, tone, and style.

4. Show a personal connection to topics introduced by professional writers.

Writing Your Argumentative Essay

1. Use a variety of prewriting techniques to explore your topic.

2. Write a thesis appropriate for an argument essay.

3. Write relevant, logical, and convincing supports to prove your thesis.

4. Use a variety of appeals.

5. Establish common ground with your audience.

6. Use research to support your argument (optional).

7. Proofread for common grammar errors.

Access grammar exercises for this section in your English CourseMate, available through CengageBrain.com.

I n your biology class, you are assigned to defend Charles Darwin's theory of evolution, using Darwin's own words and those of other renowned scientists. Having been brought up to believe in the literal truth of the biblical creation story, you are skeptical about being able to do justice to Darwin's theory, but you keep an open mind and present his arguments.

Let's Warm Up!

How many times have you questioned a requirement to take a certain course as part of your degree program? You want to be a dental assistant or an architect and don't see why you should have to take two semesters of English composition. With a fellow student, identify your respective majors and career goals, and make a brief list of the reasons for and against the English composition requirement.

Enrico Fianchini/istockphoto.com

As the director of computer services at a local community college, you must present the reasons the computer-usage policy must become more restrictive for faculty, students, and staff. You expect resistance to the new rules, such as no game playing, no access to social networking sites, and no personal e-mails on state-owned computers, but you must try to convince employees that these restrictions are for the greater good and protection of the college.

You live in a suburban neighborhood that lacks adequate recreational venues for teenagers. You hope to convince your neighborhood association and your city council that it is worth investing in a skate park on a vacant piece of land in your area. As you prepare your list of reasons for both organizations, you try to think of negatives, as well as positives, to be ready to address any objections to the proposal.

Arguments are all around us. They are part of our daily conversation, and they are part of our inner conflicts: Should I invest my money? Should I continue to pursue a specific career? Should I start a family? Whom should I vote for in this election year? To resolve these dilemmas, we weigh both sides of the issue and consider all evidence.

Previewing Your Task

Many people think of the term *argument* as having to do with out-of-control emotions, shouting matches, and longstanding hard feelings. However, true argument is one of the highest forms of the writer's, or speaker's, craft. Higher education has always focused on teaching students how to persuade others and how to be open minded enough to agree that opponents can be right now and then. But argument is just as important in other areas of life.

Writing for College

In the following essay, written for an English class, Anne, a student concerned about tattooing, makes an appeal to her peers to support regulating the tattoo industry.

Tattooing: When the Ink Gets Under Your Skin

Tattooing has become a fashionable way to permanently mark the body. This process involves puncturing small holes in the top layer of the skin and injecting pigment through them into the lower dermal skin layer. Because the pigment is injected into the dermal layer rather than the epidermis (the top layer that is constantly being replaced), tattoos are permanent and often last a lifetime with little fading or distortion.

In the last 10 years, tattooing has become popular. Even a casual observation at a public place such as the local mall confirms that tattoos are now as common as certain kinds of jeans or jewelry. Fortunately, most people who get tattoos experience few problems, but tragically, recent news stories indicate that HIV and hepatitis B have been linked to improper tattooing procedures. It is crucial that the government take steps to help prevent such consequences by regulating the tattoo industry. In doing so, we can control the composition of the pigment used in the tattooing process, ensure that tattoo artists are properly trained in the process, and prevent the diseases now associated with tattoos.

First, regulation will control the composition of the pigments used in the tattooing process. The Food and Drug Administration (FDA), which regulates all types of additives, including those in food, cosmetic, and drugs, does not regulate the pigments used for tattooing, according to my informal survey of local tattoo artists. In fact, the FDA has not approved the use of any color additives for tattooing. Although tattoo businesses fail to see the need for setting such standards, the possibility exists that harmful chemicals are present in tattoo pigments. For decades, the medical field has publicized the harmful effects of lead, and as a result, many manufacturers have removed it from their products, including paint and gasoline. Yet we hear little mentioned of the role played by the tattoo industry in protecting consumers. Properly regulating these pigments will promote the tattoo business as consumer conscious and may result in an increase in profits.

Regulation will also help set standards for training tattoo artists, thus protecting the customer and public. No doubt, most tattoo artists are conscientious and do indeed practice safe tattooing procedures. However, the fact remains that improperly trained artists can unknowingly cause the possibility of many different health problems to their customers, which can spread to the public if infectious. Under the current system, we can't be sure that all tattoo artists adhere to safe practices. Customers have observed poorly trained tattoo artists licking the needles, using the same gloves for more than one customer or not using gloves, and even pricking their hands to check the sharpness of the needles. However, a training process would set standards for the proper use and sterilization of equipment, as well as provide guidelines for a clean work area. All doctors and nurses, who are responsible for giving injections, are required to undergo a formal and stringent training period before they are permitted to practice, so why should tattoo artists, who poke the skin multiple times, be any different?

Pointing to the thousands of people who have tattoos, opponents of regulation argue that few customers have any health problems resulting from tattooing and that, therefore, regulation is not necessary. However, recent news reports from around the country indicate something different. They demonstrate that health problems associated with tattooing include the transmission of many communicable diseases, such as HIV, hepatitis C, and tuberculosis. One of my own acquaintances was recently diagnosed with hepatitis C, and her doctors believe the most likely cause was the series of tattoos she had done on her lower back over the last 2 years.

Most likely, tattooing will continue to enjoy its popularity for years to come. Therefore, people who make the decision to get tattoos should feel safe with the procedure. Regulating this industry might at first seem unnecessary, but it will promote better health for everyone: the customer, the artists, and the public. Shouldn't our health be everyone's concern?

PRACTICE 11-1

1. After reading this essay, do you have a different opinion of tattooing than you did before? Why or why not?_____

_____

_____

2. Do the body paragraphs adequately support the topic sentences? Could the author have added any additional information that might have helped her case?_____

_____

_____

Writing in Your Profession

Argument is one of the most common modes of discourse in the workplace. This doesn't mean you will always be crafting formal written arguments to address workplace concerns, but it does mean that many of the interactions you have—with coworkers, supervisors, or customers—take the form of having to convince someone that you are right about some debatable topic. The following memo is presented in terms of formal argument.

Memorandum

To: Mary McCaffery, President
CC: J. J. Villanueva, Project Manager
From: Matthew Barnes, VP for Support Services
Date: 4/10/2010
Re: Expansion into La Veta

Mary,

For the past several months, we've been debating the possibility of expanding into La Veta as part of our southern Colorado growth strategy. As you know, this subject is beginning to drain much of the energy we need to devote to other matters. It is time to recognize that our management team will probably never reach consensus on expansion; nonetheless, we can no longer postpone action. We think that despite a shaky bottom line in the near term, the La Veta expansion is necessary to preserve our long-term fiscal health.

Mark claims that the La Veta population is too small to support more than one building supply store at this time. I grant that only one hardware store has survived the years in La Veta, but it is now too outdated to support the needs of the local construction industry. We find that many custom home builders are ordering from Pueblo or even farther north to get the specialized materials and supplies they need for the niche market growing up around La Veta. A new Holmes Industries store not only would meet the needs of the current population but also would lower custom building costs and thus stimulate further development in the mountain areas surrounding the town.

Second, John and Mark believe the investment is too risky at this time given the regional downturn in the housing industry. Nothing could be further from the truth. We have encountered this same situation before—in the Woodlands community project, for instance, before you came on board. In that case, the regional picture also looked grim, but a number of factors combined to make the Woodlands project blossom— the right clientele, banks that were willing to go the extra mile, and the opening of our store in the right place at the right time. It was a risk, but look how it paid off!

Finally, John claims we are in danger of overextending our internal capacity to support an expansion project. On this point, I agree completely. Trying to expand into La Veta without opening an additional warehouse and budgeting office will prove too great a burden. That's why I'm proposing that we split the SoCo warehouse between our Pueblo and La Veta operations for now. This will involve extending the footprint of the building by one-third, but it avoids the costs of new construction. The La Veta budget staff could work in the west end of the building where Martha has her office now. When the new store is ready to become a hub of further growth, we can talk about new office space.

Mary, now is the time. Let's commit to this expansion and get it done before the end of the year. We might see slow returns for a couple of years, but when the industry takes off again, we will be in a good position to reap the rewards.

Confidential

PRACTICE 11-2

1. Is the evidence in each paragraph adequate to convince the audience and to support the purpose? Explain your answers. _____

   _____

   _____

2. Because this is an argument, what do you think of the fourth paragraph, in which the author agrees with his opponents? Does this paragraph work for or against the argument? _____

   _____

   _____

Writing in Everyday Life

Family members argue all the time. Whether successfully or not, they try to convince one another to change or accept a certain behavior or decision. The following letter from a daughter to her mom makes such an attempt.

Dear Mom,

Thanks for having me over last weekend to continue our discussion. I think we are close to an understanding, but I'm still a bit discouraged by your response. Even though you didn't come right out and say it, you let me know just how you feel. I know how much you want me to be an independent adult, living on my own. I'm working toward this goal but need to move home for a while. It seems that Dad and Sheila welcome the idea, but I have to convince you. So here goes.

First, you still need a lot of help around the house, and you know me: Housework is my favorite pastime. Dad and Sheila are such slobs, and you spend a lot of time cleaning up after them that you could be using for something more interesting. What about that drawing class you always talk about? Take it! Let me keep house! I might even be able to teach Dad and Sis to pick up after themselves for a change.

Second, since I got my new job, I can help with the budget. I won't be paying $850 a month to rent an apartment, so I'd be glad to give half that amount to you and Dad as rent. I could also buy my own food or give you a percentage toward your grocery bill. If I do contribute in these ways, I could still save close to $600 every month so that I can start college in the fall of next year. Since your house is close to my job, I could walk to work and save the gas money, which is killing me right now.

Third, I don't have a boyfriend anymore, and furthermore, I don't want one for a long time to come. You won't have to worry about my relationships this year. As I told you this weekend, I need to get serious about my future and get ready to go to school.

Despite these huge advantages, I know you'll say the same old thing: "Lisa, you're 34. When are you going to settle down on your own and stop moving back home? This is the sixth time in 10 years." The point, Mom, is that this time I'm preparing for the future. I think I'm finally growing up and realizing what it takes. This will be the last time—I promise. Just think: When I go off to college, Sheila will be a high school graduate, and we can go to school together. You and Dad will finally be empty nesters. Won't that be fun? Please give it some more thought, Mom. How can you say no?

Love,
Lisa

PRACTICE 11-3

1. What are Lisa's main strategies to convince her mother? _____

2. How effective is her letter? What might she add to successfully convince her mother? _____

_____

Understanding Argument

For many instructors, the argument essay represents the "peak" of the college writing experience and is the main reason to learn the other writing techniques. The following two main reasons make the argument essay important:

- **In our culture in general, but in academic culture especially, argument is the way knowledge is created and spread.** In colleges and universities, teachers and students engage one another's ideas by means of oral and written argument, letting their positions be refined by willingly subjecting them to the opposing ideas of others.

- **As citizens of a democracy, we conduct our best conversations—the ones that determine policies on important issues—in the form of argument.** The more you learn about the value of argument in the political context, the more you are able to fulfill your role as an educated citizen and contribute meaningfully to your community.

Too often, however, we experience argument in confrontational forms, such as when two people resort to name calling or when, in a political debate, both sides read prepared statements instead of honestly engaging in mutual discussion. Because of this situation, we've grown squeamish and hypersensitive about participating in genuine argument. One purpose of this chapter is to make you more comfortable and skilled in argumentative contexts so that you can participate in productive dialogue with your peers and coworkers.

The Elements of Argument

Most thorough and effective arguments are based on a small set of common elements:

- **A claim (your thesis) about which reasonable people can disagree.** True argument occurs when people with goodwill, adequate knowledge, and the ability to reason happen to disagree on some issue of importance to them. Reasonable people, for instance, can disagree about the claim that elderly drivers should be relicensed annually; both sides have compelling reasons to support their position.

- **Evidence to support each of your reasons.** Reasons are considered valid partly on the basis of the evidence used to support them. In writing an argument, you are not obligated to present the other side's evidence, but you are obligated to fully support your reasons with valid and sufficient evidence.

- **A logical line of reasoning.** Argument requires careful use of reasoning techniques that lead your reader to your conclusion. At any step along the way, it is easy to get off track—to contradict yourself or to write something that might support the other side of the issue instead of your own.

- **Fair acknowledgment of the other side of the debate, including (sometimes) concession of one or two points.** As a reasonable, open-minded person, you are likely to agree with your opponents about one or more of the reasons they've advanced to support their side of the argument. When this is the case, your argument becomes stronger if you concede that your opponents are right (not about the argument as a whole, just about the element you agree with). It helps you establish common ground with your opponents, and it marks you as fair and reasonable.

- **Refutation of the other side's position.** Even though you will probably concede a point or two to your opponents, you also must show that their major arguments fail to lead to their conclusion. In addition to advancing your arguments, then, you must refute some arguments of your opposition.

Types of Claims

Basically, there are four types of claims you can make in your thesis: claims of fact, claims of cause or effect, claims of value, and claims of policy.

1. **Claims of fact.** Facts are not absolute truths. People argue about them all the time. For example, most people believe it is a fact that DNA evidence is conclusive; however, lawyers constantly debate the validity of such evidence. Here are some factual questions that, when converted to claims, can be interesting, thought-provoking thesis statements:
   - Will a proposed school lunch program cost $10 million or $15 million?
   - Are rates of teen smoking decreasing or increasing in our community?
   - Does Facebook adequately protect users' privacy?
2. **Claims of cause/effect.** Because people commonly disagree about the cause/effect of particular situations, these types of claims make perfect argumentative theses: They're based on disagreement. The reader wants to know what really causes something or what really happens because of it. The following questions can lead to claims of cause/effect suitable for argumentative theses:
   - Do smoking bans in public places reduce the incidence of lung cancer?
   - Does the use of cell phones in cars increase car accidents?
3. **Claims of value.** Claims of value attempt to argue that the beliefs, behavior, customs, and traditions that we or society hold are worthwhile or undesirable. Religious, political, and moral issues are common in such claims. Examine the types of questions that may lead to claims of value:
   - Is assisted suicide morally right?
   - At what point should we curb freedom of speech?
4. **Claims of policy.** Claims of policy argue for maintaining or changing existing conditions, usually to solve a particular problem. This type of claim argues what should be done, how something should be done, and who should have the authority to do it. Here are some questions that lead to theses arguing claims of policy:
   - Should the drinking age be increased?
   - Should we spend less on the prison system?

Using Evidence to Support Your Position

To persuade your reader to accept your position, you need to back up your argument every step of the way with convincing evidence (facts and details that support your point). Fortunately, you've been practicing this skill in your other writing, so you are ready to apply it to argumentation.

In an argument, you need to make sure the evidence you present meets three standards: It must be relevant, representative, and sufficient.

1. **Your body paragraphs need evidence that is *relevant*.** Suppose you want to convince your reader that your college should start an intramural handball competition. One of your reasons to support this proposal is that your college has several racquetball courts and that they are always busy. Is this relevant to your argument? It might seem to be; after all, handball and racquetball are played on similar courts using the same basic set of rules. However, it also assumes that people who play racquetball are ready and willing to switch to handball. If this assumption turns out to be wrong, your argument is weakened. Keep in mind that you have to *prove* the relevance of your evidence. In this case, you could survey the users of the racquetball court; if they indicate a willingness to participate in handball tournaments, you've made the connection that proves the relevance of your point.

2. **The evidence you present must be *representative*.** That is, it must fairly represent the range of possible opinions and data. Sticking with the handball example, suppose you decide to conduct random interviews with three groups on campus: administrators, students, and faculty. Your results turn out to be disappointing to you: 90% of administrators are opposed, 82% of students are in favor, and 60% of faculty members indicate they are indifferent. You decide to include the 82% result but not the other two. In this case, you are not presenting a sampling of all of the available evidence. Again, this doesn't mean you can't use the data from your survey, but you need to prove that the relevant part of it is the student response, not the other two.

3. **The evidence you present must be *sufficient* to convince your reader that your reasons are valid.** A single piece of evidence, unless it is utterly convincing in itself, is rarely sufficient to convince a skeptical or hostile audience that you are correct. Try to gather several pieces of evidence to bolster each of your supporting arguments.

A Logical Line of Reasoning

An argument is a line of reasoning leading to a conclusion. The way you present your case to your reader not only helps your reader follow your thinking process but also helps establish your credibility as a writer. When organizing the evidence in your paragraphs, you can use two basic types of reasoning: deductive and inductive.

Deductive reasoning means to argue starting with general principles, usually a claim or proposition, and then move to particular observations, your evidence. For instance, the law of gravity holds that objects of a certain weight dropped from a height fall to the ground. Therefore, if I drop a bowling ball from the top of the Leaning Tower of Pisa, it will fall to the ground.

In contrast, *inductive reasoning* means to argue from specific observations to more general principles. For example, every time I drop a bowling ball from the top of the Leaning Tower of Pisa, it falls to the ground. Therefore, there must be a law by which objects of a certain weight dropped from a height will fall to the ground.

In your own writing, it can be difficult to distinguish between deductive and inductive reasoning, especially because, most of the time, you probably begin your supporting paragraphs with a general topic sentence. However, *a general topic sentence can be the opening of either a deductive or an inductive paragraph*. Look at a couple of examples of paragraphs in outline form.

UNDERSTANDING
Argument

Thesis: Voters should be demanding that our national leaders make global warming their number one priority.

A. **Topic sentence A:** The evidence is mounting that global warming is causing radical changes to our coastal ecosystems.
   1. Areas on the east coast of the United States are losing shoreline at higher rates than ever before.
   2. Water temperatures in coastal estuaries are rising measurably each year.
   3. Fishing industries are closing shop as fish begin disappearing from our waters.

   Paragraph A is inductive: The writer bases the general topic sentence on the evidence scientists have gathered previously.

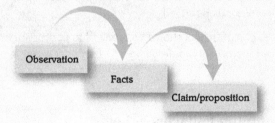

B. **Topic sentence B:** After our ocean waters reach a certain average temperature, the effects will be drastic and irreversible.

   1. Many of the largest coastal cities will be inundated, causing massive migrations to other parts of the country.
   2. Weather patterns will change in ways we don't yet understand.
   3. New diseases will begin to affect large segments of the population.

Paragraph B is deductive: On the basis of a general principle about rising water temperature, specific effects are predicted. (They haven't happened yet, so they couldn't serve as evidence.)

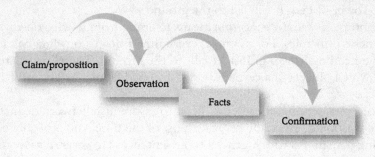

PRACTICE 11-4

In your group, pick one of the following topics. Show how you would develop two paragraphs to support it, one using deductive reasoning and the other using inductive reasoning. You don't need to write the paragraphs; simply outline them, and be ready to share your ideas.

Topic A: Smoking bans should not include bars and nightclubs. (**Hint:** One paragraph might begin with a statement about the principle of individual rights of business owners. The other might begin, "Evidence is mounting to demonstrate that smoking bans are driving many bars and restaurants out of business." The first paragraph is deductive; what kinds of points would you add to support it? The second is inductive; what kind of evidence could you use to support it?)

Topic B: Graduates of high school should be required to participate in mandatory community service for one year before being admitted to college.

Eliminating Common Fallacies in Logic

If an argument is a line of reasoning leading to a conclusion, then the types of support or evidence that can go wrong in an argument must relate to the reasoning itself. When your reasons depart from accepted rules of argument, you are committing an error known as a *logical fallacy*. On the positive side, one of the best ways to refute an opposing argument is to show that it fails to support its conclusion.

Most logical fallacies, especially in student writing, are not deliberate. Listen to political ads during election time, and you will hear many deliberate fallacies designed to mislead you into voting one way or another. Student arguments may also contain such fallacies. Examine a few of the most common fallacies:

1. **The red herring.** This phrase comes from the practice of dragging a dead fish across one's trail so that those who are in pursuit, and who have a good sense of smell, will be thrown off track. This fallacy is an attempt to throw your reader off track. Red herrings come in a number of guises; some of them should sound familiar.

WHY IS THIS STATEMENT A FALLACY?   South High School must adopt an open-campus policy during lunch because all other schools in town have it.

This is an example of the *bandwagon appeal*, or the "everybody's doing it" argument. Even if South High were the only school in the state with a closed-campus policy, this is no reason to adopt an open one.

WHY IS THIS STATEMENT A FALLACY?   If South High School doesn't adopt an open-campus policy during lunch, students will stop doing their homework, and their performance on the state assessment test will suffer drastically.

This is called *predicting a false consequence*, or a highly unlikely one, and it's not just because most of the students don't do their homework anyway. Rather, the writer simply has no basis for making this claim.

WHY IS THIS STATEMENT A FALLACY?   South High School's lunchtime restrictions are reminiscent of Hitler's regime in the 1930s.

In this case, it is clear that South High's closed-campus policy can in no way be compared with the true horrors of Hitler's reign. This type of comparison is called *false analogy*.

WHY IS THIS STATEMENT A FALLACY?   Mr. Tompkins apparently believes that even honors students are incapable of taking care of themselves off campus for 45 minutes.

This is a case of the *straw man* fallacy. In the straw man, the arguer takes the flimsiest, weakest opposition reason just to have something easy to attack. In this case, Mr. Tompkins would probably never make the claim that honors students were incapable of appropriate behavior.

2. **The black or white fallacy.** Also called the *either/or fallacy*, this is one of the most common fallacies. It usually takes the form of a statement that "the only alternative to X is Y," except that the statement is false.
   - The only alternative to the death penalty is rampant murder.
   - You've heard the reasons for restricting driving privileges of people over 75. Now is the time to act. If we don't, the alternative is streets and roads overrun by confused baby boomers who don't know which way to turn.

3. **The *ad hominem* fallacy.** This fallacy occurs when you attack the character of your opponent. Most likely, your attack against the person's character has nothing to do with the issue.
   - Mr. Tompkins has always shown himself to be an uncaring principal—unless the subject is the football team.
   - Those who believe in capital punishment are no better than the murderers they want to execute.

4. **Hasty generalization.** This common fallacy occurs when you make a large claim on the basis of a small sample that is too small to support the claim.
   - My nephew went off to college last year. All he does is skateboard during the day and party at night, yet he has a B average. Clearly, grade inflation is ruining our colleges and universities.
   - Based on a survey I conducted of my classmates in my English class, it is obvious that the requirement to take English should be abolished.

PRACTICE 11-5

Identify the type of logical fallacy illustrated in each of the following statements. Explain your answer.

1. Legalizing marijuana will result in higher rates of addiction to harder drugs such as heroin and cocaine. _____

_____

2. No wonder my opponents want to pass such a vague piece of legislation as Amendment 41—they're all lawyers! _____

_____

3. Why shouldn't we authorize casino gambling in the city? Half the towns between here and Nevada have adopted casino gambling. _____

_____

4. Do we want to allow prayer in schools, or do we want to preserve the freedoms granted to us by the founding fathers? _____

_____

5. In approving the local smoking ban last November, our city council proved itself no better than Hitler. _____

_____

6. Mr. Alvarez's support for the new recreation center is based on his notion that money grows on trees. _____

_____

7. Based on my "man-on-the-street" survey of 10 students between classes, it is clear that the majority of the student body couldn't care less about whether we have a rap or a metal band at the Spring Fling. _____

_____

Concession of Opposing Arguments

A characteristic feature of argument writing is the way it fairly and objectively represents the opposition. When you write an argument, you don't need to represent the opposition fully (that's their job), but you do need to indicate to your reader that you take your opposition seriously and that you have considered its major arguments. If you ignore your opposition or unfairly represent its position, you cause your own argument to fail. Here are the ways you may respond to your opposition:

1. **Acknowledgement.** To acknowledge your opposition is simply to state its main points and supporting reasons. The following paragraph states the major points of the opposition. Notice that the simple statement of these points gives the needed acknowledgement of the other side.

   > My opponents believe a parking garage would destroy the architectural unity of our campus. They also claim that it would cost too much and that we should use the money to build more learning center space. Furthermore, they seek to prove that even with a parking garage, students will still fight for spaces on the street and in the existing lots simply because these spaces are closer. Finally, they argue that parking garages are inherently unsafe, resulting not only in increased accident rates but also in more assaults and attempted rapes.

2. **Concession (optional).** *Concession*, also known as *accommodation*, means to admit that your opposition has a good point now and then. Concession is realistic, reasonable, and fair in the real world of conflicting ideas. It also has another advantage: It identifies you, the writer of your own argument, as realistic, reasonable, and fair. By acknowledging other opinions beyond your own, you show your reader that you are well informed on the issues and open minded. Your reader is more likely to read your essay if you acknowledge other views rather than just insist on your own reasons. Often, the balance of an argument depends on tipping the weight to one side of the scale or the other rather than obvious right and wrong ways of thinking. When your reader sees that you are trying to understand and appreciate the values and ideas of your opposition, your own argument becomes more believable. Here's an example of concession.

   > I admit that the parking garage will cost a lot of money and that we have long needed a larger learning center to accommodate our growing enrollment. In this case, my opponents have succeeded in identifying a major project that we must find a way to fund.

Refutation

Conceding one or more of your opponents' points may be optional, but an imperative element of an argument is to refute your opponents' major arguments; that is, you must show that your opponents' argument is weak in some way. For example, you might point out that the opponents' evidence is incorrect or exaggerated or show how your opponent is not seeing the entire issue. If you do not address and dispel opposing points, your reader is just as likely to accept your opponents' arguments as your own. Notice that in the following selection, the writer refutes the either/or argument of the opposition.

> However, the fact is that we need both projects if we are to move forward in serving students. One approach we can take is to divide the available money between the two projects, beginning both of them now, and then use next year's project capital budget to finish both projects. It doesn't have to be one or the other.

Patterns for Organizing an Argument

Although most thorough arguments contain many of the same elements, these elements can be arranged in different ways depending on your topic, your opponent's major reasons, your audience, and other aspects of your writing situation. Examine the three major patterns for organizing an argument.

Pattern A, shown in Figure 11.1, is probably the most commonly used method for organizing an argument. It is sometimes referred to as the *classic pattern*. In this pattern, you first present your case and then refute the most valid points of the opposition.

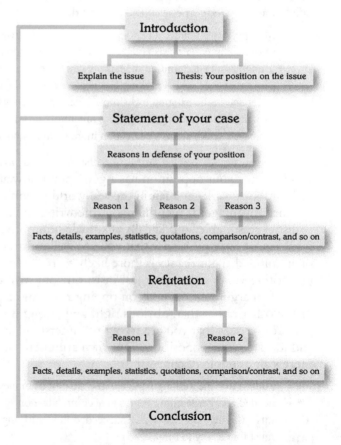

FIGURE 11.1 *Pattern A: Classic Pattern of Argument*

Pattern B is the reverse of pattern A, as shown in Figure 11.2. In this pattern, you first address your opponents' views and then present your side. One advantage of this pattern is that it permits you to deal with your opponents' arguments first so that you can focus on your own defense, leaving the reader with your points as the final impression. Another is that it reassures your opponents that you are familiar with their objections.

Pattern C, shown in Figure 11.3, focuses on opposing views. By refuting the opposition's strongest points, you make your own argument in defense of your thesis at the same time.

Consider combining the patterns to organize your argument effectively. For example, you can present each pro point followed by a con point. Feel free to present your information in the way that best fits your topic, purpose, and audience.

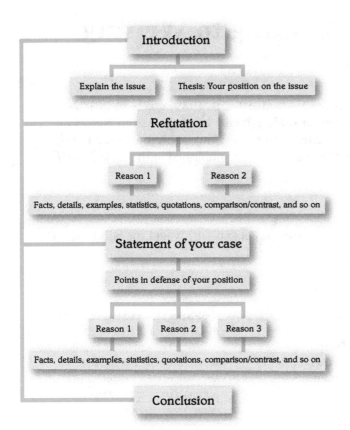

FIGURE 11.2 *Pattern B: Refute-then-Defend Pattern*

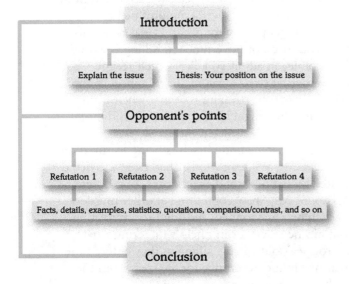

FIGURE 11.3 *Pattern C: Opposing Views Pattern*

Connecting Reading to Writing

Death and Justice

by Ed Koch

Ed Koch, mayor of New York City from 1978 to 1989, was born in 1924 in the Bronx to Polish immigrants. He earned a law degree from New York University in 1948 and has written several autobiographical tomes, a novel, and a book of essays. The following essay was published in the *New Republic* in April 1985.

Preparing to Read

If a person murders, should that person be put to death? Would you be willing to administer the lethal injection?

Increasing Your Vocabulary

- **clemency:** mercy, kindness
- **reverence:** respect
- **constituency:** a group of voters represented by a particular elected official
- **reprehensible:** worthy of blame
- **flagrant:** obvious
- **implacable:** unable to change

- **sophistic:** plausible but misleading
- **discriminatory:** prejudiced
- **painstaking:** extremely careful
- **sovereign:** power of the state
- **ambivalent:** not sure of
- **seminal:** original, beginning
- **paramount:** most important

1   Last December a man named Robert Lee Willie, who had been convicted of raping and murdering an 18-year-old woman, was executed in the Louisiana state prison. In a statement issued several minutes before his death, Mr. Willie said: "Killing people is wrong. . . . It makes no difference whether it's citizens, countries, or governments. Killing is wrong." Two weeks later in South Carolina, an admitted killer named Joseph Carl Shaw was put to death for murdering two teenagers. In an appeal to the governor for **clemency,** Mr. Shaw wrote: "Killing is wrong when I did it. Killing is wrong when you do it. I hope you have the courage and moral strength to stop the killing."

It is a curiosity of modern life that we find ourselves being lectured on morality by cold-blooded killers. Mr. Willie previously had been convicted of aggravated rape, aggravated kidnapping, and the murders of a Louisiana deputy and a man from Missouri. Mr. Shaw committed another murder a week before the two for which he was executed, and admitted mutilating the body of the 14-year-old girl he killed. I can't help wondering what prompted these murderers to speak out against killing as they entered the death-house door. Did their newfound **reverence** for life stem from the realization that they were about to lose their own?

Life is indeed precious, and I believe the death penalty helps to affirm this fact. Had the death penalty been a real possibility in the minds of these murderers, they might well have stayed their hand. They might have shown moral awareness before their victims died, and not after. Consider the tragic death of Rosa Velez, who happened to be home when a man named Luis Vera burglarized her apartment in Brooklyn. "Yeah, I shot her," Vera admitted. "She knew me, and I knew I wouldn't go to the chair."

During my 22 years in public service, I have heard the pros and cons of capital punishment expressed with special intensity. As a district leader, councilman, congressman, and mayor, I have represented **constituencies** generally thought of as liberal. Because I support the death penalty for heinous crimes of murder, I have sometimes been the subject of emotional and outraged attacks by voters who find my position **reprehensible** or worse. I have listened to their ideas. I have weighed their objections carefully. I still support the death penalty. The reasons I maintained my position can be best understood by examining the arguments most frequently heard in opposition.

5   1. *The death penalty is "barbaric."* Sometimes opponents of capital punishment horrify with tales of lingering death on the gallows, of faulty electric chairs, or of agony in the gas chamber. Partly in response to such protests, several states such as North Carolina and Texas switched to execution by lethal injection. The condemned person is put to death painlessly, without ropes, voltage, bullets, or gas. Did this answer the objections of death penalty opponents? Of course not. On June 22, 1984, the *New York Times* published an editorial that sarcastically attacked the new "hygienic" method of death by injection and stated that "execution can never be made humane through science." So it's not the method that really troubles opponents. It's the death itself they consider barbaric.

Admittedly, capital punishment is not a pleasant topic. However, one does not have to like the death penalty in order to support it any more than one must like radical surgery, radiation, or chemotherapy in order to find necessary these attempts at curing cancer. Ultimately we may learn how to cure cancer with a simple pill. Unfortunately, that day has not yet arrived. Today we are faced with the choice of letting the cancer spread or trying to cure it with the methods available, methods that one day will almost certainly be considered barbaric. But to give up and do nothing would be far more barbaric and would certainly delay the discovery of an eventual cure. The analogy between cancer and murder is imperfect, because murder is not the "disease" we are trying to cure. The disease is injustice. We may not like the death penalty, but it must be available to punish crimes of cold-blooded murder, cases in which any other form of punishment would be inadequate and, therefore, unjust. If we create a society in which injustice is not tolerated, incidents of murder—the most **flagrant** form of injustice—will diminish.

2. *No other major democracy uses the death penalty.* No other major democracy—in fact, few other countries of any description—is plagued by a murder rate such as that in the United States. Fewer and fewer Americans can remember the days when unlocked doors were the norm and murder was a rare and terrible offense. In America the murder rate climbed 122 percent between 1963 and 1980. During that same period, the murder rate in New York City increased by almost 400 percent, and the statistics are even worse in many other cities. A study at M.I.T. showed that based on 1970 homicide rates a person who lived in a large American city ran a greater risk of being murdered than an American soldier in World War II ran of being killed in combat. It is not surprising that the laws of each country differ according to differing conditions and traditions. If other countries had our murder problem, the cry for capital punishment would be just as loud as it is here. And I daresay that any other major democracy where 75 percent of the people supported the death penalty would soon enact it into law.

3. *An innocent person might be executed by mistake.* Consider the work of Adam Bedau, one of the most **implacable** foes of capital punishment in this country. According to Mr. Bedau, it is "false sentimentality to argue that the death penalty should be abolished because of the abstract possibility that an innocent person might be executed." He cites a study of the 7,000 executions in this country from 1893 to 1971 and concludes that the record fails to show that such cases occur. The main point, however, is this: If government functioned only when the possibility of error didn't exist, government wouldn't function at all. Human life deserves special protection, and one of the best ways to guarantee that protection is to assure that convicted murderers do not kill again. Only the death penalty can accomplish this end. In a recent case in New Jersey, a man named Richard Biegenwald was freed from prison after serving 18 years for murder; since his release he has been convicted of committing four murders. A prisoner named Lemuel Smith, who, while serving four life sentences for murder (plus two life sentences for kidnapping and robbery) in New York's Green Haven Prison, lured a woman corrections officer into the chaplain's office and strangled her. He then mutilated and dismembered her body. An additional life sentence for Smith is meaningless. Because New York has no death penalty statute, Smith has effectively been given a license to kill.

But the problem of multiple murder is not confined to the nation's penitentiaries. In 1981, 91 police officers were killed in the line of duty in this country. Seven percent of those arrested in the cases that have been solved had a previous arrest for murder. In New York City in 1976 and 1977, 85 persons arrested for homicide had a previous arrest for murder. Six of these individuals had two previous arrests for murder, and one had four previous murder arrests. During those two years, the New York police were arresting for murder persons with a previous arrest for murder on the average of one every 8.5 days. This is not surprising when we learn that in 1975, for example, the median time served in Massachusetts for homicide was less than two-and-a-half years. In 1976 a study sponsored by the Twentieth Century Fund found that the average time served in the United States for first-degree murder is ten years. The median time served may be considerably lower.

10 4. *Capital punishment cheapens the value of human life.* On the contrary, it can be easily demonstrated that the death penalty strengthens the value of human life. If the penalty for rape were lowered, clearly it would signal a lessened regard for the victims' suffering, humiliation, and personal integrity. It would cheapen their horrible experience and expose them to an increased danger of recurrence. When we lower the penalty for murder, it signals a lessened regard for the value of the victim's life. Some critics of capital punishment, such as columnist Jimmy Breslin, have suggested that a life sentence is actually a harsher penalty for murder than death. This is **sophistic** nonsense. A few killers may decide not to appeal a death sentence, but the overwhelming majority makes every effort to stay alive. It is by exacting the highest penalty for the taking of human life that we affirm the highest value of human life.

5. *The death penalty is applied in a* **discriminatory** *manner.* This factor no longer seems to be the problem it once was. The appeals process for a condemned prisoner is lengthy and **painstaking**. Every effort is made to see that the verdict and sentence were fairly arrived at. However, assertions of discrimination are not an argument for ending the death penalty but for extending it. It is not justice to exclude everyone from the penalty of the law if a few are found to be so favored. Justice requires that the law be applied equally to all.

6. *Thou shalt not kill.* The Bible is our greatest source of moral inspiration. Opponents of the death penalty frequently cite the sixth of the Ten Commandments in an attempt to prove that capital punishment is divinely proscribed. In the original Hebrew, however, the sixth commandment reads, "Thou shalt not commit murder," and the Torah specifies capital punishment for a variety of offenses. The biblical viewpoint has been upheld by philosophers throughout history. The greatest thinkers of the 19th century—Kant, Locke, Hobbes, Rousseau, Montesquieu, and Mill—agreed that natural law properly authorizes the **sovereign** to take life in order to vindicate justice.

Only Jeremy Bentham was **ambivalent**. Washington, Jefferson, and Franklin endorsed it. Abraham Lincoln authorized executions for deserters in wartime. Alexis de Tocqueville, who expressed profound respect for American institutions, believed that the death penalty was indispensable to the support of social order. The United States Constitution, widely admired as one of the **seminal** achievements in the history of humanity, condemns cruel and inhuman punishment but does not condemn capital punishment.

7. *The death penalty is state-sanctioned murder.* This is the defense with which Messrs. Willie and Shaw hoped to soften the resolve of those who sentenced them to death. By saying in effect, "You're no better than I am," the murderer seeks to bring his accusers down to his own level. It is also a popular argument among opponents of capital punishment, but a transparently false one. Simply put, the state has rights that the private individual does not. In a democracy, those rights are given to the state by the electorate. The execution of a lawfully condemned killer is no more an act of murder than is legal imprisonment an act of kidnapping. If an individual forces a neighbor to pay him money under threat of punishment, it's called extortion. If the state does it, it's called taxation. Rights and responsibilities surrendered by the individual are what give the state its power to govern. This contract is the foundation of civilization itself.

Everyone wants his or her rights, and will defend them jealously. Not everyone, however, wants responsibilities, especially the painful responsibilities that come with law enforcement. Twenty-one years ago a woman named Kitty Genovese was assaulted and murdered on a street in New York. Dozens of neighbors heard her cries for help but did nothing to assist her. They didn't even call the police. In such a climate, the criminal understandably grows bolder. In the presence of moral cowardice, he lectures us on our supposed failings and tries to equate his crimes with our quest for justice.

15 The death of anyone—even a convicted killer—diminishes us all. But we are diminished even more by a justice system that fails to function. It is an illusion to let ourselves believe that doing away with capital punishment removes the murderer's deed from our conscience. The rights of society are **paramount**. When we protect guilty lives, we give up innocent lives in exchange. When opponents of capital punishment say to the state: "I will not let you kill in my name," they are also saying to murderers: "You can kill in your own name as long as I have an excuse for not getting involved."

It is hard to imagine anything worse than being murdered while neighbors do nothing. But something worse exists. When those same neighbors shrink back from justly punishing the murderer, the victim dies twice.*

---

*"Death and Justice" by Edward J. Koch as appeared in *The New Republic*, April 1985. Reprinted by permission of Edward J. Koch.

Reading Connection

Understanding the Reading

1. What is Koch's position on capital punishment?
2. Review the types of appeals that Koch uses and give examples of each: emotional, ethical, and logical.
3. Which of Koch's counterarguments are the strongest? The weakest? Support your answers.

Understanding the Structure, Style, and Tone

1. How does Koch organize his argument?
2. What technique does Koch use to immediately grab the reader's interest in the beginning of the essay?
3. What logic does Koch use to order his points?
4. What analogies does Koch use, and how believable are they?
5. How would you describe Koch's tone in this essay? Is he angry, dismayed, adamant, calm, rational, belligerent?

Making a Personal Connection

1. After reading Koch's argument in favor of capital punishment, how have your views changed, and what particular points were most effective?
2. Write an essay arguing against capital punishment, using the same structure that Koch uses to support it.

Writing Your Argumentative Essay

Kent, a student majoring in social work, wrote the following essay for a political science class. This essay contains references to Kent's research sources in Modern Language Association (MLA) style. You will learn about research in Chapter 13 and 14, but we present this essay here to demonstrate that research is often necessary to build an effective argument.

The Sound of Falling Money

Cripple Creek, Colorado, was once a quiet mountain town with wooden plank sidewalks, a saddle shop, a couple of bars, and a popular general store where people would stop in on their way through town to someplace else. Today, it's the principle destination of thousands in our state who don't have the time or money to fly to Las Vegas or Reno. The low-key, charming ambience has disappeared, replaced by glitter, neon, and the jingle of falling coins. Some people, for whom gambling is the seed of all evil, lament the passing of the former era; the vast majority, however, for whom gambling is a form of recreation and, at least subconsciously, even the

WRITING Your Argumentative Essay

ultimate chance at a better tomorrow, believe we should have more Cripple Creeks around the country—a slot machine within easy reach at all times.

Gambling has long been part of our nation. Our Revolutionary War armies were funded by the original type of gambling—lotteries. As time passed, gambling took different forms, many of them illegal, or completely faded away in some communities. In the 1920s our nation was introduced to legalized horse and dog races, and in 1931 the state of Nevada changed the southwest forever by allowing casinos to open legally. Soon, states across America started reopening lotteries to help fund state projects. In 1987, the Supreme Court allowed Indian tribes to open casinos on their reservations to help combat harsh living conditions. In 1989, America's Mississippi River valley introduced riverboats that gamblers could get on and wager just as if they were in Las Vegas ("Gambling").

One fact is certain: gambling is controversial wherever it is found. Supporters claim that it is harmless and fun and that it brings wealth to communities; opponents claim that it is addictive and ruinous. Although gambling does carry with it some problems, the benefits far outweigh them, and it is time that we recognize those benefits. With its enormous direct impact on state revenues, the new jobs the industry brings, and the draw for tourism, we should no longer be arguing about this issue.

Since the late 1990s, most states in the Union have been forced to make drastic budget cuts, and they've been prevented from raising taxes by their poorly performing economies. Everyone realizes why we have taxes, but we all hate it when they are raised. But what if there were an alternative way to generate revenue? Legalized gambling offers a solution: it can generate enormous revenue for individual states. By replacing tax initiatives with legalized gambling, states would allow citizens to keep more of their money in the expectation that they would go out and gamble. If current trends continue, this expectation is completely realistic: gambling has taken over as America's favorite pastime by leaps and bounds ("Gambling"). In fact, 82% of all adult Americans gamble in one form or another (Vatz and Weinberg). Gambling could help fund public schools, pay for road improvement projects, or cover the increasing costs of caring for the elderly. Without gambling revenues, these and other needed projects will go begging as they have in the past decade.

In addition to direct revenues that gambling would produce for each state, we need to consider the creation of jobs in local communities. The gambling industry produces an enormous number of jobs. In 1987, the government ruled that Indian tribes could open casinos on reservations to help combat the poverty and unemployment levels. Today, more than 120 Indian casinos are in operation in 28 states ("Gambling"). Just think about the jobs new gambling facilities would produce. First, the casinos or racetracks would need to be built, thus creating construction jobs. Then the facilities would need to be operated and managed, necessitating upper-level management positions, gaming positions, maintenance positions, and so on. Mandalay Resort Group President Glenn Schaeffer put it best when he said casino jobs "are not fast-food jobs" but "jobs you can grow in and support a family on" (qtd. in Smith).

Another benefit of legalized gambling is an increase in tourism. With states putting their residents to work creating spectacular new gambling industries, people from other states would rush in to spend money, thus expanding tourism. Imagine a Las Vegas or Atlantic City in every state, each with its own character and a special offering for the recreational gambler who likes to travel. With more tourism, everyone benefits, from local communities to the state budget.

Even with all the benefits gambling would bring states, adversaries of gambling complain about the so-called pathological or compulsive gamblers. Opponents of gambling tell stories about how it leads to bankruptcy, which in turn leads individuals into a life of crime to pay for their debts and then eventually to suicide because they just can't handle the pressure anymore ("Gambling"). The federal government was so worried about these issues in 1999 that it formed a group called the National Gambling Impact Study Commission (NGISC) with the mission to investigate whether gambling was having a negative effect on society. The NGISC determined through a telephone survey that only 1.4% of gamblers were compulsive gamblers (Vatz and Weinberg). This number is quite low, much lower than even most gamblers would have predicted. However, recognizing that compulsive gambling concerns many, every gaming plan should offer programs, funded from gambling revenues, to help those who appear to be harming themselves through gambling.

Anytime a proposed idea involves gambling, the word *crime* is not far behind. Gambling opponents are quick to point out that Las Vegas did not get its "Sin City" nickname for gambling alone. In the 1880s, the prevalence of unsound money practices caused all state lotteries to be terminated ("Gambling"). Today, big gambling towns are associated with the mob, "fixed" sporting events, and the sex and drug trades. It should be obvious, however, that these associations are the result of the long history of illegal gambling in our country. When gambling is made legal everywhere, crime will cease to be part of its aura over time. If we legalize gambling, it should be easier for police departments to focus their energies on truly criminal activities.

Free people in a free country should be free to gamble—for the vast majority of gamblers, it is a harmless recreational activity. However, if legalization is haphazard or poorly planned and regulated, we will continue to lose out on the many public benefits gambling offers. It is time for states across the United States to take a coordinated look at legalization: they need the revenues to support important public projects, their communities need the tourism dollars that gambling can bring, and their citizens need the high-paying jobs. Let's take a bold step: legalize gambling so that we can all enjoy the winnings.

Works Cited

"Gambling." *Enotes.com*. Enotes, 2004. Web. 5 July 2010.

Smith, Rod. "Casino Proliferation as Key Is Consensus at Global Expo in Las Vegas." *Las Vegas Review-Journal* 18 Sept. 2003: n. pag. *Newspaper Source*. Web. 5 July 2010.

Vatz, Richard E., and Lee S. Weinberg. "Gambling, Psychology and State Politics." *USA Today Magazine* May 2003: n. pag. *Academic Search Premier*. Web. 8 July 2010.

   This argument demonstrates a number of strengths: It employs a variety of writing techniques—cause/effect analysis (common in arguments), as well as description and illustration; it provides plenty of evidence to back up its more general assertions; and it uses transitional devices expertly to connect parts of the argument.

Prewriting

To maximize the effectiveness of your prewriting experience, use as many techniques as you can to give you the best results. Whenever you can't think of additional or interesting information, stop to use another prewriting technique that you feel would be useful.

Discovering and Limiting Your Topic: Combination of Techniques

You may want to start using listing to generate ideas for your claim. To help increase the variety of possible topics, try a more focused listing by dividing your paper into four areas, dedicating each area to a type of claim. Here's how Kent filled out his prewriting chart.

Claims of Fact	Claims of Cause/Effect
The true state of climate change is . . .	Effects of global warming on the West.
Israeli-Palestinian peace talks are productive.	Causes of obesity among the young.
Women are underpaid.	Causes of workplace stress.
Schools have dumbed down education.	Effects of sleep deprivation over time.
Claims of Value	**Claims of Policy**
Our media culture is a good thing.	Attendance policies should be stricter.
The book is still the best way to learn.	Gambling should be legalized.
Digital literacy is an important skill.	Marijuana should be legalized.
Parenting skills are undervalued.	No speed limits should be set on interstate highways.
Mentoring is the best volunteer activity.	Lottery funds should go to education.

Kent identified the following claims during his initial prewriting activity.

1. Schools have dumbed down education.
2. Parenting skills are undervalued.
3. Gambling should be legalized.

WRITING 11-1

Fill in as many claims as possible, spending 5 to 10 minutes on each type of claim. If you get stuck, ask friends and family members for ideas.

Claims of Fact	Claims of Cause/Effect

Claims of Value	Claims of Policy

After you have generated a good list of possible claims, circle the three you feel most interested in and most connected to. Don't worry about making the wrong choice; you can always come back to this list if you change your mind.

Now that you have identified possible issues and claims to write about, choose the one you find most interesting and use freewriting, looping, clustering, branching, diagramming, or a combination of these to generate ideas, recall knowledge you have about your topic, identify arguments for both sides of the issue, and predict what information you may have to research to prove your claim. If you get stuck or lose interest, go on to your next claim, and start generating ideas.

WRITING Your
Argumentative Essay

TOPICS TO CONSIDER

If you're experiencing writer's block, review the following list of topics. If you choose from this list, be sure to narrow the topic and make a claim so that you can create your thesis.

Writing for College		
▪ U.S. involvement in an-other country ▪ Censorship of the arts	▪ A national DNA databank ▪ Immigration reforms	▪ Media's effect on elections ▪ NAFTA

Writing in Your Profession			
BUSINESS	▪ Corporate responsibility ▪ Surveillance of employees	▪ Pay based on performance ▪ Marketing to children	▪ Government bailouts ▪ CEO compensation
CRIMINAL JUSTICE	▪ Plea bargaining ▪ Prisoners' rights	▪ Education for prisoners ▪ Racial profiling	▪ Early-release programs ▪ Miranda rule
EDUCATION	▪ School uniforms ▪ Scholarships based on ethnicity	▪ Drug testing in schools ▪ Decisions based on stan-dardized tests	▪ Metal detectors in public schools ▪ School vouchers
HEALTH	▪ Universal health care ▪ Smoking banned from all public places	▪ Physician-assisted suicide ▪ Vegetarianism	▪ Obesity ▪ Alternative medicine
SOCIAL WORK/ PSYCHOLOGY	▪ Mentally handicapped tried for murder ▪ Violence in the Media	▪ Gay marriages or adoptions ▪ Use of drugs to treat depression	▪ Welfare policies and practices
TECHNICAL	▪ Internet regulation, taxa-tion, or censorship ▪ V-chip curbing children's viewing of television violence	▪ Downloading or intellectual property, music, and videos ▪ Video games depicting vio-lence controversy	▪ Outsourcing of computer techni-cian jobs ▪ Cell phones
OTHERS	▪ Hate-crime laws ▪ English as the official language	▪ Opening of the borders to immigrants ▪ Electoral College	▪ Social networking ▪ English-only law

Writing in Everyday Life		
▪ A letter to your congress-man encouraging support of a certain issue	▪ A letter to the editor pro-testing a change in a city ordinance	▪ A letter to a family member arguing for more equitable distri-bution of a rela-tive's legacy

Identifying Your Audience

For the argumentative essay, you might start by classifying the audiences into four general types; each type requires a personal approach, as shown in Figure 11.4. An important aspect of crafting an effective argument is to consider the ways that you can connect with your audience. Of course, evidence combined with reasoning is your main tool for convincing your reader of the strength of your argument, but appeals to character and emotion can also be powerful when used effectively.

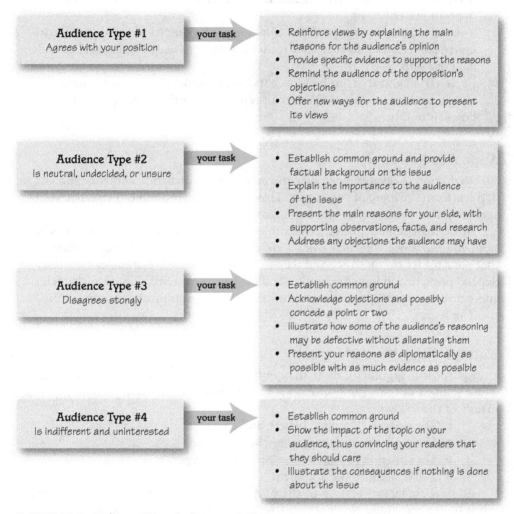

Audience Type #1
Agrees with your position

your task

- Reinforce views by explaining the main reasons for the audience's opinion
- Provide specific evidence to support the reasons
- Remind the audience of the opposition's objections
- Offer new ways for the audience to present its views

Audience Type #2
Is neutral, undecided, or unsure

your task

- Establish common ground and provide factual background on the issue
- Explain the importance to the audience of the issue
- Present the main reasons for your side, with supporting observations, facts, and research
- Address any objections the audience may have

Audience Type #3
Disagrees stongly

your task

- Establish common ground
- Acknowledge objections and possibly concede a point or two
- Illustrate how some of the audience's reasoning may be defective without alienating them
- Present your reasons as diplomatically as possible with as much evidence as possible

Audience Type #4
Is indifferent and uninterested

your task

- Establish common ground
- Show the impact of the topic on your audience, thus convincing your readers that they should care
- Illustrate the consequences if nothing is done about the issue

FIGURE 11.4 *Audience Types in Argumentation*

Appeal to Character

When you appeal to character, you show yourself to be a writer and thinker who is fair minded, objective, thoughtful, and caring about a topic. You establish your credibility with the following:

1. **Language.** Avoid overly emotional or inflammatory language. For example, don't refer to the opposition, or their views, as *ignorant* and *stupid*. Instead, discuss them as people who need to examine the totality of the issue to understand its complexity.

2. **Addressing objections to your side.** Avoid just dismissing your opposition's objections as unimportant. Instead, take them seriously, concede a point if necessary, and reassure your reader that you have thought carefully about the opposition's concerns.
3. **Tone.** Tone ties in with your use of language. Be sure to adopt a conciliatory, understanding tone so that your reader is willing to keep reading and considering your side.
4. **Style.** Tone and style go hand in hand. Use formal diction to maintain an educated tone, and use variety in sentence length so that the essay flows smoothly.

Appeal to Emotion

An overly emotional argument alienates an educated, analytical audience and detracts from the logic of your paper. However, some emotion can enhance your argument if you use it sparingly and appropriately.

By dramatizing an idea or situation, especially in the introduction or conclusion, you can move your idea from a mere abstraction to a level of concreteness that your reader can both see and feel. Although an effective argument should depend primarily on logic (reasoning and evidence), you may appeal to character and emotion at appropriate times. Your skills in description and narration can come in handy.

Establishing Your Purpose

Your purpose in argument, more than in other types of writing, depends on the whole context of the writing situation. The elements of the writing context consist mainly of the following:

- The writer's thoughts, beliefs, and concerns
- The reader's thoughts, beliefs, and concerns
- The situation in which the writing is presented
- The content of the argument

All of these factors add up to the purpose of the argument, and the writer's job is to connect these elements into a coherent whole. As you plan your essay, keep in mind that the more in depth is your analysis of each of these elements, the more confident you will feel about the effectiveness and the success of your paper.

WRITING   11-2

Look at your writing context and answer the following questions.

Your claim: _____

You the Writer

1. Why is this topic important to you? Why does it interest you? _____
   _____

2. On a scale of 1–10, how strongly do you feel about your claim? _____
   _____

3. Do you already have assumptions or opinions about the topic you plan to
   research? _____
   _____

4. What is your attitude or opinion about this topic? _____
   _____

5. How much do you already know about this topic? _____
   _____

6. Do you know your reader personally? _____
   _____

7. What do you and your reader have in common? _____
   _____

Your Reader

1. What audience (person or group) would benefit most from your writing? _____
   _____

2. How agreeable is your audience to your claim? Is your audience against it?
   _____

3. What would your reader gain from your essay? _____
   _____

4. What previous knowledge does the audience have of your topic? _____
   _____

5. What information does your audience need? _____
   _____

Your Writing Situation

1. Is this topic related to another class, a particular project, a strongly held personal belief, or something else? _____

_____

2. What format, requirements, or constraints must you observe? _____

_____

Your Content

1. What kind of sources do you need to consult? _____

_____

2. What information do you need first? _____

_____

3. What kind of source is likely to supply it? _____

4. Review your answers and reflect on your writing context. At this point, what strategies do you feel can help make your essay effective: illustration, process, classification, cause/effect, comparison/contrast, definition? _____

_____

5. What pattern should you use to organize your essay? _____

Your Purpose

1. What effect do you want your essay to have on your audience? _____

_____

Setting Your Tone

After you have chosen an audience, you must keep that audience in mind as you are crafting your sentences to avoid alienating, insulting, or offending them.

- **Use appropriate language.** Although you most likely feel passionate and emotional about your topic, don't let your word choice reflect such emotions as anger, impatience, or intolerance. As a reasonable thinker, use tactful, courteous language.
- **Establish common ground.** Most argument topics have reasons with which most people can agree. For example, if you are discussing whether the death penalty should be allowed, you could certainly mention that we all value human life. If the topic is whether a specific class should be a re-quirement, couldn't we all agree that we value knowledge and education?

Formulating Your Thesis

Your thesis, also known as your claim or proposition, should have the following characteristics:

1. **Your thesis should express your opinion.** Not all opinions make good argumentative topics. For example, the statements "This is the best spaghetti sauce this side of the Mississippi" or "After 50 years of rock n' roll, Elvis is still my favorite performer" are definitely opinions; however, they would not be suitable as an argumentative thesis because they are merely personal preferences.

2. **Your thesis should be debatable.** If you can't imagine someone disagreeing with your claim, you have no argument. Which of the following statements would make a good thesis?

    - Building more prisons is the best way to deal with our growing prison population.
    - The prison population continues to increase annually.

   If you chose the first statement, you're correct. A large audience would disagree with this claim. Your opponents may well argue that we should, instead, reduce the penalties for victimless crimes to create prison space for major felony convictions. The point is that such statements create disagreement and can, therefore, engage the reader in a debate. The second example is a simple statement of fact requiring no proof; therefore, there is no issue to debate.

3. **Your thesis should be focused.** As you are deciding on a topic, be careful that you don't take on too broad of a topic, not allowing you to convince your reader of anything. For example, a popular topic for argument is whether or not children should have to wear uniforms to school. To focus the topic, ask yourself the following questions:

    - What age group could I concentrate on?
    - What location or types of schools could be discussed—urban, suburban, rural, charter public, private?
    - To whom should I write this argument?

4. **Your thesis should include three main parts:**

    - The topic
    - The claim (opinion)
    - The reasons to support your opinion

   Examine the following thesis statements:

    - Children of illegal immigrants should be provided with basic human services such as health care and schooling so that they don't miss out on important aspects of their development.
    - The arts should be required as core classes in K–12 because they help students develop self-esteem, thinking and listening skills, discipline, and coordination.

Armed with a good claim and a good awareness of the writing context, you can confidently write your thesis. Don't forget the equation:

Thesis = Topic/Issue + Claim/Position + Focus (Reason for Claim)

Here is how Kent phrased his thesis initially.

> Gambling's destructive and addictive side is not sufficient reason to keep gambling illegal; gambling should be legalized in every state in the Union.

As you can see from Kent's working thesis, your thesis doesn't need to be perfect at this stage. If you are bothered by his beginning with the negative "destructive and addictive behavior," you are correct because this phrase actually works against his claim in the minds of some readers. As Kent drafts and revises his essay, he has plenty of opportunities to polish his thesis statement. But for now, he has a debatable issue, a claim that he feels strongly about, and a focus.

WRITING   11-3

Take a few minutes to review your analysis of your own writing context, as well as some ideas you generated from your prewriting activities, and then write your thesis here.

Working thesis: _____

_____

Outlining Your Ideas

Before you start your outline, create a list of arguments on both sides of your topic. Such a list is called a *pro/con list* because it lists arguments in favor of your thesis (pro) and arguments against your thesis (con). Draw arrows from the argument in the Pro column to its matching argument in the Con column. If there's no match, leave it alone.

This can help you determine how you can best organize the information in your outline. For example, you can use the points that match in the refutation section of your paper: You argue against them to prove your claim. If all points match, you might consider using pattern C to organize your essay (see page 363). However, if you have stand-alone points, you may want to handle those separately, in which case, perhaps pattern A or B may be your choice. Examine Kent's pro/con list.

Topic: Legalized gambling

Thesis: Every state should legalize gambling.

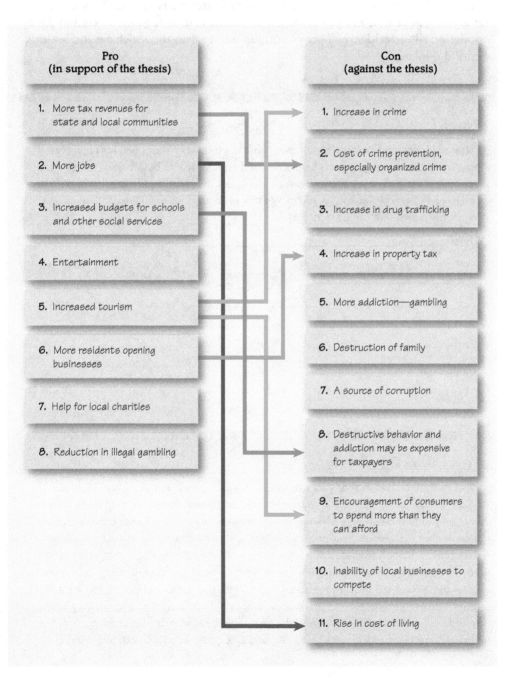

Pro (in support of the thesis)	Con (against the thesis)
1. More tax revenues for state and local communities	1. Increase in crime
2. More jobs	2. Cost of crime prevention, especially organized crime
3. Increased budgets for schools and other social services	3. Increase in drug trafficking
4. Entertainment	4. Increase in property tax
5. Increased tourism	5. More addiction—gambling
6. More residents opening businesses	6. Destruction of family
7. Help for local charities	7. A source of corruption
8. Reduction in illegal gambling	8. Destructive behavior and addiction may be expensive for taxpayers
	9. Encouragement of consumers to spend more than they can afford
	10. Inability of local businesses to compete
	11. Rise in cost of living

Creating a pro/con list is a good way of testing whether you have sufficient evidence to argue your case, at the same time permitting you to anticipate opposing arguments. If during this activity you discover a better focus for your thesis, don't hesitate to change it; it's not uncommon for students to change their position after considering all the evidence. There's nothing wrong with this. Such are the rewards of critical thinking.

WRITING 11-4

You should feel ready to create your own pro/con list on your issue. See how many valid points you can come up with on both sides of the issue. Talk to others who can give you good arguments. First ask them how they feel about the issue, and then ask why. When you have as many arguments as you can gather on both sides of your topic, use arrows to match the points that can be matched.

Thesis: _____

Pro	Con
1.	1.
2.	2.
3.	3.
4.	4.
5.	5.

WRITING 11-5

What pattern works best for your audience, purpose, and writing situation? Refresh your memory of the patterns on pages 362–363. Choose the outline that works best for you, and write it down on a separate piece of paper. As you write your outline, don't assume that each point takes only one paragraph to discuss. If you need to use more than one paragraph to discuss a particular topic sentence, make sure that your transitions establish the relationship between or among those paragraphs. Let your reader know that you're still proving the same point. Also, the number of points you want to include in your argument is up to you. Although it's unlikely that one or two points would be sufficient evidence (unless the evidence is indisputable and convincing), always consider your audience, purpose, and writing situation when determining the content of your paper.

Drafting

As you enter the drafting stage of the writing process, keep in mind the parts of the argumentative essay shown in Figure 11.5.

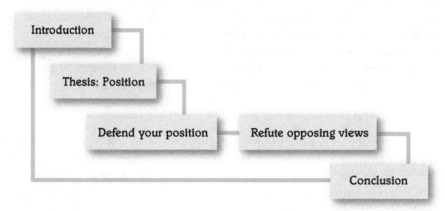

FIGURE 11.5 *Parts of the Argumentative Essay*

Writing Your Introduction

In your introduction, you want to grab the reader's attention, establish your credibility and authority, and provide background information on the issue.

In addition to other lead-in techniques, you should supply some background on the topic so that your reader understands the basics. Don't assume that your reader fully understands the topic or shares your level of knowledge before you start supporting a particular stance. As you define the issue, be as objective as possible. Don't argue in your introduction; save your argument for the body of your paper. Your goal in the introduction is to introduce your thesis, not to defend your position.

Examine Kent's first draft of his introduction and his working thesis.

> **Computer Tip!** As you draft, revise, or proofread, keep a journal page open, and write down questions and concerns as they occur to you throughout the writing process. At the end of each writing assignment, attempt to answer these questions yourself, ask your peers, or ask your instructor.

Gambling is a practice that dates back to the start of our nation. Our Revolutionary War armies were funded by the original type of gambling, lotteries ("Gambling"). As time passed, gambling evolved and at times faded away. In the 1920s our nation was introduced to horse races and dog races; then in 1931 the state of Nevada would change the southwest forever by allowing casinos to open. Soon states all across America started reopening lotteries to help fund state projects.

WRITING Your Argumentative Essay

> In 1987, the Supreme Court allowed Native American tribes to open casinos on
> their reservations to help combat harsh living conditions. In 1989, America's
> Mississippi River valley introduced riverboats that gamblers could get on and
> wager just as if they were in Las Vegas ("Gambling"). Gambling's destructive and
> addictive side is not sufficient reason to keep gambling illegal; gambling should be
> legalized in every state in the Union. With the enormous amount of new revenue
> for states, all the new jobs the industry brings, the draw for tourism, and simply
> because we live in a free nation and gambling is fun, this shouldn't even be an
> issue. Every state should legalize and expand its gambling practices.

Kent's introduction is a brief history of gambling. This information may be important, but Kent fails to establish its importance to the thesis. His working thesis definitely limits and focuses the issue, but there is little connection to the history that Kent offers to introduce the thesis. By limiting his lead-in to just the history, Kent seems to imply that his only argument is that "gambling has always been and will continue to be, so get over it." It is not likely that many readers would be interested in reading further.

Start writing your introduction for your argumentative essay by completing the next activity.

WRITING 11-6

Start drafting your introduction. As you create the draft, consider the following qualities:

1. Your introduction should engage your reader, making the reader want to read more.
2. Your introduction should establish the tone of your paper and assert your character as a reasonable, critical thinker.
3. If necessary, use your introduction to build common ground.
4. Your introduction should make your topic clear and let the reader know why your topic is important.
5. Through your introduction, you should give your reader all information necessary to understand the issue, the controversy, and your position on the controversy.
6. Your introduction should contain a thesis that lets the reader know the position you are defending, gives the reader an idea of how you organize the information, and helps the reader understand the type of evidence you provide.

Writing Your Body Paragraphs

Examine these two body paragraphs from Kent's essay: the third pro from his first draft that defends his position and one con refuting a point of opposition.

Pro #3

In addition, people from other states would be rushing to gambling states to spend money, thus expanding tourism. Believe it or not, Nevada is hoping for gambling expansion itself. Since many of the slot machines are made in Nevada and since the Nevada market is mostly tapped out, state officials are hoping for some out-of-state customers. Imagine a Las Vegas in every state, each with a special offering for the recreational gambler who likes to travel. Therefore, gambling needs to be leveled across the board so that the high rollers could land anywhere and have a casino or racetrack where they can lay their money down. With more tourism, everyone benefits: local communities and Uncle Sam as well.

In this paragraph, Kent starts with a transition and a topic sentence—not a bad first attempt. He can still come back and improve his topic sentence and opening transition. He can also build on his examples and details and provide stronger evidence. The point is that Kent has the foundation of an essay when he starts to revise it.

Con #1

Even with all the great things that gambling would bring states, opponents of gambling cry out about the so-called pathological or compulsive gamblers. Anti-gamblers tell stories that gambling may easily lead to bankruptcy, which in turn leads individuals into a life of crime to pay for their debts, eventually ending in suicide because they just can't handle the pressure anymore. The government was so worried about it in 1999 that it put together a group called the National Gambling Impact Study Commission (NGISC). The commission was to investigate whether gambling was having a negative effect on society (Vatz and Weinberg). This is where reality sets in. For something to be addictive, it has to change the composition of your body in some way. Gambling does no such thing (Vatz and Weinberg). Life is full of "adult decisions" and gambling is one of them. If individuals gamble themselves into bankruptcy, they are not addicts; they are choosing to act recklessly (Vatz and Weinberg). But to appease the weak minded, every gaming plan should have programs put in place and money set aside from revenue to finance these programs that council and help these so-called addicts.

Kent draws heavily from his sources in this paragraph refuting the opposition's claim. He may need to rethink the value of some of his information. Does he need to go into more history? What information do you feel is irrelevant? Initially, there's never too much information. Always remember that it's easier to cut information than to add it.

Coherence: Using Transitions

The following list of transitions focuses on two areas that help your argument flow smoothly: emphasizing key points and granting points to opposing arguments. As you consider the most effective and appropriate transitions to connect your ideas, keep in mind that your transitions must appear naturally and help your essay read smoothly. If you feel that your paper sounds choppy, refer to this and other lists of transitions in previous chapters to help glue your ideas together.

Transitions to Help Emphasize Key Points		
above all	in truth	there is no question that
again	main problem, issue, concern	to add to that
as a matter of fact	major point, reason, argument for	to clarify
as noted	more importantly	to emphasize
certainly	most dramatic	to repeat
chiefly	obviously	to stress
definitely	of course	to underscore
in any case	of greater concern	truly
in any event	of greater consequence	unquestionably
indeed	once again	without doubt
in effect	surely	without fail
in fact	that is	without question
Transitions to Help Grant or Concede a Point		
after all	naturally	to agree
although	no doubt	to concur
although this may be true	of course	unfortunately
at the same time	to acknowledge	while it is true
granted (that)	to admit	

WRITING 11-7

Start creating the body of your first draft. Your goal is to prove your thesis. Follow these guidelines.

1. Follow your outline. Make any changes to the outline that you feel help your essay.
2. Choose the most effective pattern for organizing your argument. Consider your purpose in light of your writing context. Again, you can always change your mind. The goal now is to start.
3. Start each of your body paragraphs with a clear topic sentence. During the revising stage, you may change the position of your topic sentence but, for now, keeping it as the first sentence may keep you focused on the main point of the paragraph as you provide supporting evidence.
4. Use appeals to character and emotions effectively.
5. Add transitions to keep your ideas flowing smoothly and to guide your audience through your information.
6. If you run out of ideas in any of your paragraphs, stop and use one or more prewriting techniques to get your creative juices flowing.

Writing Your Conclusion

In his conclusion, Kent attempts to do three things: emphasize his claim, give his essay a sense of closure by summing up his key points, and leave the reader with something to think about. He doesn't want the reader to end the essay wondering, "So what?" He wants to show that his essay is meaningful, leaves a lasting impression, and perhaps incites the reader to action.

> Between the enjoyment of gambling and the chance of hitting it big, free people in a free country should be free to gamble. If you take away the fact that the generated revenue would be a gigantic help to state budgets and the industry would employ countless number of people, and take away that gamers wouldn't be able to wait for their next trip to a new town to try their luck, then gambling simply adds a fun element to life. So before states start cutting money from public schools or nursing home budgets, we need to support legalized gambling.

Kent has made a bold start; you see in his final draft how he builds on his strengths during revision.

WRITING 11-8

Write a conclusion for your argumentative essay. Here are some ideas:

1. Let the reader understand the importance and significance of your topic.
2. If you choose to summarize your key points, don't just repeat the same points mechanically. You can be sure that your reader hasn't forgotten them. Instead, show how these points are vital evidence in proving your thesis.
3. Consider using an emotional appeal, but be careful not to overdo it.
4. Pose a question so that you leave your reader pondering something.
5. Emphasize the urgency of the issue by making a call for action.
6. Build on or refer to a scenario, example, description, or anecdote that may have been in your introduction. This approach not only gives cohesiveness to your essay but also lets the reader know that you have accomplished your goal.
7. Read your introduction and then your conclusion to make sure that there's a smooth connection between both.

Revising

Start the revising stage with this question: Do you feel you have accomplished your goal? Review your first draft; circle the strengths and underline the weaknesses as you perceive them. How can you build on your strengths?

Style Tip: Use Appropriate Levels of Formality

When you communicate with friends, you may rely on slang, clipped words, and even made-up words in conversation. Your use of language in this case is informal. In contrast, when you speak to an instructor, an employer, or a government official, you tend to be more formal. In writing, you also choose levels of formality based on your audience.

Bridging Knowledge

For more information about levels of formality, go to Handbook Chapter 9b, 9c, 9d.

As you edit your argumentative essay, pay close attention to your word choice. Because the audience for an argument tends to be precise and critical, using a style that is too informal hurts your credibility as a writer. Avoid slang and colloquial expressions, and beware of words that don't convey precise meaning, such as the following:

awesome	great	thing
bad	incredible	well ("Well, the next effect is even more incredible.")
fantastic	nice	
good	terrible	back in the day

WRITING

My introduction seems dull, vague, undeveloped, and/ or not engaging.

→

1. Did you analyze your writing context? Argumentative essays usually address audiences who may not be receptive to your point of view. Try building common ground in your introduction.

2. Is the background information you offered meaningful? You need to show your reader that you understand the issue, so offer relevant background information that leads to the purpose of your argument.

3. Does your introduction grab the reader's attention? When you have a clear idea of your audience, use a strategy that is most likely to interest that reader. Review the various strategies for developing your lead-in.

4. Did you establish an appropriate tone for your audience and purpose? Your reader needs to see you as a reasonable and credible writer. Don't start with a combative tone or with emotional outbursts that alienate your reader. That first impression is crucial.

5. Is your thesis clearly stated and placed in a logical position? Nothing bothers a reader more than not knowing what to expect.

WRITING

My paragraphs don't seem to be developed enough, nor does my evidence seem too convincing. What should I add?

→

1. Employ any technique that effectively proves your point:

   a. **Illustration.** What examples can you give to illustrate your points?

   b. **Classification.** In any of your paragraphs, can you explain your points by breaking down your idea into categories?

   c. **Comparison/contrast.** Discuss similarities, differences, or both. Compare an idea, concept, or practice to one with which your audience can easily identify. Offer a simile to connect the familiar with the unfamiliar.

   d. **Definition.** Are there any abstract or technical terms that you should define? Perhaps there's a term that you are using differently from how it's normally used.

   e. **Cause/effect.** Are there reasons, consequences (results), or both that you need to explain or clarify?

   f. **Process.** In any of your paragraphs, would it help to explain how something occurred or how a situation developed?

2. Do you offer sufficient, relevant, accurate information? Make sure that you have enough evidence to prove your topic sentences and to help your reader follow your argument. If your instructor approves, conduct research.

WRITING Your Argumentative Essay

<table>
<tr><td>

WRITING

My conclusion is too brief and abrupt.

</td><td>

1. Does your conclusion effectively wrap up your process? If not, see how you can make your conclusion meaningful by stressing the importance of your thesis, referring to some point or example that you made in your introduction, or both, thus bringing your reader full circle.

2. Does your conclusion attempt to connect with the reader? Try to show how the issue can impact the reader's life, challenge the reader to be part of the solution, or urge action. You might also leave your reader with a profound question that lingers.

</td></tr>
<tr><td>

ARGUMENT

My refutation doesn't seem just right. Also, I seem to rely less on evidence and reasoning in some places and more on just stating my feelings and beliefs.

</td><td>

1. If appropriate, use a transitional paragraph to introduce your refutation. Review your main arguments, and then end with a sentence or two that indicates you are moving to the refutation, for example, "But these points are not readily accepted. Opponents of this policy offer three main objections: X, Y, and Z."

2. Make sure that when you introduce your opponents' points, your transitions and lead-ins make the distinction that these are not your arguments but your counterarguments. Without proper transitions, your reader might start a paragraph believing that you changed your position.

3. Are the points you're refuting important claims made by your opponents or just easy claims to refute? Your opponents want you to address their questions to their satisfaction; don't run away from the hard questions.

4. Do you remain focused on your opponents' issue? Check carefully for logical fallacies, especially red herrings. It's easy to stray from points that you don't believe in and go more into emotional appeals than into reason and logic. Get the facts. Facts are what eventually prove your case.

</td></tr>
</table>

WRITING 11-9

Start your revision. Don't leave any part of your essay untouched.

- Be sure your evidence is relevant, representative, and sufficient.
- Be sure to respond to opposing arguments that are valid.
- Check for coherence. Make sure you offer enough transitions to help guide your reader.
- Be sure that your tone or diction doesn't alienate your reader.
- Review your paper carefully to remove any logical fallacies it may contain.
- Use a variety of sentence types to spice up your paper.

Collaborative Critical Thinking

Asking Your Peers

After you have completed the writing process and have a polished final draft, exchange papers with a classmate for peer review. Use the following form to answer questions about your peer's paper.

1. Who is the writer? Who is the peer reviewer?
2. Briefly describe the method or methods the writer uses to introduce the thesis. Do these methods of introduction grab your interest? Explain.
3. Underline the thesis statement in the essay. Is the thesis clear? Does the writer limit the topic? What is the writer's position on the topic?
4. Where does the writer give background information on the topic? Is the information clear and relevant?
5. What additional information do you feel the writer should supply in the introduction?
6. How does the writer support his or her views (examples, statistics, facts, testimony, and so on)? Is the support sufficient?
7. Which point has the least support? What might the writer add?
8. Is the majority of the support based on research? Is it effective?
9. Should the writer include more research? Is the research well integrated?
10. Has all information that is not the writer's personal experiences or observations been properly documented?
11. Does the writer refute at least two opposing views? How convincing is the refutation? Explain.
12. What might the writer add?
13. Circle any points that are illogical, confusing, or ambiguous.
14. Give examples of how the writer appeals to the reader (reason, ethics, emotions, and character).
15. Is the conclusion effective?
16. If you were neutral or opposed to this opinion, would you be convinced or at least have an understanding of this opinion after reading this essay? Why or why not?

Proofreading

One of the more difficult grammatical concepts to understand, much less execute correctly, is the use of commas with modifying phrases or clauses. As you continue editing for the major errors covered in this book, add the following to your grammar toolkit.

Common Error #12: Misusing Commas with Restrictive or Nonrestrictive Elements

A *restrictive element* is necessary to the meaning of a sentence. It "restricts" or limits the meaning of the noun it modifies.

RESTRICTIVE ELEMENT: The woman wearing the blue dress got up to leave.

The phrase "wearing the blue dress" is restrictive because it restricts the meaning of the sentence to one particular woman. The other women present in this case, presumably, did not get up to leave.

Do not use commas to separate restrictive elements from the rest of the sentence:

INCORRECT: The collie, sitting near the back of the cage, is the one she wants.

CORRECT: The collie sitting near the back of the cage is the one she wants.

A *nonrestrictive element* may look like a restrictive element, but it does not restrict the meaning of the sentence. It simply adds additional information; if you were to remove a nonrestrictive element, the meaning of the sentence would be the same.

NONRESTRICTIVE ELEMENT: That gentleman, who graduated with my father, has made a fortune in the car business.

Use commas to separate nonrestrictive elements from the rest of the sentence.

Bridging Knowledge

See Handbook Chapter 12a for complete information on the use of commas to set off nonrestrictive elements.

INCORRECT: Her son's present which had dropped from her hand was run over by a bus.

CORRECT: Her son's present, which had dropped from her hand, was run over by a bus.

Applying Previous Knowledge

Be sure to check your essay for the most common errors presented in previous chapters.

Common Error #1	Sentence Fragments	
handbook H-1b	**fragment:** Because he was angry.	☐
	better: I left early because he was angry.	

Common Error #2	Shifts in Verb Tense
handbook **H-5c**	She got off the bus and then ~~walks~~ **walked** to the corner. ☐

Common Error #3	Fused Sentences
handbook **H-2a**	**fused:** I left early they_were angry. **better:** I left early. They were angry. ☐

Common Error #4	Comma Splices
handbook **H-2b**	**comma splice:** I left early, they were angry. **better:** I left early. They were angry. ☐

Common Error #5	Commas after Introductory Clauses and Phrases

handbook **H-12a**	■ When you start a sentence with a subordinate conjunction—*although, as, because, before, even though, if, since, unless, when, while,* and so on—use a comma **after the introductory clause.** ☐
	  <u>Because I was late,</u> they left me behind.
	■ When you start with a long prepositional phrase or two or more prepositional phrases, use a comma. ☐
	  <u>Near the park by the elementary school,</u> the officer found the stolen car.
	■ When you start with a participial phrase (-*ing*, -*ed*, -irregular past participle), use a comma. ☐
	  ● <u>Throwing the glass against the wall,</u> John left angrily.
	  ● <u>Wanted by the FBI,</u> the fugitive left the country.
	  ● <u>Written in 1802,</u> the novel was a success.

Common Error #6	Shift in Person
handbook **H-4d**	**shift from third to second person:** A <u>student</u> should get a topic approved so **you** don't waste time. ☐ **better:** <u>Students</u> should get a topic approved so **they** don't waste time.

Common Error #7	Pronoun–Antecedent Agreement
handbook H-4a	A **person** should know what ~~they are~~ **she or he is** doing. Be careful with indefinite pronouns (*everyone, everybody, somebody, something, each, every,* and so on); they take singular pronouns. **Everyone** decided to go ~~their~~ **his or her** separate way. ☐

Common Error #8	Pronoun Reference
handbook H-4b	● Rita skis and plays tennis. ~~This~~ **Her participation in these sports** shows her interest in sports. ● At the flea market, ~~they~~ **the vendors** sold new and used merchandise. ☐

Common Error #9	Pronoun Case
handbook H-4c	● The president, treasurer, and ~~me~~ **I** examined the proposal. ☐

Common Error #10	Lack of Agreement between Subject and Verb
handbook H-3	Each of the candidates ~~have~~ **has** addressed the issue. ☐

Common Error #11	Missing or Misplaced Apostrophe
handbook H-13a	● The ~~speakers~~ **speaker's** assumptions irritated the audience. ● The **painter's** ~~painters~~ did not want the ladder removed form ~~it's~~ **its** present position. ☐

WRITING 11-10

Start proofreading your own essay. Check for and correct any grammatical errors. Look for other obvious errors in spelling, punctuation, and so on.

Final Checklist

1. Does your introduction define the issue and offer essential background information? Does it lead smoothly to the thesis? ☐

2. Does the thesis assert a position on an issue that is clear and arguable? ☐

3. Is the organization of your essay effective? ☐

4. Does the essay offer sufficient evidence for each reason? Is the evidence informative and persuasive? ☐

5. Does your essay consider valid opposing arguments and offer logical responses to each counterargument or effectively concede a point? ☐

6. Is the tone, diction, or manner of expression appropriate and effective for your audience? ☐

7. Does your essay provide sufficient and effective transitional devices to guide the reader through the argument, particularly when you shift from your side to the opposition's reasoning? ☐

8. Does your paper demonstrate mastery over the basics in sentence completeness (no fragments), structure (no fused sentences or comma splices), sentence variety, and word choice? ☐

9. Did you edit carefully for possible errors in grammar, spelling, and punctuation? ☐

Reflecting

You are completing one of the most difficult writing assignments in this course, the argument. It has involved all of the skills you learned in previous chapters plus several additional ones. Take some time to reflect on what you have accomplished.

WRITING 11-11

Self-Reflection

Before you hand in your paper, write a brief paragraph in which you reflect on your final draft. Include your feelings on the following questions:

1. What peer suggestions do you find most useful? What should you change to address the suggestions?
2. What are you most proud of in this essay?
3. What is the weakest aspect of the essay?
4. What type of comments or feedback on this essay do you think would be most helpful to your writing progress?
5. What should you do differently as you write the next essay?

After you have completed this self-reflection, carefully review your instructor's comments. How are they similar or different from your own answers to the self-reflection? Make a list of your grammar, punctuation, and spelling errors so that you can follow up on the ones that recur. Consider what strategies you will employ to address your challenges or weaknesses and to improve the quality of your essay.

How might you use argument outside of this English course? Look back at the writing samples in Previewing Your Task in this chapter.

- **College:** _____
- **Your profession:** _____
- **Everyday life:** _____

Making Choices: Developing an Integrated Essay

"Writing became such a process of discovery that I couldn't wait to get to work in the morning: I wanted to know what I was going to say."

— Sharon O'Brien

YOUR GOALS

Understanding the Integrated Essay

1. Demonstrate an understanding of the choices necessary for an effective integrated essay.
2. Analyze the interrelationship among audience, purpose, and writing situation.

Connecting Reading to Writing

1. Demonstrate an understanding of effective reading strategies.
2. Increase your vocabulary.
3. Analyze readings for comprehension, structure, tone, and style.
4. Show a personal connection to topics introduced by professional writers.

Writing Your Integrated Essay

1. Use visual approaches to determine topics and strategies.
2. Mix and match writing techniques creatively.
3. Create various drafts to produce a more effective and polished final draft.
4. Review your draft for style, grammar, and punctuation.
5. Write an essay that demonstrates unity, coherence, and completeness.
6. Proofread for common grammar errors.

Access grammar exercises for this section in your English CourseMate, available through CengageBrain.com.

Y ou are assigned different papers to write for different courses, each with different expectations. Some instructors have clear guidelines; for example, your history instructor asks you to write on the consequences of a certain treaty, making your choice of strategy easier because you are given the primary pattern of development—effects. However, some instructors allow you to choose any topic relevant to the course, unit, or period. You've studied many patterns of organizing your essay. But how do you approach such open-ended writing tasks?

Let's Warm Up!

You have already gained a lot of experience in writing essays. You are also aware that good writing is the result of careful planning and revision. Nonetheless, there's always a degree of uncertainty and at times apprehension about whether your writing is worth submitting to your instructor. Reflect for a few minutes on the essays you've written in this and other courses, and then write a paragraph in which you discuss the qualities of an effective essay. What makes an essay work?

Banana Stock/Jupiter Images

You have some ideas to make your workplace more effective. Your supervisor likes your ideas and asks you to write them up and submit them to management. Should you just list your ideas? Should you explain the events that led to your ideas? Should you recommend how your ideas can be implemented efficiently? Should you compare your plan to what is currently being done?

Your growing appreciation for writing as a way of thinking has prompted you to write regularly at home. Each evening, you sit down at the computer and work on blogs, e-mails, or discussion boards that you participate in for your own enjoyment. Your writing takes many forms, combining and recombining all the techniques you have learned in your composition class. Nonetheless, each evening as you sit down to write, your first questions are "How should I begin, what's my topic today, and how will I approach it?"

In this chapter, we focus on the variety of choices you have as a writer and suggest ways you can sharpen your critical thinking skills by applying previous knowledge to new writing situations. This chapter follows a different pattern from previous writing chapters. Its purpose is to challenge your creative side and cause you to think in new ways about your writing.

Previewing Your Task

As you plan your writing, you're faced with many choices. To highlight and illustrate some of these choices, we preview one integrated essay whose author makes some interesting decisions to achieve his purpose.

Angered and frustrated by his peers' passivity on social issues, Claude, a non-traditional student majoring in computer information systems, writes an essay on political involvement using a variety of tools to explain his thesis. After analyzing his writing context, he establishes the following audience, purpose, and effect:

Audience: People who feel powerless and disenfranchised and those passive critics who don't exercise their right to vote

Purpose: To convince my audience that each individual can make a difference

Effect: Make my audience feel empowered, show them that they can make a difference, and, hopefully, have them take action

Approach: I want my audience to feel that I'm one of them, and like them, I can make a difference. In a sense, I'd like to be their conscience. I also want them to see me as someone who's been there, is knowledgeable, and is now aware of his social responsibilities.

As you read Claude's essay, refer to the explanatory notes provided in the margin. Also, note the use of the following tools that you've been learning about:

- Choice of tone, style, diction, and point of view
- Combination of patterns: illustration, narrative, comparison/contrast, cause/effect, and process
- Use of analogy

$(1+1)^2$

Have you ever felt like a penny? Know what I mean—the common, ordinary, everyday penny? You've seen these coins. They are everywhere, easy to find and even easier to overlook. A penny has value, but the value is not all that great. What can you buy with a penny? Not much! Lose a $100 bill and you worry until you find it. But lose a penny—who really cares? It's hardly missed.

So there you are—a common, ordinary, everyday person. You have value, and you know it because you hear that from all kinds

Introduction

- Claude starts with rhetorical questions.

- He uses second person to engage the reader. Although his instructor prefers third person, Claude sees the benefit of using second person to achieve the desired effect.

- Claude identifies the type of audience he's trying to reach and states the thesis—"You have value"—and implies through his questions that we often underestimate our value.

of speakers and read it in all kinds of books and magazines. But how much do you see yourself being worth? Like a penny, is your value unimportant in the scheme of life? If you die, how much would you be missed? The "hundred dollar" heroes and heroines who died made headlines, evoked millions of tears, and touched continents of people with their passing. But how badly would your own loss impact the world?

Look at your life through the symbol of a penny—the common, ordinary, easily over-looked, and limited-value penny. Pull two pennies out of your pocket and look at them. One of them is you; the other is just another ordinary, everyday person like yourself: it could be anyone in our world of 6 billion pennies. See a differ-ence? One may be a little more polished, be older or younger, or show evidence of greater wear and use than the other. But the fact re-mains that for all practical intents and purposes, they are both similar and almost identical. Pick the one that best represents you and lay it down. Now, let me tell you about the remaining penny in your hand.

Perhaps the other penny came from a different mint (background) than did the penny representing you. Perhaps it was a common, everyday person from Atlanta, Georgia, back in 1929. Perhaps he was the son of a Baptist minister, and there was nothing to make his penny stand out from the thousands of other pennies born in that city in that year. However, this ordinary penny found himself suddenly making a world of difference in the econom-ics of human dignity because he refused to see himself as only being worth a small amount. This penny dreamed of investing him-self in a dream that exceeded the impact of the $100 bill. How do we know? This penny told us so. On August 28, 1963, this penny stood on the steps of the Lincoln Memorial in Washington, D.C., to tell 200,000 other ordinary pennies like

- By posing more questions, Claude gets the reader to start thinking of the value of an individual.

- In both paragraphs, he compares a person to a penny, establishing the extended analogy he uses through-out the essay.

Body

- Claude starts his analogy, one which he carries from one paragraph to the next. Although most analogies when carried too far become logical fallacy—false analogy—an analogy, nonetheless, can be an effective rhe-torical strategy:

  1. It grabs the reader's attention.

  2. It adds creativity to your writing.

  3. It helps the reader understand a difficult or abstract topic more easily and eagerly.

- The tone is friendly, and the diction is informal. Claude realizes that to be persuasive, connect with the reader, and maint ain the reader's attention, he has to make sure that the reader perceives him as a knowledgeable person, one the reader can trust.

- By using Dr. Martin Luther King Jr. as an example in the analogy, Claude has given his analogy concrete-ness and has strengthened his the-sis—we have value; we can make a difference.

himself, "I have a dream." The *Chronicles of America* records that Dr. Martin Luther King Jr.'s speech "turned the tone of the event from a party into a crusade" (800). One ordinary penny, when joined with 200,000 others, is no "chump change."

There are those who would argue that there was nothing ordinary about Dr. King since he was a man of manifest destiny. But Dr. King began life just as we all do, endured obstacles many of us may never face, and succeeded not so much for who he was but for what he accomplished. He found the value in himself to prove that one penny can make a big difference. This fact is true of not only the father of American Civil Rights but of every other individual (penny) in human history who has made an impact on our world. In every such example, the "movers and shakers" were ordinary people with a dream, coupled with the belief that they could make a difference. The difference was not in the person but in the attitude toward personal value. There is nothing wrong with being common and ordinary; it simply proves that we are human like everyone else.

Okay, so much for the concept of being common and ordinary. We can accept that fact cheerfully. Still, it's hard to imagine our own personal value on par with that of Dr. King, Abraham Lincoln, or Bill Gates. Consider then the age-old saying:

> For the loss of a button, a uniform was lost.
> For the loss of a uniform, a soldier was lost.
> For the loss of a soldier, a battle was lost,
> And all for the loss of a button.

This simple but profound statement tells us not only that one person can make a difference but also that the loss of one ordinary soldier makes a difference. We tend to think that the sergeants and generals decide the outcome of major events when it is the effort of the common and ordinary soldier that really matters.

- Claude refutes a possible objection to his previous point. In doing so, he shows his understanding for those who hesitate to agree with him and, at the same time, illustrates his point by presenting two additional examples with which his reader may be familiar, thus making his idea vivid and concrete.

- He uses comparison to make his point that we all have a dream.

- He uses contrast to show that one quality alone differentiates his audience from historical giants.

- The use of transition is informal. Again, Claude feels that this technique is necessary to achieve his purpose. Before you attempt a style this informal, check with your instructor.

- The short verse offers the reader time to think about Claude's comparison and acts as transition to the next point.

Consider one of the $100 bills of human history, Helen Keller. The impact of this ordinary person in demonstrating the value of people with disabilities is beyond question. Stricken with blindness and deafness when she was only 19 months, at the age of 24 Ms. Keller graduated with honors from Radcliffe College. After World War II, she visited wounded veterans in U.S. hospitals to inspire them to live life beyond their own war-inflicted disabilities. During her lifetime, she authored numerous widely acclaimed books, including an autobiography. The story of Ms. Keller has inspired generations and changed our world. Indeed, if we are pennies, she must have been a $1,000 bill.

● Claude uses illustration, narrative, and effect as support.

Ms. Keller changed the world, but Anne Sullivan was the penny who changed the life of Ms. Keller. It was Ms. Sullivan who took the time to teach the young Ms. Keller to read and write. Without Ms. Sullivan, perhaps there would be no "thousand dollar" difference from Ms. Keller. When considering value and personal wealth, we may never fully understand the long-range impact or value of our participation in the process called life.

● Claude starts the paragraph with effect and uses illustration and effects as support.

This might be a stretch when we think of our own importance in the overall scheme. "I'm just one person. What difference does my effort make?" Have you ever heard someone say, "My vote doesn't count; I'm only one person"? Such erroneous thinking is easy to adopt and equally simple to disprove. The *Chronicle of America* points out that John Adams defeated Thomas Jefferson by only a 3-vote margin (71–68 electoral votes) to become our second president. In 1868, the U.S. House of Representatives voted 126 to 47 to impeach President Andrew Johnson, "one vote shy of the required two-thirds majority" (Calabresi and Yoo 757). How much difference does one vote make? It made all the difference in the world.

● Claude adds a transitional paragraph to reinforce his thesis.

● Research helps establish the writer's credibility where personal experience is lacking.

Are you feeling the power of the ordinary, everyday person yet? This is only the beginning.

● Again, Claude's transition is informal. Most readers may equate this

Take a look at the power of a penny. Looking back at the penny as a way to understand our own self-worth and potential impact on our world, we begin to apply the power of exponential value. Start with that one penny and double it tomorrow. When you go to bed tomorrow night, you will have two pennies. This amount won't buy much, but the value has doubled. Double it again the next day. In 4 days, you are now 8 cents rich! Wow!

Now plan to double your pennies every day for 2 weeks. How hard can that be? By the end of 14 days what started as just 1 ordinary cent has multiplied itself into $81.92. Now you have some buying power. See how easy it is for one penny to come close to making the $100 difference in just 2 weeks? Now apply this principle to your own life. Imagine that each day is 1 year and that each penny represents one person in your world. How hard can it be for you to find enough value in your life to touch one other life in a positive way each year? When you apply the principle of exponential value (remember how Anne Sullivan touched one life and the impact that one life had on others), in 14 years, your impact on one person can affect or influence 8,192 other lives. Clearly, you are influential!

Day 1	$0.01	Day 8	1.28
Day 2	0.02	Day 9	2.56
Day 3	0.04	Day 10	5.12
Day 4	0.08	Day 11	10.24
Day 5	0.16	Day 12	20.48
Day 6	0.32	Day 13	40.96
Day 7	0.64	Day 14	81.92

At this point, if the average life span lasted only 14 years, I could conclude this analogy, and you could settle for making an impact on just less than 10,000 other lives. Fortunately,

as a motivational piece of writing, but how will Claude's reader react? That's the risk Claude is taking, but it should work if he did a careful analysis of his audience.

● He presents a process, and reestablishes his extended analogy of the penny to further his thesis and to maintain the unity and coherence of the essay.

our life spans generally exceed 14 years, so the exponential values continue. Go back to that penny and see what happens over another 2 weeks. Simply by starting with one penny and doubling it every day, by the end of 3 weeks, that penny will have translated its value into more than $10,000. At the end of 4 weeks, just 28 days, that one penny will make you a millionaire. Now, just how powerful and influential is that common, ordinary penny?

Day 15	$163.84	Day 22	20,971.52
Day 16	327.68	Day 23	41,943.04
Day 17	655.36	Day 24	83,886.08
Day 18	1,310.72	Day 25	167,772.16
Day 19	2,621.44	Day 26	335,544.32
Day 20	5,242.88	Day 27	671,088.64
Day 21	10,485.76	Day 28	1,342,177.28

But let's get back to real life. If that first penny is your life and each day represents 1 year in your life, imagine your own impact. If you can so influence one life every year in so positive a fashion that the influenced individual in turn passes that on to one person every year, in a 30-year span you directly and indirectly influence more than 134 million people. Now, how much value does your life hold?

● Claude brings his analogy to an end and emphasizes the point of the analogy to the importance to his thesis.

History is made, influenced, and changed for better or worse by ordinary people, people just like you and me. Sometimes the process is long, and often, like Anne Sullivan, we may never realize during our lifetime the full impact of our efforts. However, it is important to remember, regardless of how ordinary we feel we may be or how small we estimate our personal value and worth, in the long run, each of us makes a difference. If we could carry on our exponential values for only another 4 years, 32 in all, we would find that the number of lives we have in some way touched would exceed 4 billion. That, my friend, means you have changed the whole world.

Conclusion

● The conclusion starts by emphasizing the meaningfulness and importance of the topic and thesis of the essay.

● Claude brings up previous examples to give the essay closure and reinforce its unity.

● He ends with a challenge to the reader and a call for action.

PRACTICE 12-1

1. Does Claude accomplish his established goal? Explain. _____

   _____

   _____

   _____

2. What is your impression of Claude's style and diction? _____

   _____

   _____

   _____

3. Claude uses a variety of techniques in his essay. What other patterns could he use? For example, how and where would classification work in this essay?

   _____

   _____

   _____

Understanding the Integrated Essay

Your ability to incorporate a variety of writing modes not only reflects your growth as a writer but also reveals your awareness of a basic fact about writing: Most writing strategies can be used to the writer's advantage in any particular essay.

Making Choices

Writing requires that you make choices, and making choices requires you to think critically and creatively about your topic and to examine your options and possibilities. Your first step, then, is to explore the most appropriate and effective approach for your essay based on the most important questions you want to answer. As you develop your topic, you will find that sentences and paragraphs can use different patterns: illustration, comparison/contrast, process, cause/effect, classification/division, and argumentation. You have many choices before you, and choosing among them can be an exciting, creative act, as you can see in Figure 12.1.

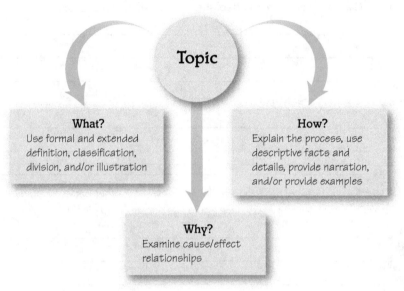

Topic

What?
Use formal and extended definition, classification, division, and/or illustration

How?
Explain the process, use descriptive facts and details, provide narration, and/or provide examples

Why?
Examine cause/effect relationships

FIGURE 12.1 *Writing Choices*

Although most short papers may employ one primary pattern with other patterns woven throughout, longer papers may have two or more primary patterns of development. For example, if you are writing a paper on the causes and effects of child abuse in the foster care system, you might, after the causal analysis, shift the primary focus of the essay to prevention, thus continuing the essay with a process analysis of what the state might do to prevent child abuse. You might end the essay by addressing the objections from those defending the system, shifting the focus of the essay to argumentation. Your decision to include other primary patterns depends on your purpose and audience. Your thesis makes your purpose clear to your reader. As you develop your essay, you then may integrate other patterns into your paragraphs.

Figure 12.2 illustrates the writer's options in combining modes. Keep in mind that this is just one of many possibilities.

An essay with the plan outlined in Figure 12.2 would definitely be longer than three or four pages; therefore, if length is important to your audience, whether your instructor, your peers, or a civic or workplace audience—make length a criterion in your choice of structure and content. In a shorter essay, you may not have space to develop more than one primary method of development.

Examine the many choices you have. From this point on, to stimulate your creative thinking processes, we provide visuals to help you create your ideas rather than give you topics from which to select.

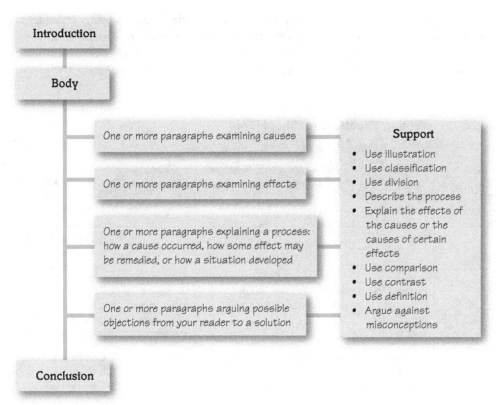

FIGURE 12.2 *Combining Patterns of Development in Writing*

Reacting to Your World

First, examine the following photo of a person shoplifting. What's going on? What topics for writing does this photo suggest?

An initial reaction to this photo might be, "Gosh, that's awful. Why would anyone shoplift?" An essay answering this question might prove interesting, but you can expect others to write essays on basically your same idea and most likely your same points. So how do you make your essay meaningful? Would research help you understand this person's motivation? What other topics does this scene suggest? Start by exploring your options.

Table 12.1 examines the many choices that the writing situation offers. Evidently, the table does not cover all possible approaches. That's the beauty of writing: Whether academic or technical, all writing is creative. Every day, you draw conclusions, make decisions, and respond positively

or negatively to what you see, hear, or read. Your everyday activities bring fresh ideas and new questions that translate into exciting and meaningful topics for writing. It's all a matter of looking deeper and questioning what's in front of you. As you consider your topic, think critically and creatively by exploring your many choices.

TABLE 12.1 **Writing Situations for Shoplifting**

Writing Situation	Purpose and Focus	Possible Audience	Intended Effect on Audience	Primary Pattern(s)	Possible Additional Modes
Criminal justice	Explain types of shoplifters	New police officers New security personnel	Educate to increase skills in identifying	Classification	Cause/effect, comparison/contrast, definition, description, illustration, narration, process
	Propose an effective surveillance system	Store managers	Accept suggestion	Persuasive focus: cause/effect, process, argument	Argumentation, cause/effect, comparison/contrast, illustration, narration
	Explain the effects of shoplifting on businesses	Consumers Store personnel Stakeholders	Raise awareness of consumers; urge closer observation; justify or explain loss to stakeholders	Effects	Comparison/contrast, cause, illustration, process
	Propose a way of reorganizing the store to prevent shoplifting	Managers	Consider investing in changes	Persuasive focus: cause/effect, process, argument	Cause/effect, classification, comparison/contrast, definition, description, illustration, narration
Business	Explain why some people resort to shoplifting	Peers Law enforcement	Educate peers; help law enforcement officers understand motives	Causes Narrative	Classification, comparison/contrast, definition, description, effect, illustration, narration, process
	Develop a profile of people most likely to shoplift	Law enforcement Security	Identify possible shoplifters	Description Classification	Cause/effect, classification, comparison/contrast, description, illustration, narration, process

(*Continued*)

Writing Situation	Purpose and Focus	Possible Audience	Intended Effect on Audience	Primary Pattern(s)	Possible Additional Modes
Psychology	Explain why consumers fail to report incidences of shoplifting	Consumers	Change attitudes	Causes	Classification, comparison/contrast, description, effect, illustration, narration, process
	Convince the reader that it's everyone's duty to report shoplifters	Consumers	Be more proactive in crime prevention	Argument Narrative	Cause/effect, comparison/contrast, description, illustration, narration

PRACTICE 12-2

Examine the following photos. What connections, issues, or problems do these visuals conjure up?

Kevin Winter/Getty Images

© Emmanuel LATTES/Alamy

Using two writing situations based on one of the photos, list possible purposes, audiences, intended effects, primary patterns, and additional modes. Use the chart on page 408 as an example. Return to your chosen photo repeatedly. The more times you examine it, the more ideas you associate with it.

Collaborative Critical Thinking

Form groups according to the photo you chose for Practice 12-2. In groups of three or four, compare the different possibilities that you have for essays about the photo. Answer the following questions.

1.   How many different focuses (ideas for essays) did the group generate?

2.   Which focuses did you find unique, approaching the topic from a different angle than most people would think of?

3.   Which topics require research?

4.   Examine and discuss the intended effect you want each focus to have on the audience. Are the effects reasonable and realistic? Are they appropriate for the focus and the audience? What advice can you give one another?

5.   Examine and discuss the primary pattern(s) and additional modes. Are they appropriate? What would you change?

Share your answers with other groups. Apply this activity by discussing any ideas or major changes you would consider in your own writing assignments.

Connecting Reading to Writing

Veiled Intentions: Don't Judge a Muslim Girl by Her Covering

by Maysan Haydar

Maysan Haydar, a New York City social worker, has written articles for *Spin*, *The Nation*, and *Venus*. This essay first appeared in *Body Outlaws: Rewriting the Rules of Beauty and Body Image*.

Preparing to Read

When you see a veiled woman on TV or in public, what is your initial reaction? What assumptions do you make about her?

Increasing Your Vocabulary

- **donned:** put on
- **antithetical:** completely opposite
- **turbulent:** unsettled, disturbed
- **chagrin:** dismay
- **monotheistic:** believing that there is only one God
- **ensemble:** outfit
- **degradation:** dishonor, disgrace
- **compulsion:** forcing, compelling
- **absolves:** frees
- **posturing:** assuming an unnatural attitude
- **solidify:** make concrete
- **coerced:** forced

- **fawned over:** flattered
- **subjugate:** control, dominate
- **swathed:** surrounded by
- **extol:** praise
- **discretion:** choice
- **utopic:** perfect, ideal
- **grapple:** deal with
- **hummus:** a Mediterranean dip of garbanzo beans and peanut oil
- **patriarchy:** male dominance
- **resurgence:** renewal
- **egalitarian:** equal
- **unscathed:** unhurt

O Prophet! Tell thy wives and daughters and the believing women that they should cast their outer garments over their persons. That is most convenient that they should be known and not be molested.

– THE QURAN, Chapter 33, Verse 59

And say to the believing women that they should lower their gaze and guard their modesty: that they should not display their beauty and ornaments except what ordinarily appears thereof; that they should draw their veils over their bosoms and not display their beauty…

–THE QURAN, Chapter 24, Verse 30–31

1   I have a confession to make.

2   I've been covering my hair, as is prescribed for Muslim women, since I was twelve years old. And while there are many good reasons for doing so, I wasn't motivated by a desire to be different, to honor tradition, or to make a political statement.

3   I wanted the board game Girl Talk

4   When girls from our small, Midwestern Muslim community **donned** their first *hijab* (headscarf), their families rewarded them with parties and monetary gifts. At twelve, I wasn't nearly as physically developed as a Muslim girl is supposed to be when she starts covering, but I desperately wanted Girl Talk. I knew that if I announced my intention to begin veiling in the board game aisle at Kmart, I could ask for anything and receive it.

5   My choice of Girl Talk as reward for taking on a religious responsibility is amusing to me now, because it's so **antithetical** to what veiling is supposed to represent. Girl Talk was the ultimate slumber party game, where players performed gags or revealed embarrassing secrets, then got to choose from four kinds of fortune cards as a prize. My favorite cards hooked me up with the class president, the football captain, or a hunky lifeguard who saved me from drowning. And I still have a sheet of "zit stickers," which were meant to punish gamers who failed to share their dirt.

6   Now that I'm twenty-five and have worn a veil for more than half my life, I can admit to this shallow beginning, which is so far from my reason for veiling today. As an adult, I embrace the veil's modesty, which allows me to be seen as a whole person instead of a twenty-piece chicken dinner. In spite of the seeming contradictions of my life—I'm married to a white man who was raised Catholic, I love heavy metal, I consider myself a feminist, and I sport a few well-disguised piercings—I follow my religion's standard of modesty and appearance. It's only now, after comparing my **turbulent** teen experiences with those of other women, that I can fully appreciate how much of a saving grace this small piece of cloth was.

7   Much to my **chagrin**, many Americans see veiling as an oppressive tool forced on Muslim women by the men in our culture. Yet, the practice of covering hair and body is a choice for many women—and it is not specific to Islam. All the **monotheistic** religious (Christianity, Judaism, and Islam) advocate modesty in dress, though the interpretation of "modesty" varies

greatly. Ironically, the population that spends millions on beauty products, plastic surgery, and self-help guides is the same one that takes pity on me for being so "helpless" and "oppressed." On a New York City bus a couple weeks ago, I sat with another woman, also veiled, but wearing a traditional *jilbab* (a cloak that women wear over their clothing). A girl two seats over remarked to her friend, while flipping her hair for effect, that she couldn't understand how we could dress this way. "Me, I got to be *free*."

8   To my eyes, her idea of freedom involved a complicated hairstyle, loads of makeup and jeans she probably had to sew herself into. If anything, I would find that **ensemble** more caging, more oppressive and more painful than clothes that allow me to walk in front of construction sites confidently, with minimal risk of harassment. (Construction workers may feel obligated to say something to every passing woman, but I often get things like "I like your skirt!" or "Girl, I would marry you!"—harmless compared to the **degradation** I've heard many women complain about.)

9   As for freedom, my parents have a healthy understanding of Islam, especially the Quranic verse "Let there be no **compulsion** in religion" (2:256). Having been raised in religiously different homes themselves (Mom: very liberal, European-minded, not so religious: Dad: religious, culturally structured gender roles and expectations), they only practiced traditions that they understood, accepted, and believed. Thus, my mother knew the best way to introduce veiling to me was to emphasize its feminist, forward-thinking reasons: Covering removes that first level of being judged, of being assessed based on my measurements, and it **absolves** me of the need or desire to be wanted solely for my looks. My choice of Girl Talk didn't showcase a deep understanding of that idea. But reflecting back, I see that wearing a scarf greatly influenced how people viewed me and my goals, before I could ever appreciate that it was having that effect.

10   In high school, my interactions with the opposite sex were different than the norm. If I hadn't yet been inclined to deal with boys in an unpressured, ungiggly, un-made-up way, the scarf shoved me in that direction. So, without being given handbooks or informative flyers about how they should curb their **posturing** and come-ons, guys sensed that they should treat me with respect.

11   I didn't watch boys and girls learn about each other from the sidelines. I have many rich friendships with men, and over the years a good number of them have made a go at becoming "more than friends." I didn't participate in dating games, but I was flattered by the attention, especially since I knew I was being liked for who I was beyond my body. What made me attractive was my ability to relate to everyone in a very natural way, without all the confusing sexual pressure. The weirdness that normally clouds boy-girl interactions was lifted, because most guys automatically assumed I wasn't available for dating. Of course, girls deserve to be treated with respect no matter what they wear. But since we live in a world of mixed messages, I got to bypass a lot of damaging experiences.

12   The veil bestowed other experiences upon me that I wouldn't quite classify as negative, but definitely educational. Like anyone else who's visibly different from the norm, I encountered ridiculous ideas about what a covered person should be, do, and enjoy. If someone overheard me talking about my interests, which included karate and skateboarding, I grew to enjoy their disbelief and shock. I didn't pick my hobbies to prove that stereotypes are often false, but it was nice to make people reconsider their notions of a Muslim girl.

13   Moving to New York City right after college and living alone was the most affirming thing I've done to **solidify** my resolve and truly understand what veiling means. Here, for the first time, people believed that I was wearing a scarf because I wanted to, not because my family **coerced** me into it. On the other hand, New York exemplifies what's wrong with our image-obsessed society. I worked for a couple of magazines and saw the way women acted out to draw attention to themselves. It was especially apparent at my anything-goes dot-com job, where women showed up to work in backless halter tops and were **fawned over** by male coworkers.

14   And now, as I write this, I can watch women **subjugate** themselves on reality dating shows. On a show about aspiring models I heard a woman say that her greatest goal would be to appear in *Stuff* magazine. I can't imagine centering my life on something as fleeting and meaningless as being admired simply for my body.

15   You might assume that because Muslim women traditionally don't display our bodies, we don't hold them as important or feel connected to them—or that we don't value ourselves as sexual beings. Guess again. While our degree of modesty is high, the value Muslim women place on the bodies underneath our veils is higher. In Sunday school, girls are taught that our bodies are beautiful ("God is beautiful and loves beauty" is a *hadith*, or saying, of the prophet Muhammad) and that they're so valuable that they're only meant to be shared in an intimate relationship: husband and wife, mother and baby, among women, and in clinical or safe spaces (for example, with your doctor, among family members). Historically, the most severe-looking coverings used to be limited to the richest women in Arab society; being **swathed** in so much cloth was regarded as a sign of status.

16   People who have written about being in the secluded quarters of Arab homes or at their parties often express surprise at the degree to which these cloaked women maintain themselves via fitness, style, and decadent rituals. (Let's not even get started on the body hair-removal process in the Middle East.) I'm not one for creams and blushes, but I understand that there are women who enjoy the beauty process, and I see no harm in indulging it for the right reasons. Feminist author Geraldine Brooks, in her book *Nine Parts of Desire*, quotes women across the Middle East who **extol** the virtues of prettying up for their loved ones. To me, this demonstrates that Western priorities are out of line: American women spend hours getting ready for strangers to see them but don't give the same effort to those who see them in intimate settings.

[17]   As for the variation in Muslim women's dress, it demonstrates the wide-ranging interpretations of modesty. I often get asked what the most "right" version is: the Afighani *burqah*, the Iranian *chador*, the Pakistani *salwar kameez*,[1] the Arab *jilbab*, or a sweatshirt and jeans. The short answer is that the recommendations for modesty are to be interpreted and applied at the **discretion** of the woman picking her clothes.

[18]   All through high school, I wore a *jilbab* exclusively because I didn't have to spend any effort worrying about what was in season or what I would be expected to wear to fit in. I now cover my hair, but generally wear jeans and a long-sleeved shirt. My once-strict interpretation of modesty has been adapted to my urban lifestyle. Is wearing an *abaya* (the head-to-toe gown that completely covers the wearer) and a face veil a good idea in New York City? Probably not, since the *abaya* would likely get stuck in a subway door or pick up the dust off any floor you glide across. But not wearing an *abaya* in Saudi Arabia would probably make getting around very difficult for a woman.

[19]   It's **utopic** and ridiculous to assert that looks don't matter and that by veiling I'm avoiding the messiness—particularly after September 11th. Now some people hold their breath a bit longer, assuming I'm a fundamentalist or wondering if I'm there to cause them harm. I sense people studying me on the trains, reading the cover of the book in my hand and trying to gauge if I'm one of "us" or one of "them." I **grapple** with the frustration that I can't reassure everyone individually that my goals have everything to do with social justice and nothing to do with holy war. But I have seen suspicions fade in the eyes of the pregnant woman to whom I've given my subway seat, or the Hasidic[2] man whose elbow I've taken to help him up the stairs.

[20]   Though many of the stereotypes and incorrect assumptions people had while I was growing up still prevail (that Muslim equals backwards/oppressed/fundamentalist/terrorist), current events have pedestrians describing their secondhand "expertise" of Islam—the history of Wahhabi Islam,[3] the export of Sayyid Qutb[4] and the Muslim Brotherhood's[5] ideas—or trying to argue that the Quranic requirements for modesty don't include veiling. It's much harder to explain why I cover to those who think they have a full understanding of the culture and the faith than those whose "knowledge" of the Middle East is limited to *Aladdin* and **hummus**.

---

[1] *burqah...salwar kameez:* The *burqah* covers a women from head to toe, with a mesh strip in front of the eyes to allow some vision; the *chador* also drapes the head and body, but not the face; the *salwar kameez* is a tunie-and-trouser set.

[2] *Hasidie:* Hasidism is a form of Jewish mysticism; Hasidie men typically wear long black coats and wide-brimmed black hats, while women cover their hair and wear long skirts and long sleeves for modesty.

[3] *Wahhabi Islam:* A Sunni fundamentalist form of Islam founded by Muhammad ibn Abdel al Wahhab (1703–1792), Wahhabism is the majority faith of Saudi Arabia and Qatar.

[4] *Sayyid Qutb:* Egyptian writer and intellectual (1906–1966) who condemned western values and promoted the idea of a fundamentalist Islamic state; affiliated with the Muslim Brotherhood.

[5] *Muslim Brotherhood:* Worldwide movement, founded in Egypt in 1928, that advocates government imposition of strict Islamic law.

21   I do appreciate the status Islam and the Middle East have in the news these days—the interest has generated new scholarship on Arabia's history and anthropology and on Islamic law, all of which I'm interested in and am relieved is being researched. This research includes a pool of female scholars reexamining Islamic texts with a feminist lens, and separating actual religious commands from their long-held, culturally laden interpretations, which often smack of **patriarchy**.

22   Forcing women to veil or unveil usually has the opposite effect. When I attended elementary school in Saudi Arabia and flew home to Michigan each summer, a parade of women swathed in black *abayas* would head to the airplane bathrooms once we were safely in the air and emerge wearing short, tight ensembles. Conversely, banning the veil in Syria and Turkey sparked a **resurgence** in its popularity.

23   The question of veiling comes up once someone finds out that I've married into a family that celebrates Christmas, with my full participation. "If you have a daughter, what will she wear?" they ask. I haven't yet cracked a pregnancy or parenting book, but I hope that my policy will be similar to the **egalitarian** way I was raised. If she wants to, she can; if she doesn't want to, then she won't. It's far more important for her to respect herself, her body, and her life.

24   At the heart of my veiling is personal freedom. I dress this way because it has made it easier to get through adolescent phases and New York City streets with no self-loathing, body hang-ups, or sexual harassment. I wish more women emerged **unscathed**; no one should suffer for what they look like or what they wear.*

Understanding the Reading

1. Why did Haydar initially decide to wear the veil when she was 12?
2. Why does she wear it as an adult?
3. What negative attitudes or assumptions about the veil do many Americans have?
4. What attitudes do Muslim women have about their bodies?
5. How does Haydar think that many modern women subjugate themselves in the way that they dress?
6. What happens when societies force women to veil or unveil?

Understanding the Structure, Style, and Tone

1. How does Haydar organize her essay?
2. Where does Haydar integrate the following types of development:
   - Narration
   - Cause or reasons
   - Effects
   - Comparison/contrast
   - Illustration
   - Definition

*From *Body Outlaws: Rewriting the Rules of Beauty and Body Image*, edited by Ophira Edut (Seal Press, 2003), pp. 258–265. Copyright © 2004 Ophira Edut, Rebecca Walker. Reprinted by permission of Seal Press, a member of the Perseus Books Group

3. What is the effect of the Quranic quotations at the beginning of the essay?
4. How do the references to types of Muslim coverings and Muslim and Jewish organiza-tions, historic figures, and food contribute to the essay?
5. To whom is Haydar writing?
6. What is Haydar's attitude or tone? Is she angry, resigned, puzzled, determined?

Making a Personal Connection

1. Think of a certain style of dress that you find particularly obnoxious or offensive. What characteristics of the apparel do you dislike and why? What factors shaped your negative attitude?
2. Women are not the only ones who veil. In the Saharan region of North Africa, the custom of the Tuaregs, a nomadic people, is for men to veil, whereas women traditionally don't. Why is covering certain parts of the body so embedded in particular societies?

Writing Your Integrated Essay

To guide you through your integrated essay, we include an essay by Deborah, a social work major taking her first composition course. As you read her essay, note the various techniques and patterns she uses to support her thesis. Also, at various points of this essay, consider other choices Deborah could have made to enhance this essay.

Multicolored Leaves

The crisp autumn leaves had begun to fall, signaling the start of another school year for me and every other school-age child in Southern California. It was 1976, and after a turbulent decade of fighting for equal rights for all, we had finally begun to embrace our dif-ferences. But I knew it wasn't over yet. Even at the tender age of 11, I knew that racism was still alive and well in America. As I trudged to my new school for the first time, absentmind-edly crunching leaves of red and gold as I walked, I prepared myself for the inevitable moment when another kid would ask me yet another version of the question I had come to dread—"WHAT! Your brother is a N——R?"

Whatever one's definition, racism is an ugly word. Microsoft Encarta defines racism as "making the race of other people a factor in attitudes or actions concerning them. . . .

Introduction
- Deborah uses description.
- She gives brief background.

- She presents her topic.

- She uses narrative.

- Deborah gives a literal definition.

[It] implies a belief in the superiority of one's own race." To me, the word evokes feelings of frustration, hurt, embarrassment, anger, and injustice. Although I'm not biracial, I grew up as a white child in a family where Mama was white and Daddy was black.

There has been surprisingly little research conducted on the issue of prejudice toward the biracial, according to Francis Wardle, executive director of the Center for the Study of Biracial Children. However, I know from my own family's experience that it is a bigotry that differs from the traditional view of racism. Many people who don't consider themselves racially biased show a real hostility when asked for their views on interracial marriage and biracial children. This tendency to react with aggression seems to transcend both race and ethnic background (Wardle). I personally have found more acceptance from my step-father's family than from my mother's or my biological father's family. It's as if the biracial family is an insult and introduces a threat to the ordinary view of the world as it should be.

If facing prejudice is hard for an adult, it's all the more difficult for a child. Adults know that children haven't yet acquired the life skills and sense of self that are necessary to deal with serious issues successfully; however, they subject the biracial child to extreme emotional pain. At such a young age, the child faces hostility at the hands of those who oppose "mixing races." Even more troubling, the pain may be inflicted by people the child looks up to, such as a teacher or a minister. The biracial child must silently work out her feelings of anger, hurt, and injustice that result from being shunned and ridiculed since these are feelings that she can't share, express, or define. Who is there to turn to?

Although the majority of children can identify and fit in with one group, biracial children face the problem of not being white

- She makes a statement of authority.

Body
- Deborah introduces an authority to support her claim.
- Her thesis, or primary focus, is to define.
- She cites an authority to give weight to her own claim.

- Deborah uses effect.

- Deborah uses illustration.

or black enough. Biracial children constantly must deal with the taunts from their peers of either race. Such words as Oreo, half-breed, and mutt become part of their early vocabulary. Kelly Burrello, Diversity Training Group senior associate, points out that the belief in separate but equal rights is so ingrained in some societies that "the homes of interracial families have reportedly been targets of hate crimes by members of their communities who do not accept mixed race households." However, as difficult as these external forces may be, many biracial children do survive. I saw my brother grow up to be a person of great fortitude, resilience, and compassion, and these are priceless character traits. But he is more fortunate than most. He has a strong family to support him.

There's really no secret to raising a happy, healthy biracial child. Some parents wait helplessly to comfort the child. However, parents need to see this situation and climate for what it is: racism, bigotry, and ignorance. My parents found that the most important factor in raising a biracial child is to exemplify the kind of adult they hope their children to be. My parents showed my brother and me what we can be. From my brother's earliest years, they reminded him often how beautiful and unique he is. As he grew older, they let him know that he could come to them to talk about any and all feelings he had about being biracial. In addition, my parents encouraged my brother to explore as much of each parent's culture as he wished. My brother, as well as I, inherited a devotion to family and an appreciation for diversity that embodies a standard of a global society. Yet in a society where we have seen the number of inter-racial couples quadrupled in the last 35 years (Burrello), it's difficult to explain how such scorn from diverse groups continues to exist.

● Deborah uses process.

The autumn leaves are falling once again. It is now 2007, and the school-age kids, including my young son, have started school. I don't know what sort of struggles my son will be going through for having a black daddy and a white mommy, but I want to hope that we as a society have evolved. Unfortunately, I can't help but sense that we will continue down the wrong path: it's still not over. I still sense the hate in this world for what people can't understand. After all, it wasn't too long ago that the Twin Towers were destroyed in a horrible terrorist act, and in an effort to retaliate against a faceless enemy, some Americans have become terrorists themselves by persecuting and killing our fellow citizens who happen to be Muslims.

As I ponder such events, I occasionally look out of my window to admire the Colorado mountainside now covered in a multitude of colors, shades of gold and brick, and the most vibrant red and orange imaginable. They paint a kind of mosaic with their beautiful colors, colors that would be diminished if not for the colors that contrast and complement them. In our diversity and beauty, humanity has the opportunity to be just as magnificent as the leaves with their collective brilliance. Can we learn from the multicolored leaves?

Conclusion

● Bringing the essay to a close, Deborah goes back to the beginning by describing a similar scene: the season, the leaves, a child going to school, and the feeling that the problem persists.

● She uses comparison to illustrate the senselessness of bigotry, which also echoes the historical events in her introduction.

● She uses description to make a point and as an appeal to emotion. She returns to the leaves as a picture of harmony and unity and then challenges her audience to be receptive.

Prewriting

Choosing the right topic is crucial when writing any essay because your topic shapes the organization and development of your essay. If you have a strong interest or personal connection to the topic, the topic meets the standards set by your instructor or your workplace, or both, you're on your way to an excellent paper. It all starts with your topic.

Discovering and Limiting Your Topic
Prewriting Strategy: Responding to Visual Cues

Before we move to your own writing, do the following activity to sharpen the power of the senses and relate your sensual impressions to your thinking. Try to "see the whole picture." This exercise is just a warm-up activity for the rest of the chapter.

PRACTICE 12-3

Examine the following photo and answer the questions that follow.

Calvin Klein Jeans

LM Otero/AP photo

1. What is your overall impression of this photo? _____
   _____
   _____
   _____

2. Give a brief description of the photo. _____
   _____
   _____
   _____

3. Think of ways to develop themes based on this photo.

   a. If you were using classification to develop an essay on an idea based on this photo, what would you classify? Write a possible thesis, and add an essay map to indicate the categories. _____
   _____
   _____

b. Write a thesis in which you consider effect analysis of your primary pattern of development. _____

_____

_____

c. Write a thesis in which you make an argument about an issue that you associate with the photo. _____

_____

_____

Photos capture moments in time and are packed with the emotions and passion of those moments. The following photos are divided into four themes: seeing our changing values, seeking a better world, changing our future, and building bridges. The photos in each theme reflect issues in our lives as a nation and as global citizens. Focus on each theme separately. You are probably familiar with and may have your personal views on most, if not all, of these issues. If you are unfamiliar with the subject of a photo, attempt it anyway. Think creatively with no limits.

Theme 1: Seeing our changing values. Take a moment to examine the following photos. Respond to each photo by raising questions that can result in thesis statements or even research questions for a possible research paper for this or other courses. For each photo, raise two important questions. Don't limit yourself: View each photo from different angles, and consider the vast possibilities of what you are observing. Every time you write a question, come back and examine the photo; try to discover something new each time.

1. _____

_____

_____

_____

2. _____

_____

_____

_____

Joe Giblin/AP photo

3. _____

_____

_____

_____

Matt Dunn/Superstock

4. _____

_____

_____

_____

5. _____

_____

_____

_____

Queerstock

6. _____

_____

_____

_____

WRITING **12-1**

Look over your questions. In the space provided, write two questions that you feel would lead to interesting thesis statements. Make additions, clarifications, or changes as you feel necessary.

1. _____

2. _____

Theme 2: Seeking a better world. When you feel personally connected to your ideas, your essay has a stronger voice. Examine the next set of photos. React to what you're seeing in the same way as you did for theme 1. React also to what you're not seeing but feel should be part of the scene. Omissions of details can generate judgments.

1. _____
   _____
   _____
   _____

2. _____
   _____
   _____
   _____

Eric Feferberg/Getty Images

3. _____
   _____
   _____
   _____
   _____

4. _____
   _____
   _____
   _____
   _____

Anna Gowthorpe/PA Wire URN:5466425 (Press Association via AP Images)

5. _____
   _____
   _____
   _____

6. _____
   _____
   _____
   _____

The Paducah Sun/Steve Nagy/AP/Wide World Photos

WRITING 12-2

Again, look over your questions and choose two that you feel you would be interested in writing about. Don't forget to make any additions, clarifications, or changes that you feel are necessary.

1. _____

2. _____

Theme 3: Changing our future. Examine the next series of photos. Think critically about these events.

1. _____

_____

_____

_____

_____

2. _____

_____

_____

_____

_____

Ben Cawthra/Photoshot/Newscom

3. _____

_____

_____

_____

_____

4. _____

_____

_____

_____

_____

Daryl Estrine/Photo Library

5. _____
   _____
   _____
   _____
   _____

6. _____
   _____
   _____
   _____
   _____

WRITING 12-3

Review your questions and pick two you are interested in writing about. You should make any additions, clarifications, or changes that you feel are necessary.

1. _____

2. _____

Theme 4: Building bridges. Use your power of observation and your critical thinking skills to respond to the following final set of events.

1. _____
   _____
   _____
   _____
   _____

2. _____
   _____
   _____
   _____
   _____

3. _____
  _____
  _____
  _____
  _____

4. _____
  _____
  _____
  _____
  _____

David McNew/Getty Images

5. _____
  _____
  _____
  _____
  _____

6. _____
  _____
  _____
  _____
  _____

John Moore/Getty Images

WRITING   12-4

Pick two of your questions from the final theme that you feel you would be interested in writing about. If necessary, make any additions, clarifications, or changes to the questions.

1. _____

2. _____

You should now have eight stimulating questions for possible theses. Review each one. This is the hard part: Narrow your list to your top two questions, and write them in the space that follows in your order of preference.

1. _____

2. _____

After you have selected your questions, take the first one and choose any combination of prewriting techniques you feel would generate the most ideas. Your goal at this point is to search for a focus for your thesis and uncover possible supporting details.

Identifying Your Audience, Establishing Your Purpose, and Setting Your Tone

Most likely, you have a good idea who your audience is, but it is still helpful to complete a formal analysis because the more you know about your audience, the more effective you can be in making the right choices in developing your essay.

Deborah does an audience analysis to find the most effective approach for her essay. She then establishes the following aims:

Audience: People who don't realize the extent of bigotry and the consequences of their own behavior

Purpose: To convince my audience that we need to embrace differences in spite of our environment

Effect: Appeal to my audience's sense of humanity and have them question the soundness of their personal judgments

Approach: I'd like to establish a compassionate, nonjudgmental tone. To prevent the essay from appearing too emotional (which I am), I'll use some research to support my assertions. I'll use description as a way to appeal to my audience and at the same time make an analogy using nature to reflect the point that what people judge is part of the natural order of life. My own experiences serve as examples to illustrate my points.

WRITING 12-5

Record your observations about your audience, purpose, and tone by filling out the following form.

Audience, Purpose, and Tone Analysis

Topic: _____

I. Audience

   1. Who is your reader? _____

     Age: _____   Gender: _____

2. What is your audience's educational background? _____
    _____

3. Who would be the most interested in your topic? _____
    _____

4. What does your reader know or assume about your topic? _____
    _____

5. What are your reader's social or cultural interests? _____
    _____

6. Why would your reader be interested in your topic? _____
    _____

7. What connection do you have with this audience? _____
    _____

II. Purpose

1. What do you want your audience to understand? _____
    _____

2. Why is this topic important to your audience? _____
    _____

3. What does your reader expect when reading your writing? _____
    _____

4. How do you expect your audience to react? _____
    _____

III. Tone

1. What tone do you hope to establish? _____
    _____

2. What can you realistically achieve through this writing? _____
    _____

Review what you have written, and then identify your audience, purpose, effect, and approach.

Audience: _____

Purpose: _____

Effect: _____

Approach: _____

Formulating Your Thesis

Review your question again to formulate your tentative thesis. Whatever form your thesis takes, make sure it clearly states what you intend to prove.

Deborah felt a personal connection to the theme "changing our future" and formulates the following tentative thesis:

> Biracial children struggle silently trying to make sense of the bigotry that surrounds them.

Outlining Your Ideas

Outlining is itself a creative process. As you jot down the elements of your essay, you are still brainstorming, associating ideas, and revising your approach. You can use a rough "scratch outline" to get you started, or you can choose one of the patterns presented in earlier chapters of *Bridges to Better Writing* that offer a close model of the type of essay you might be writing. For example, if you plan to use classification as the primary pattern, go to Chapter 9 for a sample outline. However, if you have no set pattern of development, like Deborah's essay, consider drawing up your own plan for your essay. Don't forget that effective writing is a product of careful planning. Examine Deborah's outline.

ESSAY OUTLINE

I. **Introduction**
  A. Start with a description to set the scene and establish an analogy to nature using the different colors and shapes of leaves.
  B. Give the accepted definition of racism to focus on another type of racism.
  C. Support my focus on racism with a statement of authority, and mention the limited research on effects of prejudice on biracial children.
  D. To set the scene, introduce my topic, and establish credibility, I need three or four paragraphs for my introduction.
  E. Thesis: Biracial children struggle silently trying to make sense of the bigotry that surrounds them.

II. **Body**
  A. Start with the difficulties and emotional effects the biracial child must endure.
  B. Explain the feelings of the child, and describe how the child deals with these feelings in silence.
  C. Show that the biracial child is split between two worlds and does not seem to fit in either world.

D. Show that there is hope; explain how my parents helped my brother appreciate both worlds and helped me understand my role in this new environment.

E. Maintain an upbeat tone throughout the development.

III. Conclusion

A. Return to the description and the scenario in the introduction.

B. Continue the analogy of the multicolored leaves.

C. Bring the scenario to the present and show that much hasn't changed, especially with the current world situation.

D. Close with an appeal to emotions.

WRITING 12-6

Write your outline. As you determine the information that helps explain your thesis, consider all the choices you have. Design the outline format that is best for your particular essay. However, if you choose to use a specific pattern of development as your primary pattern, go to the appropriate chapter in this book for an outline form.

Drafting

Look at your outline and start drafting any section of your essay: beginning, middle, or end. As you draft sections of your essay, feel free to change your outline. What seemed logical earlier may not be such a good idea now.

WRITING 12-7

On a separate sheet of paper, start drafting your essay.

1. Make sure your introduction and conclusion are not merely decorations to fulfill a requirement. Your introduction and conclusion must serve some meaningful purpose.
2. Make sure that each of your paragraphs develops one main idea.
3. Use a variety of patterns and methods to explain, argue, or prove your ideas.
4. Add transitions to keep your ideas flowing smoothly and to guide your audience through your information.
5. Above all, don't lose sight of your audience and purpose.

Revising

Revise! Revise! Revise! Leave nothing untouched. We can't emphasize this stage of the process enough. Rethink every part of your essay. Go back to your audience and purpose analysis, and rethink some more. Talk to others about your topic, and rethink again.

To solve specific problems in your paper, refer to the troubleshooting sections in chapters of this textbook that pertain to your topic and approach.

WRITING 12-8

Start your revision. Again don't leave any part of your essay untouched. Revise, revise, and revise again.

- Make sure your essay provides specific, purposeful, and creative information (examples, details, observations, combinations of patterns) to explain your topic fully, demonstrating an understanding of the complexity of the topic. Overall, check that your essay has a sense of completeness.

- Check your use of transitions carefully between and within your paragraphs.

- If your essay contains secondary evidence, make sure your sources are integrated smoothly into the text. Your sources should be varied, reliable, and correctly cited using the correct style of documentation. Refer to Chapter 13 for guidance on using sources. Follow your instructor's guidelines.

Collaborative Critical Thinking

Asking Your Peers

Get feedback from your peers. Exchange papers with a classmate, and review the paper by responding to these questions.

1. Who is the writer? Who is the peer reviewer?

2. What method or methods of introduction did the writer use (humor, anecdote, startling fact, rhetorical question, narration, and so on)?

3. Is the introduction effective? (Is it interesting? Does it grab your attention?)

4. Is the introduction fully developed? What can you suggest to improve the introduction?

5. Is the thesis statement clear, and does the introduction lead smoothly to this thesis statement? What should the writer add?

6. Do the body paragraphs have clear topic sentences? Identify any weaknesses, and make suggestions to strengthen these sentences.

7. Read the supporting details of each paragraph. Does the writer give you sufficient details, facts, and/or examples to explain topic sentences or general ideas in the various paragraphs? Where do you feel the essay can use additional support?

8. Does the writer use a combination of patterns to develop the thesis? What suggestions can you make?

9. Make suggestions or comments, and circle any unclear or irrelevant information directly on the essay.

10. How does the writer establish credibility: personal experience, research, or both? Is it effective?

11. Is the conclusion meaningful? What can you suggest to improve the conclusion?

12. Give your overall impression of the essay's diction (language). Is it too pompous or elaborate, making the ideas unclear and confusing? Are the sentences too choppy, or is the word order confusing? Is it appropriate for the audience?

13. What did you enjoy most about the essay?

Proofreading

Start proofreading your draft by focusing on the most common grammar errors. Review these rules if necessary.

Applying Previous Knowledge

Be sure to check your essay for the most common errors presented in previous chapters.

Common Error #1	Sentence Fragments	
handbook H-1b	**fragment:** Because he was angry.	☐
	better: I left early because he was angry.	

Common Error #2	Shifts in Verb Tense	
handbook H-5c	She got off the bus and then ~~walks~~ **walked** to the corner.	☐

Common Error #3	Fused Sentences	
handbook H-2a	**fused:** I left early they were angry.	☐
	better: I left early. They were angry.	

Common Error #4	Comma Splices	
handbook H-2b	**comma splice:** I left early, they were angry.	☐
	better: I left early. They were angry.	

Common Error #5	Commas after Introductory Clauses and Phrases

handbook
H-12a

- When you start a sentence with a subordinate conjunction—*although, as, because, before, even though, if, since, unless, when, while,* and so on—use a comma **after the introductory clause**.
  <u>Because I was late</u>, they left me behind.
- When you start with a long prepositional phrase or two or more prepositional phrases, use a comma.
  <u>Near the park by the elementary school</u>, the officer found the stolen car.
- When you start with a participial phrase (*-ing, -ed,* -irregular past participle), use a comma.
  - <u>Throwing the glass against the wall</u>, John left angrily.
  - <u>Wanted by the FBI</u>, the fugitive left the country.
  - <u>Written in 1802</u>, the novel was a success.

Common Error #6	Shift in person

handbook
H-4d

shift from third to second person: A **student** should get a topic approved so **you** don't waste time.

better: **Students** should get a topic approved so **they** don't waste time.

Common Error #7	Pronoun–Antecedent Agreement

handbook
H-4a

A **person** should know what ~~they are~~ **she or he is** doing. Be careful with indefinite pronouns (*everyone, everybody, somebody, something, each, every,* and so on); they take singular pronouns.
Everyone decided to go ~~their~~ **his or her** separate way.

Common Error #8	Pronoun Reference

handbook
H-4b

- Rita skis and plays tennis. ~~This~~ **Her participation in these sports** shows her interest in sports.
- At the flea market, ~~they~~ **the vendors** sold new and used merchandise.

Common Error #9	Pronoun Case

handbook
H-4c

- The president, treasurer, and ~~me~~ **I** examined the proposal.

WRITING
Your Integrated Essay

Common Error #10	Lack of Agreement between Subject and Verb	
handbook **H-3**	Each of the candidates ~~have~~ **has** addressed the issue.	☐

Common Error #11	Missing or Misplaced Apostrophe	
handbook **H-13a**	● The ~~speakers~~ **speaker's** assumptions irritated the audience. ● The ~~painter's~~ **painters** did not want the ladder removed form ~~it's~~ **its** present position.	☐

Common Error #12	Misused Commas with Restrictive or Nonrestrictive Elements	
handbook **H-12a**	● Employees who come in late are unprofessional. ● Our manager, who is constantly late, is unprofessional.	☐

WRITING 12-9

By now, you're probably aware of the grammar, usage, and punctuation rules that you consistently violate. Proofread specifically for your problem areas.

Final Checklist

1. Does the introduction have a strong and clear purpose statement (suggesting new, broader insights into the topic) that captivates the audience and clearly addresses the complexity of the issue? ☐

2. Does the thesis clearly state the main point of your essay? Does it control the entire essay? Is it smoothly integrated into the introduction? ☐

3. Does each main body paragraph contain a strong, clear topic sentence that supports the thesis? ☐

4. Does your essay provide sufficient information (examples, details, observations, combinations of patterns) to explain your topic fully? ☐

5. Does your essay contain appropriate and smooth transitions between paragraphs and sentences? ☐

6. Does the conclusion bring closure to the essay? Does it emphasize the importance of your topic and give the reader something to think about? ☐

7. Does your essay provide the essential information, tone, and level of formality appropriate to the essay's purpose and audience? ☐

8. Does your essay have varied sentence structures, complete sentences (no fragments, comma splices, or fused sentences), and minor or no errors in spelling, usage, and punctuation? ☐

Reflecting

In this chapter, you have explored a more creative way of making choices about developing your essay. We believe that an open-ended, questioning, yet logical and informed approach can yield the best results, especially as you become more comfortable and fluent as a writer. Use the following activity to help you reflect on your writing process in this chapter.

WRITING 12-10

Self-Reflection

Before you hand in your paper, write a brief paragraph in which you reflect on your final draft. Include your feelings on the following questions:

1. What do you feel you did best?
2. What part of your paper was most challenging to you?
3. In which areas do you feel you need the most practice?
4. What strategies could you employ to address your challenges or weaknesses, to improve the quality of your essay, or both?

After you have completed this self-reflection, carefully review your instructor's comments. How are they similar or different from your own answers to the self-reflection? Make a list of your grammar, punctuation, and spelling errors so that you can follow up on the ones that recur. Consider what strategies you will employ to address your challenges or weaknesses and to improve the quality of your essay.

How might you exercise your many choices as a writer outside of this English course?

- **College:** _____

- **Your profession:** _____

- **Everyday life:** _____

WRITING WITH SOURCES

© Peter Adams/Corbis

Working with Sources

"Plagiarists are always suspicious of being stolen from."
— Samuel Taylor Coleridge

YOUR GOALS

Understanding Sources

1. Annotate sources as a way to gather and extract information
2. Distinguish between primary and secondary sources
3. Use, punctuate, and integrate direct quotations into your essays
4. Use paraphrase to integrate source information smoothly into your essays
5. Use summarization to integrate source information smoothly into your essays
6. Use signal phrases to introduce and to end source information
7. Recognize and avoid plagiarism

Documenting Sources

1. Use in-text citations
2. Prepare a works cited list

Access grammar exercises for this section in your English
CourseMate, available through CengageBrain.com.

In a recent assignment, your friend "borrowed" information from an on-line encyclopedia and simply inserted it word for word into the text of his report, believing that because he included a reference to the source at the end of the paper, he was fulfilling his requirement to document the source. When you try to use this technique in your college history class, your instructor accuses you of plagiarism. Confused, you find that you have no choice but to drop the class. Where did you go wrong?

As a newly hired technical writer for an engineering firm, you are told that "it's okay to swipe information from the Internet" to put in a proposal for city funding to construct portable childproof barriers for parade routes. When you realize you need some additional evidence, you copy and paste information from another firm's successful proposal in another city. A city staff person researching your proposal discovers the original source of the information, and your firm loses the bid.

While writing an e-mail to a current romantic interest, you decide to borrow some helpful ideas from Shakespeare's sonnets. In such a personal situation, there can be no legal or practical consequence of this borrowing, so you select freely from Shakespeare's stock of descriptive and figurative ideas—although you are careful not to use his actual language. As it turns out, the object of your desire has been reading the sonnets from an early age and recognizes the fraud in your approach.

The misuse of source material is unacceptable in any context, including college. It violates the rules of academic integrity that most institutions of higher learning adhere to. This chapter shows that using sources means more than just dropping them into your paper. Your goal is to show your instructor not that you have found sources

Let's Warm Up!

As a college student, you may feel at times like the image seen here—surrounded by books and needing somehow to use all that valuable source material to create something of your own. How do you go about it? What are the "rules" for extracting ideas and information from your reading so that you can use them in your own research and writing? What does the term *plagiarism* mean, and how can you avoid plagiarizing an author's work?

Take a moment to write a short paragraph that explains your current understanding of the term *plagiarism*. Have you ever known someone who was accused of plagiarism? Have you ever unintentionally plagiarized information only to realize it later? Write about these circumstances.

Todd Davidson/Getty Images

related to the topic at hand but rather that you understand your sources—and their relationship to the thesis and purpose of your paper—and that you can skillfully use your sources to support your ideas and claims.

Understanding Sources

Being a college student is all about learning to interact with published materials—in other words, reading. It is about discussing what you read with others and applying what you read to solve problems or think through important issues. In sum, being a college student is about writing and speaking your own ideas in the context of what you and your classmates have read.

Reading for College

Although this course is concerned mainly with writing, students who read thoughtfully and understand what they read make better writers. To grow as a writer—in terms of the ideas you are able to analyze, as well as your writing style—you must make serious reading a regular part of your life. Your success depends on how accurately and thoroughly you understand what others say about the topics you investigate. Understanding and incorporating source material into your own writing is a high-level critical-thinking skill that you practice not only in this course but throughout your college education.

In college, you read so that you can give back—contribute your own ideas and reasoning—to the general conversation going on around you. Your ethical obligation, therefore, is to make sure you understand other people's ideas as they were intended to be understood and to report those ideas accurately to your own audiences, giving proper credit where it is due. Part of this responsibility involves your ability to comprehend what you read, and part of it involves your honesty.

PRACTICE 13-1

Read the following passage taken from an article by Yvonne Bynoe called "Don't Dismiss Hip-Hop," which appeared in *ColorLines Magazine: Race, Action, Culture* in Spring 2003, and then answer the questions that follow.

Hip-Hop Culture Left Adrift

Much of the Black Nationalist rhetoric of rap music takes its cues from the Black Power Movement. However, unlike the Black Arts Movement, which was the cultural arm of the Black Power Movement, hip-hop culture never developed as part of any political or economic movement. Although the middle 1980s were populated with politically conscious rap artists such as Public Enemy, X-Clan, Paris, and KRS-One, who highlighted the injustices being experienced by young and poor people of color, they got no love from the civil rights crowd. The civil rights establishment, by failing to critically analyze and distinguish "political" rap from the merely trite and materialistic, missed a significant opportunity to use hip-hop to engage and politicize young people around the reactionary policies of the Reagan/ Bush administrations.

Hip-hop culture—abandoned and left to the dictates of multinational corporations—has largely metastasized into apolitical entertainment. Essayist Christopher Tyson states, "Alienated and underestimated, hip-hop became vulnerable to mainstream influence. Since social integrationist philosophy identifies white reality as the default cultural, political, and social norm, hip-hop became in some measure a reflection of the 'American' culture. Therefore, partying and leisure activities were esteemed above the more serious occupations of collective responsibility and organization."

"Hip Hop Culture Left Adrift" by Yvonne Bynoe from Colorlines.com, Spring 2003. Reprinted by permission of Colorlines.com.

1. Does the author admire hip-hop? _____

_____

_____

_____

2. How does the quotation from Tyson support the point of the second paragraph?

_____

_____

_____

3. If you were asked to restate this passage in your own words (in conversation, not writing), what would you say? _____

_____

_____

_____

The way you answer such questions depends on how you approach the task of reading. One thing is certain: You probably couldn't give satisfactory answers to these questions after just one quick reading. You had to slow down, reread, and give yourself time to think about what you were reading. At this point, a few strategies for critical reading can enable you to work successfully with sources (and to become a better student generally):

1. **Annotate your reading.** To annotate means to make notes about what you read, usually by writing notes right in the passage itself. Annotation reinforces every response, intellectual or emotional, that you have as you read through a piece of writing. It is like having a conversation with the author: Your brain is stimulated to go beyond just taking in meaning and begins to create meaning of its own as you begin to understand more about what you have read. Look at how a student has annotated the passage we introduced earlier.

Hip-Hop Culture Left Adrift

Much of the Black Nationalist rhetoric of rap music takes its cues from the Black Power Movement. However, unlike the Black Arts Movement, which was the cultural arm of the Black Power Movement, hip-hop culture never developed as part of any political or economic movement. Although the middle 1980s were populated with politically conscious rap artists such as Public Enemy, X-Clan, Paris, and KRS-One, who highlighted the injustices being experienced by young and poor people of color, they got no love from the civil rights crowd. The civil rights establishment, by failing to critically analyze and distinguish "political" rap from the merely trite and materialistic, missed a significant opportunity to use hip-hop to engage and politicize young people around the reactionary policies of the Reagan/Bush administrations. Hip-hop culture—abandoned and left to the dictates of multinational corporations—has largely metastasized into apolitical entertainment. Essayist Christopher Tyson states, "Alienated and

I wasn't aware of this political connection. I thought it was just street slang. How did rap start to separate itself from other movements in the black community?

Don't know if I like the idea of being "used" as a fan of rap. But, I see her point. Wasn't rock used for political purposes by the antiwar movement in the sixties?

Rap is big these days. Is that so bad? Doesn't that mean that its message is spread among a wider audience, with more awareness and sympathy along with it? Or are we all being fooled?

underestimated, hip-hop became vulnerable to mainstream influence. Since social integrationist philosophy identifies white reality as the default cultural, political, and social norm, hip-hop became in some measure a reflection of the 'American' culture. Therefore, partying and leisure activities were esteemed above the more serious occupations of collective responsibility and organization."

2. **Respond in writing, reread the passage, and then respond again.** After you've read a passage and annotated it, write down your overall reaction to the piece briefly but in complete sentences. You can respond in many ways:
   - State the main point, and then write about whether you agree or disagree (and why).
   - Discuss the author's choice of language or logical development.
   - Put the whole passage in your own words.

   After you have your thoughts down on paper, reread the original passage again. Has your understanding deepened or changed in some other way? Are there parts of the passage you need to think about more carefully? What words do you need to look up to get at the subtle aspects of the author's meaning? Here's how one student responds in writing to the preceding passage.

   I've never thought about rap in this way. I always think of it describing life on the street or in the neighborhood, but it didn't occur to me that rap could be political. The author seems to be saying here that rap's language comes from the radical politics of the civil rights movement but that it has been taken over by the music industry just to make money. We rap fans are being led to believe that listening to rap is an important act that makes a statement when really we are just playing into the hands of the multinational corporations, who are quite happy with the status quo. Anyway, I don't like the idea that whether it's for a good cause or a bad one— politics or big business—there is an assumption that rap fans can be "used" at will by powers that are more conscious than we are about the purposes of the music.

   Notice that part of the response is devoted to stating the meaning of the passage, another part to evaluating the author's ideas, and yet another part to applying those ideas to the reader's own life.

3. **Converse with a partner.** Talking about a reading with someone lets you get your partner's input on the meaning, logic, and expression of the original, and you get to contribute your own reactions to your partner's understanding of the piece.

Learning to read actively makes you a better researcher and writer, helping you use others' ideas properly and without misrepresenting those ideas to your own reader.

Why Use Source Material?

Suppose you've been given a short writing assignment in your history class. You are to write a four-page essay on some aspect of the civil rights movement in the decades following the 1960s. Your instructor's handout says, "Your essay must incorporate two recent sources."

What does it mean to incorporate sources into your writing? "Incorporate sources" is a phrase that opens the world to you as a thinker and a writer. Imagine writing a four-page paper about the civil rights movement based on what you now know. What would you say? Could you give a brief historical summary of the movement? Could you name its major leaders or describe its lasting effects? Could you evaluate the changes it brought to our country? Without exploring source material on your own and reading thoughtfully what you find, chances are you simply don't know enough at this point to write a four-page paper. By incorporating sources, you are synthesizing the published ideas of other writers to create your own personal contribution to the topic you are writing about.

Types of Source Materials

You can rely on two major types of sources: primary and secondary sources.

Primary Sources

Primary sources are those with which you interact personally, without the intervention of another researcher or scholar. Whether you observe the evidence, speak to people knowledgeable about the issue, or read original documents or files, the evidence is the result of your own interpretation of these experiences, not someone else's. Your research paper benefits from three types of primary evidence:

1. **Personal observation or experience.** It is appropriate to use your own observations and experience to convince your reader that your main point is valid. This kind of evidence might be sufficient for certain topics; however, you might have to supplement it with other kinds of support.

2. **Interviews or surveys you conduct.** Sometimes you are fortunate to be able to interview someone who knows a lot about your topic. You don't want to

interview or survey just anybody, of course, because your interview material must be considered valid by your reader. (Students often want to interview or survey their classmates about certain topics—this might work if the topic concerns a classroom issue, but it won't adequately support a broader topic.)

3. **Original documents.** If you go directly to published historical documents for quotable material—the U.S. Constitution or the Magna Carta, for example, or the text of a speech by Martin Luther King Jr. or Winston Churchill—you are relying on primary documentary evidence.

When you incorporate evidence from primary documents into your writing, you must obey the rules for documenting your sources, which are discussed later in this chapter.

Secondary Evidence

Secondary evidence is the information you get from reading the work of other researchers: articles published in newspapers, magazines, journals, or encyclopedias; news broadcasts or documentary films; books written by scholars—the list goes on. This kind of evidence is called secondary because it is written or produced by people who have relied on their own observation or experience, their own research into primary historical documents, or their own reading of other secondary material. When you use secondary sources, you are relying on other people's interpretation; therefore, you must be cautious and check that the evidence is valid.

PRACTICE 13-2

For each of the following sources, write P if the source is primary evidence or S if the source is secondary evidence.

_____ 1. An article that appears in *Newsweek* magazine

_____ 2. An article from a medical journal

_____ 3. A speech by a major political figure

_____ 4. An article from a local newspaper

_____ 5. An article from an international newspaper such as the *New York Times*

_____ 6. Your analysis of a novel by Toni Morrison

_____ 7. An informal survey you conducted

_____ 8. A class lecture given by your history teacher

_____ 9. Information from people's personal letters that you use to form judgments

_____ 10. A trial transcript you review

How Do I Use Source Material?

Given that you have spent some time in the library or online to locate source material that pertains to your project, you can use one or all of the following methods to incorporate information into your text: quote directly, paraphrase, or summarize.

Bridging Knowledge

See Chapter 14, pages 492–494, for instructions on evaluating the reliability of your sources.

Quoting Source Material

When most students think of using source material in their papers, they think of quoting it, taking it word for word from the original. However, quotation is not the most recommended or commonly used method of incorporating secondary source material. You can easily overuse this technique so that your paper becomes a mass of disconnected quotations. When you do need to quote, follow these guidelines:

1. Quote when the material is so well stated that to change it in any way would diminish its power.
2. Limit your use of quotation from secondary sources to a small percentage of the source material you incorporate, perhaps 10–15%.
3. Enclose the quoted information within quotation marks. All information within the quotation marks *must* be exactly as the source states it, including any errors in grammar, spelling, or punctuation.
4. Quote interview sources if you feel it is important to present their exact words. In most interviews you conduct, you are most likely limited to note taking unless the interviewee permits you to tape the discussion. Thus, make sure you distinguish a direct quotation—exactly as the person said it—from your own reconstruction of the conversation from notes. Don't treat your reconstruction as a direct quotation by enclosing the information in quotation marks.
5. In theory, you can quote all you want from primary sources, but you should obey some principle of balance when you do so: If you are writing a four-page paper, you wouldn't want to quote an entire page or more of a speech of Martin Luther King Jr.
6. Within your paragraphs, make your quotations brief, such as a phrase or short sentence integrated into your own writing.
7. If you need to include a long quotation, consisting of more than four lines of text, set it off from your text, indenting it 10 spaces from the left margin. Don't build a whole paragraph in your own essay by using a long quotation composed of various paragraphs or several quotations from various sources.
8. When you quote, document the source according to the appropriate citation style.

Look at the following example of quotation. The original passage comes from a *New Yorker* article by Jeffrey Goldberg titled "Selling Wal-Mart," published April 2, 2007.

> **ORIGINAL PASSAGE:** "Ethical ambidexterity is not a barrier to success in the public-relations field, particularly in Washington. Many prominent Democrats spend the years between national elections representing corporate clients." (36)*

Notice that the first sentence of Goldberg's paragraph is particularly well stated; in this case, you could easily write a paraphrase of the sentence, but you might not catch the same ironic tone as the original. Therefore, quotation is a reasonable choice. Here is how you could do it in the context of your own essay:

> **YOUR QUOTATION:** According to Goldberg, "Ethical ambidexterity is not a barrier to success in the public-relations field, particularly in Washington" (36).

Paraphrasing Source Material

When a passage is too long to quote or not "quote-worthy" in terms of its language or style, you should paraphrase it. To *paraphrase* source material means to put it into your own words in approximately the same length as the original. The purpose of paraphrasing is to capture the main point and supporting ideas of the passage. Here are some guidelines for paraphrasing:

1. **To paraphrase source material, you have to understand it thoroughly in its own context, as well as in the context of your own ideas.** Therefore, make sure you read the source critically and actively before you begin trying to paraphrase it.
2. **Reread the passage with even more attention and focus than you already have.** You need to understand the main point and supporting ideas of the passage so well that you can readily put them into your own words.
3. **Put the original passage aside or cover it up; then try to state the main point and supporting ideas in your own words.** Don't just substitute your own individual words for the original author's. Rethink the sentence structures, as well as the words and phrases, of the original. Note that substituting your own words for the author's words is a form of plagiarism in which you "steal" the author's sentence structures. Make sure you completely rewrite the passage.
4. **Check your paraphrase against the original.** Make sure you have captured the same meaning with the same level of detail and that you have not plagiarized the author's words or sentence structures.
5. **Acknowledge the source from which you are paraphrasing.** Even though you've put the passage into your own words, you still must indicate to your reader that you are borrowing the ideas from another author.

*From "Selling Wal-Mart" by Jeffrey Goldberg, *New Yorker*, April 2, 2007. Reprinted by permission of International Creative Management, Inc. Copyright © 2007 by Jeffrey Goldberg.

Warning: Sometimes when you are faced with a particularly challenging text with words or phrases that are unclear, it is tempting to just copy the information. Not only is this outright plagiarism, or stealing, but it's also relatively easy for your instructor to spot. The change in style from your own writing to a more complex, sophisticated wording interrupts the flow of the paper and makes it apparent that the material is copied from the original source.

To get an idea of how paraphrase works, look at the following example. (The original is taken from the Goldberg article excerpted earlier):

ORIGINAL PASSAGE: "When Walton retired in 1988 (he died in 1992), the company had revenues of sixteen billion dollars. Today, Wal-Mart is the second-largest company in the world in terms of revenue—only Exxon-Mobil is bigger." (Goldberg 32).

YOUR PARAPHRASE: In 1988, when Walton retired, Wal-Mart made $16 billion. Now the company is the second biggest in the world in relation to revenue; only Exxon-Mobil is larger (Goldberg 32).

Does this paraphrase follow all the paraphrase guidelines? Reread point 3 and you realize that you have plagiarized the sentence structure of the original article. So you try again, this time rereading the sentence several times and then covering up the passage. Here is your improved paraphrase:

YOUR PARAPHRASE: Wal-Mart took in $16 billion of revenue in 1988, the year that its founder, Sam Walton, retired. Today, only one company, Exxon-Mobil, is larger than Wal-Mart (Goldberg 32).

Note that in the improved paraphrase, the sentence structure, as well as the phrasing, changed. Also note that you must credit the source of the information. *Don't commit the common mistake of believing that just because you used your own words, you do not need to cite the source.* Whether you use direct quotation, paraphrase, or summary, you *must* cite your source. Not doing so constitutes plagiarism.

PRACTICE 13-3

Practice paraphrasing with a longer passage from the same article. Before starting your paraphrase, circle the words or phrases that are distinctive to this particular writer so that you remember to either rephrase them or put quotes around them. Compare your choices with those of your fellow students. After reading this passage several times and annotating it, cover it up, and write your own paraphrase of the passage. Check your paraphrase against the original to be sure that you haven't plagiarized any information.

The job of the Edelman people—there are about twenty, along with more than three dozen in-house public-relations specialists—is to help Wal-Mart scrub its muddied image. Edelman specializes in helping industries with image problems; another important client is the American Petroleum Institute, a Washington lobbying group that seeks to convince Americans that oil companies care about the environment and that their profits are reasonable. Edelman does its work by cultivating contacts among the country's opinion elites, with whom it emphasizes the good news, and spins the bad; by such tactics as establishing "Astroturf" groups, seemingly grassroots organizations that are actually fronts for industry; and, as I deduced from my own visit to Bentonville, by advising corporate executives on how to speak like risk-averse politicians. (34)

Your paraphrase: _____

_____

_____

_____

_____

_____

_____

Summarizing Source Material

Summarizing source material is much like paraphrasing except that a summary is significantly shorter than a paraphrase. When you summarize, you capture the main point of a long passage, an article, or even a book in a much shorter expression— even in a single sentence, if it suits your purpose.

With summary, you have much less chance of plagiarizing the author's sentence structures, but you still have to be careful not to plagiarize any of the author's substantive words. A summary should be composed of your own words and sentence structures.

1. **Be sure that you thoroughly understand the original and that your expression of its main point is accurate.** Make sure to express the main point of the original—its overall thesis, accomplishment, or contribution to the topic you are researching.

2. **In the case of longer pieces, summarize some supporting ideas that back up the main point, but be careful not to write too much.** A summary should be much shorter than the original and short enough to fit naturally into your paper.

PRACTICE 13-4

Read the following passage from the Wal-Mart article and write a brief (two–three sentence) summary of the author's main points.

More recently, the company experienced a run of bad publicity when it announced new scheduling policies for its store workers (known as "associates"). Under what critics call the "open availability" policy, workers must make themselves available for different shifts from month to month or risk losing hours. Kathleen MacDonald, a cosmetics-counter manager at a Wal-Mart in Aiken, South Carolina, explained to me, "It's simple. They say you have to be there when the computer says the customers will be there. So if you have kids at home you can't show up, but then your hours are being cut."

The company is facing more consequential challenges over its treatment of women. A class-action lawsuit filed in San Francisco in 2001 by six female Wal-Mart employees, alleging that the company has denied promotions and equal pay to women, is proceeding steadily to trial; by some estimates, the suit could cost the company as much as five billion dollars. Wal-Mart has denied that it discriminates against women. Kathleen MacDonald joined the suit after she learned that a male counterpart, who, like her, was stocking shelves, earned more than she did. When she raised the issue, she told me, "My immediate supervisor said, 'Well, God made Adam first, and Eve came from him.' I was, like, what? That's when I decided enough was enough."

Your summary: _____

_____

_____

_____

_____

Extracting Information from a Source

Look at how a student has extracted information from an article for use in her own paper. In this case, the student is researching the worldwide political response to the global warming crisis and has found an article by Michael Glantz, a senior scientist at the National Center for Atmospheric Research in Boulder, Colorado, which appeared in *Geotimes* in April 2005. She has read and annotated the article, and she has highlighted the sections she might use in her paper. Now her job is to extract the material she needs by using paraphrase, summary, quotation, or an appropriate mixture of these.

Global Warming: Whose Problem Is It Anyway?

It no longer seems to make a difference who started the global warming problem, and by "problem," I am referring to the likely enhancement of the naturally occurring greenhouse effect as a result of human activities. Those activities primarily center on the release of carbon dioxide through the burning of fossil fuels such as coal, oil and natural gas. Other heat-trapping greenhouse gases include methane, nitrous oxide and chlorofluorocarbons (CFCs). [. . .]

As we settle into the 21st century, new major greenhouse-gas-producing nations are appearing on the scene, such as India and China. They want to develop their economies, and they have a right, as well as a responsibility, to their citizens to do so. But they are also going to be emitting a larger share of heat-trapping gases, overtaking the industrialized countries that have been the dominant producers of greenhouse gases in the past. Now what? [. . .]

Since 1985, however, another category has emerged: the ostrich. The ostriches include those who refuse to think about global warming as a problem, who refuse to consider any new scientific research, and who think that someone somewhere will solve this problem before it becomes a crisis. [. . .]

Global warming is not a hoax. It actually happens naturally. Industrialization processes in rich countries and now in developing ones are abetting the naturally occurring greenhouse effect. [. . .]

But although we talk a lot about doing something about global warming, we do not have a whole lot of meaningful action. "Let them eat carbon dioxide" seems to be the current response of various governments,

Use this to show that whatever we in the West do, it's the emerging economies of Asia and Latin America that will be hardest to rein in. They say, "You did it—why shouldn't we?"

What will it take to convince naysayers of the seriousness of the problem? This is a task of education.

despite words of concern. Is anyone trying to cut back on carbon dioxide emissions?

The business community, at-risk cities and island nations are increasingly calling for action to combat human-induced global warming. What is needed? Only an active government policy around which a coalition can rally will thoroughly address the complex issue.

Alas, the issue demands government leadership from the "bully pulpit" that calls for and wholeheartedly supports an all-out "war on global warming." In my view, it is the only way to address the global warming problem with some sense of optimism. [. . .]

The war on global warming should begin now. With government support (moral and financial) and a search for new ways to keep our industries progressing without adding greenhouse gases to the atmosphere, there is a real chance for the global community to pull together. [. . .]

The Dutch have successfully fought off the floods of the North Sea for centuries, with few breaches in recent times (1953 comes to mind). The Netherlands have even contracted with the U.S. federal government for a few hundred million dollars, to assist in developing levees that can withstand certain intensities of tropical storms around New Orleans.

Despite their levee-making skills, however, the Dutch know their limits. The Netherlands is now working to develop a "Hydropole," a city that can live on the rising waters. They know they need to do something to protect the 70 percent of the country that is below sea level, when a warmer atmosphere leads to rising seas.

Other countries need to follow by accepting the potential changes that lie ahead, and working now to plan for those changes and to curb actions that

---

Well, if the business community sees the risk, it must be real, and it must be bad. I'm not sure how optimistic we can be given that we haven't slowed our production of harmful emissions. How long will it take?

Use this to show that some countries are at least planning to protect their populations.

> would otherwise fuel more change. Only with an aggressive war on global warming, supported by the entire international community of nations and with participation of the United States, can we learn to live within the guidelines of nature, respecting her thresholds of change by choosing not to cross them.*

Here, the student summarizes a portion of the article:

> In his article, Glantz describes the efforts of the Netherlands to protect its low-lying populations by developing cities that can survive as waters rise around them.

Here are two paraphrases from the article.

PARAPHRASE 1:
According to Glantz, the only way we will begin addressing the problem of global warming with any hope for success is for governments to take leadership roles and begin developing policies that lead the way. He notes that the pressure for change is coming from a range of interests, including business, coastal cities, and nations situated on islands.

PARAPHRASE 2:
(INCORPORATING QUOTATION)
Glantz writes that the newly developing nations of India and China, just to name two, will be increasing contributors to the problem. After all, he claims, "they want to develop their economies, and they have a right, as well as a responsibility, to their citizens to do so." However, this natural desire for economic growth will propel them to overtake Western countries in their production of greenhouse gasses. Glantz wonders how we will approach this difficulty.

And here is a quotation, which the student believes will make a good basis for a hopeful conclusion in her own paper.

> Glantz states, "The war on global warming should begin now. With government support (moral and financial) and a search for new ways to keep our industries progressing without adding greenhouse gases to the atmosphere, there is a real chance for the global community to pull together."

---

*From Michael Glantz, Global Warming: Whose Problem is it Anyway? From Geotimes, June 2006. © 2006 American Geological Institute. All rights reserved. Reprinted by permission.

How Do I Integrate Sources?

Whenever you use borrowed material in your own work, you must indicate to your reader where the borrowed material begins and ends. Your reader should never be left wondering which words and ideas belong to you and which come from your sources. You also need to integrate borrowed material naturally into your own work so that it reads smoothly as part of your paper. In addition, you must identify the source adequately as part of the integration of the material into your own text, using a *signal phrase.*

A signal phrase is a short phrase you use in your own writing to introduce borrowed material. You've seen several of these phrases already in this chapter: "According to Goldberg, . . .," "Glantz states, . . .," and "Glantz writes that . . .."

> According to Goldberg, "Ethical ambidexterity is not a barrier to success in the public-relations field, particularly in Washington" (36).

You might think it's sufficient just to begin the borrowed material with the open quotation mark, which signals to your reader that you are introducing borrowed material. However, this practice wouldn't fulfill the other requirements of integration: The borrowed material must fit smoothly into your paper, and you must identify the source adequately as part of the integration. Leaving the signal phrase out results in an error known as *dropped quotation.* Dropped quotations appear out of nowhere. They can confuse your reader and interrupt the flow of your own writing.

DROPPED QUOTATION:	Newspapers need to be more innovative in how they deliver news if they hope to capture the youth market. "Younger readers are gleaning their news elsewhere, whether *The Daily Show* or Google's news Web site" (Steinberg). Teens find such methods less time consuming and more entertaining, two important elements of their lifestyles.
SAME QUOTATION INTEGRATED WITH APPROPRIATE SIGNAL PHRASE (LEAD-IN):	Newspapers need to be more innovative in how they deliver news if they hope to capture the youth market. According to Brian Steinberg, the new generation of readers "are gleaning their news elsewhere, whether *The Daily Show* or Google's news Web site." Teens find such methods less time consuming and more entertaining, two important elements of their lifestyles.

The following list should help you choose signal phrases to integrate your direct quotations or paraphrased material.

Signal Words to Integrate Quotations or Paraphrased Material into Writing

according to	comments	explains	refutes
acknowledges	compares	grants	rejects
adds	confirms	illustrates	reports
admits	considers (that)	implies	responds
affirms	contends	insists	states
agrees	declares	in the words of	suggests
alleges	demonstrates	notes	thinks
argues	denies	maintains	underlines
asserts	disputes	observes	writes
believes	emphasizes	points out	
claims	endorses	reasons	

Here are some examples of signal phrases in action:
- As one critic points out, ". . ." (Smith 13).
- Jean-Paul Sartre believed that ". . ." (87).
- In the words of St. Thomas Aquinas, ". . ." (35).
- According to most critics, the lyrics suggest that ". . ." (Cooper 34–35).

Besides using signal phrases, you can integrate direct quotations as follows:

1. Make your direct quotation a grammatical component of your sentence.
   - One of the most affecting comments from *The Diary of Anne Frank* was that she still believes that "all people are basically good at heart."
   - In defense, Mandalay Resort Group President Glenn Schaeffer states that casino jobs are not "fast-food jobs" but jobs "you can grow in and support a family" on (qtd. in Smith 35).

2. Use a form of the word *follow* or a verb (and a colon) to introduce your direct quotation.
   - Carrie Russell, a surrogate mother who decided to help others, made the following claim: "I knew I could do it because there were no genetic ties to me" (qtd. in Katz).
   - Chad Hills, reporter for *Focus on Social Issues,* writes: "A 73-year-old retired Colorado man gambled away his entire life savings, $63,000, at the nickel slots."

As you incorporate your direct quotations into your paper, remember to integrate each smoothly into your text. You should move the reader from your own thoughts to your sources' ideas and then back again to your discussion. Dropped quotations disrupt the smooth transition of ideas.

Punctuating Quotations

Some students find that punctuating direct quotations can be confusing. However, by applying six simple rules and editing your writing carefully, you should not have difficulty punctuating direct quotations.

1. When introducing a quotation with a signal phrase, use a comma to introduce a quotation that can stand alone.

   According to Glenn Welker, "The Mayan culture was not one unified empire but rather a multitude of separate entities with a common cultural background."

2. If the quotation is a grammatical component of your sentence (a part of your sentence structure), don't use a comma, and don't capitalize the first letter of the direct quotation.

   Recent studies indicate that the Mayan civilization developed an elaborate system of writing "to record the transition of power through the generations" (Welker).

3. Place commas and periods inside quotation marks.

   "In both the priesthood and the ruling class," reports Glenn Welker, "nepotism was apparently the prevailing system under which new members were chosen."

4. Unlike commas and periods, which go inside the quotation marks, semicolons and colons should be placed outside the quotation marks unless they are part of the quotation.

> Glenn Welker further reports that after the birth of an heir, a Maya ruler "performed a blood sacrifice": The sacrifice consisted of "drawing blood from his own body and offering it to his ancestors"; however, Welker adds that "a human sacrifice was then offered at the time of the new king's installation in office."

5. If the quotation is in the form of a question, then place the question mark inside the quotation mark; however, if you are raising a question and adding a quotation that wasn't originally presented in the source in question form, then place the question mark outside the quotation mark.

> To encourage reliable research, John Keyser raises the following question: "Why are modern ethnologists and archeologists so confused?" He claims that modern researchers have abandoned their inquiry into the culture of the people to pursue the theory of evolution. However, will these researchers really "lose the tools that would enable them to unravel the mystery of the Maya"?

6. As a general rule, you should quote only as much as you need from a sentence, not necessarily the entire sentence. When you break up your source's sentence, you need to let the reader know that the quotation is not complete and that you have left out part of the passage. Ellipsis points serve this purpose. Ellipsis points are three spaced dots (. . .) signaling to the reader that part of the source's information has been left out. Be careful not to join parts that do not form a complete sentence.

> Michael D. Lemonick further maintains that "four new Maya sites have been uncovered in the jungle-clad mountains of southern Belize . . . that experts assumed the Maya would have shunned."

Paraphrasing

Look again at the student paraphrase from the global warming article.

> Glantz writes that the newly developing nations of India and China, just to name two, will be increasing contributors to the problem. After all, he claims, "they want to develop their economies, and they have a right, as well as a responsibility, to their citizens to do so." However, this natural desire for economic growth will propel them to overtake Western countries in their production of greenhouse gasses. Glantz wonders how we will approach this difficulty.

The difficulty of indicating the beginning and end of paraphrased selections is that paraphrases can be fairly long—a whole paragraph or even longer. When you present a longer paraphrase, you not only need to indicate where it begins but you also need occasionally to remind your reader *during* your paraphrase that you are still presenting borrowed material. Notice that the student used a signal phrase to introduce Glantz at the beginning of the paraphrase, then the pronoun *he* to introduce the quotation (otherwise, she would have a dropped quotation), and then Glantz's name at the end to remind the reader that she is still presenting Glantz's ideas in the form of paraphrase. Notice that this is an example of a paraphrase that includes a direct quotation.

Summarizing

In the student's summary of the global warming article, she needs to integrate the source.

> In his article, Glantz describes the efforts of the Netherlands to protect its low-lying populations by developing cities that can survive as waters rise around them.

Because the purpose of summary is to present a short statement about what one of the sources contributes to the paper, it's natural to want to identify that source; doing so usually lends weight and authority to the point the writer is trying to make. Again, you can accomplish this purpose in the signal phrase.

Bringing Borrowed Material to an End

If you use signal phrases to introduce borrowed material, you also need to indicate to your reader that the borrowed material has ended.

1. Use a parenthetical citation as you have seen several times already in this chapter.

> Heiml reports that the Haitian leaders were at first hesitant to act (465). This is just the kind of restraint the country could have used in later years, but there was no such luck.

2. Let the borrowed passage end one of your own paragraphs. When you indent for a new paragraph, your reader understands that you're beginning anew with your own words and ideas.

Frothermeyer argues that because of their evolutionary past, humans are biologically unable to process large amounts of starchy carbohydrates; furthermore, he claims, almost all diagnosed obesity could be eliminated through dietary changes.

Another inheritance of our biological past is the need for fairly consistent, if not constant, exercise.

3. Start the next sentence with a new signal phrase, indicating the beginning of another borrowed passage or a transition to your own words and ideas.

MacElwey writes that American education in the 21st century must abandon its traditional way of doing business and adopt models from overseas. According to Galen, the German model of secondary education offers the best hope for our failing system (54).

PRACTICE 13-5

Read the following passages from student research papers. In the space provided, evaluate the integration of source materials, and briefly explain your evaluation.

1. Alarmingly, millions of children are being treated for a disease that does not actually exist. Attention deficit/hyperactivity disorder is not a biological disease. "ADHD genetic researchers cannot determine a convincing body of evidence pointing toward genetic factors" (Breggin 126). The list of potential symptoms is rather lengthy and somewhat vague.

   Acceptable _____ **Unacceptable** _____ **Explanation:** _____

   _____

   _____

2. The once-active child becomes less spontaneous and more compliant. However, these children are not learning to become more disciplined; the drugs are merely inhibiting brain function (Breggin 20). Children taking Ritalin certainly become more compliant and passive.

   Acceptable _____ **Unacceptable** _____ **Explanation:** _____

   _____

   _____

3. A national survey reveals interesting data: "Of 1,261 school administrators, 97% indicated that school violence was increasing across the United States and in their neighboring school districts" (Furlong and Morrison).

Acceptable _____ **Unacceptable** _____ **Explanation:** _____
_____
_____

4. Opinion is fairly evenly split across the country. Supporters believe the generous coverage supplied by employers and national health programs causes individuals to ignore high costs of health care, implying that under the circumstances of paying for health care out of pocket people would shop for cheaper health plans, which in turn would put pressure on suppliers (Bailey).

Acceptable _____ **Unacceptable** _____ **Explanation:** _____
_____
_____

5. In a radio address, President Clinton emphasized the importance of keeping track of sexual predators, thereby reducing crimes against children. He made the following commitment: "Above all, we must move forward to the day when we are no longer numb to acts of violence against children, when their appearance on the evening news is both shocking and rare. Our approach is working. . . . More and more, our children can learn and play and dream without risk of harm. That is an America that is moving in the right direction" (91).

Acceptable _____ **Unacceptable** _____ **Explanation:** _____
_____
_____

How Do I Avoid Plagiarism?

If you aren't quoting, paraphrasing, or summarizing your source material correctly, chances are you are plagiarizing it. When you plagiarize, you are stealing someone else's words or ideas and passing them off as your own. Sometimes, students plagiarize unintentionally, especially when they are first learning how to work with sources. At other times, students are tempted to plagiarize deliberately. Plagiarism is a serious offense against academic integrity and can result in failure in a course, disciplinary action, or expulsion from a college or university. You have an important ethical obligation when you work with other people's words and ideas.

Common Types of Plagiarism

● You plagiarize when you "lift" passages from a source word for word and place them into your own writing without quoting and citing them.
● You plagiarize when you put others' ideas into your own words (even when you do it correctly) but don't cite the source.
● You plagiarize when, in a paraphrase or summary, you use *any* of the author's stylistically characteristic words or phrases without quotation marks, or mimic the author's sentence structures, whether or not you cite the source.

Strategies to Prevent Plagiarism

If you employ the integrating techniques introduced in this chapter, you can avoid plagiarizing from your sources. That is, if you paraphrase correctly, summarize correctly, and quote correctly—and if you cite every source from which you borrow—you won't be guilty of plagiarism. As a summary of this chapter's advice, here are some helpful hints you can use to guide your thinking as you extract words and ideas from your sources.

1. When paraphrasing, remember the following:
   ● Read the original actively and critically. Make sure you really understand the material before trying to paraphrase it.
   ● Put the original aside, and do your best to capture the main and supporting points without referring back to the original.
   ● Use short sentences to capture the meaning of the original, and then combine your short sentences into longer ones.
   ● After you've written a paraphrase, check it against the original to make sure you haven't used any of the author's distinctive words or sentence structures. If you are still too close to the original, try paraphrasing your own paraphrase. Repeat this process several times to gradually move away from the original. Check to make sure that you are retaining the meaning of the original.
2. When summarizing, remember the following:
   ● Write a sentence that states your own understanding of the source's contribution to the topic you are writing about. Don't take your summary from the introduction of the article or from a book jacket.
   ● If you are summarizing a longer piece, such as a long research article or a book, your summary may contain additional material. Again, this material must be in your own words and sentence structures.
3. When quoting, remember the following:
   ● Extract the material verbatim (word for word) from your source.
   ● Put quotation marks around all quoted material, and punctuate your quotations correctly.

UNDERSTANDING
Sources

Finally, whether you are paraphrasing, summarizing, or quoting, you must document the source of any borrowed material. If you fail to document the source, you could easily be accused of deliberate plagiarism.

How Do I Document My Sources?

Although we use MLA documentation style in this chapter, you are not limited to just this style. Your instructor will let you know the style most appropriate for the course. Different purposes may require different styles. The following are the four most common types of documentation styles:

1. Generally, Modern Language Association (MLA) style is used in the humanities in such courses as English, philosophy, and art. It's probably one of the simplest documentation styles to use.
2. American Psychological Association (APA) style is often, although not exclusively, used in the social sciences: psychology, sociology, and anthropology. It's not unusual for an instructor in business management, education, or biology to require APA style.
3. *The Chicago Manual of Style* (CMS) is often used in the humanities and the social sciences. However, it's more complex than MLA and APA. Again, your instructor or your employer should have the final word.
4. Council of Science Editors (CSE) is a scientific style. This system is used to document information in the biological sciences, as well as other scientific classes.

Regardless of the particular citation style they use, all researchers must abide by strict rules to document their use of sources. Documentation consists of two components:

1. In-text citations, which you insert throughout your paper to indicate exactly where you are using source material
2. A list of all sources, or references, that you use in your paper (called *works cited* in MLA style)

These two components work closely together to inform your reader about your use of sources.

Understanding In-Text Citations

Every time you use information or ideas from a source—whether paraphrased, summarized, or quoted—you must acknowledge the source by inserting a reference in your text that credits the source. You can either mention the source in a signal phrase or indicate the source in parentheses at the end of the information. These in-text citations serve three purposes:

1. They credit your sources for their input to your paper. As you already know, failing to credit your sources is considered plagiarism.
2. They give your reader enough information to locate a complete description of your sources on the works cited page.

3. They provide page numbers to let the reader find in the original text the specific passage you are referencing if your source is a print source or a PDF file. The following paraphrase illustrates this purpose:

> Recent studies have found that several regions of the brain of a person with autism are different from the norm, but unfortunately, none of these differences alone can account for this condition (Carmichael 53).

Look at some characteristics of this citation:

- Through the parenthetical citation at the end, you immediately know that this information comes from someone other than the student writer.
- Because there are no quotation marks, you can conclude that this passage is a paraphrase, that is, the student's own interpretation of the source.
- The author's last name is Carmichael. To find out more about the Carmichael source, you need only to go to "C" in the works cited list, where you can find a full description of the source.
- The page number tells you that the information appears on page 53 in the article.

When using MLA documentation style, follow these basic rules of parenthetical citation:

1. **Place your citation right after the source's information.** Place your own commentaries after the citation to keep your own ideas and knowledge separate from your source's ideas.

> INCORRECT: According to Freud, we go through five stages of development, known as psychosexual stages. In each stage, a person faces a crisis that must be worked out or else become fixated in that stage of development. For example, a Freudian psychologist might explain my brother's smoking and overeating as a result of a fixation in the oral stage (Rivera 102).

Rivera didn't know your brother; furthermore, Rivera might not have agreed with your example. Place your citations in a manner that distinguishes your interpretations and experiences, although valuable to the paper, from the source's information.

> CORRECT: According to Freud, we go through five stages of development, known as psychosexual stages. In each stage, a person faces a crisis that must be worked out or else become fixated in that stage of development (Rivera 102). For example, a Freudian psychologist might explain my brother's smoking and overeating as a result of a fixation in the oral stage.

2. **Credit all authors.** Don't just credit the first author listed in a source. You must credit all coauthors as well. Also, when crediting coauthors, don't change the order in which the authors are listed in a document. Follow these rules for crediting authors:

> One author: (Smith 13)
> Two authors: (Smith and Jackson 13)
> Three authors: (Smith, Jackson, and Johnson 13)
> Four or more authors: (Smith et al. 13); the abbreviation *et al.* is short for *et alii,*
> which is Latin for "and others."

3. **Make your parenthetical citations clear without distracting the reader from the task of reading your paper.** The goal is to provide enough information to refer the reader to the works cited entry, so limit your information to the essentials. Sometimes the page number may not be available. For example, many Internet sources don't supply page numbers unless the document is in a PDF file. If the page number is not available, omit it. (When you print your sources from the Internet, your printer numbers your pages, but you should not use these numbers as the source's page numbers.)

4. **Permit your reader to locate your source in the works cited list without having to search.** Your works cited list should be in strict alphabetical order so that your in-text citation takes the reader directly to the correct entry in the list.

> CORRECT: The Small Business Development Center in Maine reports that more than four dollars in state revenue are generated annually for each taxpayer dollar that state residents invest in the S.B.D.C. (Turkel).

The reader needs merely to go to "T" in the works cited list to find the entire information about the source.

5. **Don't clutter your parenthetical citations.** Keep your citations clear and to the point.
   a. If you name the source in your text, don't repeat it in the parenthetical citation.

> INCORRECT: Marie Valdez writes that recent studies indicate that 5 out of every 100 high school students enrolled in October 1999 dropped out of school before October 2000 (Valdez 23).

> CORRECT: Marie Valdez writes that recent studies indicate that 5 out of every 100 high school students enrolled in October 1999 dropped out of school before October 2000 (23).

> OR

> CORRECT: Recent studies indicate that 5 out of every 100 high school students enrolled in October 1999 dropped out of school before October 2000 (Valdez 23).

b. Do not break up the parenthetical citation by inserting a comma, *p.*, or *page* between the source and its page number.

> **INCORRECT:** (Shanstrom, 46) OR (Shanstrom p. 46) OR (Shanstrom page 46)
>
> **CORRECT:** (Shanstrom 46)

6. **If the author is unknown, move to the next available unit of information.** Obtaining sources without an author's name is not uncommon. In sources from periodicals or from the Internet, the next unit of information is usually the title of the article or the title of the book.

> **ARTICLE:** Numerous studies and surveys indicate that occupational pressures are the primary source of stress ("Job Stress" 13).

Note that the quotation marks indicate the title is the name of the article. Don't omit the quotation marks in your citations. The reader can find this source under "J" in the works cited list.

> **BOOK:** The human body has a natural stress reaction that increases "the energy levels to prepare the body for a predicament and then drops the energy level when the situation is over" (*Nutrition and You* 75).

a. Just as with names of authors, if you name the title of the article or the title of the book in the text, you don't need to repeat it in the citation.

> **CORRECT:** The *Gazette's* article "Downtown Retailers Hope to Win Holiday Shoppers" points out that most retailers want to attract new customers, and to be successful they realize that they must "combine marketing dollars and promote downtown together" (12).

b. Again, make your parenthetical citations as simple and elegant as possible. It's acceptable to shorten long titles of either books or articles. Just provide enough information so that your reader can locate the source in the works cited list.

> **INCORRECT:** Most retailers want to attract new customers, and to be successful they realize that they must "combine marketing dollars and promote downtown together" ("Downtown Retailers Hope to Win Holiday Shoppers" 12).
>
> **CORRECT:** Most retailers want to attract new customers, and to be successful they realize that they must "combine marketing dollars and promote downtown together" ("Downtown" 12).

7. **If you use a quotation that was quoted in another source, indicate this in your parenthetical citation.** For example, suppose that your source is Martha Johnson. As you read the information, you find that Johnson quotes

a prominent economist by the name of Benjamin Randall. You want to use Randall's exact quotation for your paper. You have two choices: Go to the original source, Randall, or use Johnson as the source, and indicate that Randall is the indirect source. Here's how you would cite this source:

> Economist Benjamin Randall states, "America's current immigration policies . . . fail to recognize the importance of Mexican workers to the national economy" (qtd. in Johnson 18).

By using *qtd. in* (meaning "quoted in"), you're letting the reader know that Randall is not listed in the works cited list and that the information appears under Johnson.

8. **If you use two or more sources by the same author, be sure to identify which source you are using.** If you simply give the author's name, the reader looks at the works cited list and finds that you have the author listed more than once. Without additional clues, your reader does not know which source contains the information. You can identify the source in several ways:

a. Name the author in the text and the article in the parenthetical citation.

> CORRECT: We hesitate to increase our police force because of budget constraints, yet we fail to consider the cost of crime. Raymond Diaz reports that personal crimes alone are "estimated to cost $105 billion annually in medical costs, lost earnings, and public program costs related to victim assistance" ("Rethinking" 61).

b. Name the title of the article in the text and the author in the parenthetical citation.

> CORRECT: We hesitate to increase our police force because of budget constraints, yet we fail to consider the cost of crime. The article titled "Rethinking the Cost of Crime in America" states that personal crimes alone are "estimated to cost $105 billion annually in medical costs, lost earnings, and public program costs related to victim assistance" (Diaz 61).

c. Name the author and the title of the article in the text.

> CORRECT: We hesitate to increase our police force because of budget constraints, yet we fail to consider the cost of crime. In his article titled "Rethinking the Cost of Crime in America," Raymond Diaz reports that personal crimes alone are "estimated to cost $105 billion annually in medical costs, lost earnings, and public program costs related to victim assistance" (61).

d. Place all information in the parenthetical citation and not in the text.

> CORRECT: We hesitate to increase our police force because of budget constraints, yet we fail to consider the cost of crime. Personal crimes alone are "estimated to cost $105 billion annually in medical costs, lost earnings, and public program costs related to victim assistance" (Diaz, "Rethinking" 61).

PRACTICE 13-6

For each set of source information, give a parenthetical citation using the necessary information provided in the bracket. *Do not* edit the text; supply the parenthetical citations only.

1. According to a 2002 article in *The Economist*, "Schools are responsible for instilling in our youths a strong sense of civic responsibilities." [No author is given. The title of the article is "Looking into the Future," which appeared in the September 23, 2002 issue of *The Economist*.] _____

2. Brian Lawson predicts that the dropout rate would decrease if parents were held more accountable. [This information appeared on page 56 of an article by Brian Lawson titled "The Educational Crisis," published in *Education Outlook* in the April 2007 issue.] _____

3. Recent surveys indicate that 4 out of 10 high school seniors "in both urban and suburban schools have used illegal drugs." [This was written by Jay Green and Greg Forster. The article, titled "Sex, Drug, and Delinquency in Urban and Suburban Public Schools," was published in January 2004. It appeared on the Manhattan Institute for Policy Research website.] _____

4. The trend continues. Twelve seniors from Willington High School admitted having used prescription drugs they either purchased in Mexico or took from their parent's medicine chests. [The author is unknown; the article, titled "High School Assessment of Drug Use among Seniors," was published on April 25, 2004. It appeared on *The Havendale Update*, a website.] _____

5. Leslie Drier, executive director of United for a Drug Free America, states that the use of prescription drugs is "engrained in teen culture and not enough parents are aware of the existing trend." [This information, written by Leonard Rios, appears in an article titled "High School and Drugs." It was published in the October 2005 issue of *Issues in Education*. The information appears on page 73.]

_____

Understanding the Works Cited List

The final page of your research paper is your list of sources. If you're using MLA documentation style, this list is called *Works Cited*. In this section, we discuss the most common sources you are likely to document in most classes. If you use sources other than those listed here, refer to the most recent edition of the *MLA Handbook for Writers of Research Papers*.

Your first step is to identify the type of source you're using. For example, is it a book, a periodical (newspaper, magazine, or journal), a website, or an interview? After you identify the source, you can then focus on the required units of information to document that source. For example, most sources require that you start with the name of the author. A source written by **one author** looks like this:

> Carter, Lana.

Note that you invert the name of the author: last name, then a comma, first name, and a period. If you have **two authors,** you must also include the name of the coauthor but don't invert it.

> Morales, Juan, and Michael Engle.

A source by **three authors** is similar.

> Kingrey, Gail, Nick Alfonso, and Rose H. Santiago.

However, if you have **four or more authors,** list only the first author and use *et al.* (Latin for "and others") to indicate the rest of the coauthors.

> McKinnon, Sara, et al.

If **no author** is listed, jump to the next unit—the title of the book or the title of the article in a periodical, depending on the source you're documenting.

Documenting Books

In the following figure, each box represents a unit. Pay close attention to punctuation.

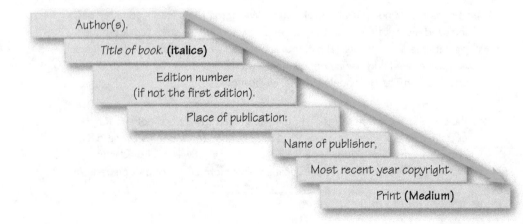

Author(s).

Title of book. **(italics)**

Edition number
(if not the first edition).

Place of publication:

Name of publisher,

Most recent year copyright.

Print **(Medium)**

For publisher's names, omit articles (*A*, *An*, *The*); abbreviations such as *Co.*, *Inc.*, *Ltd.*; and parts of the publisher's name, such as *House*, *Publishers*, or *Press*. However, if referring to university presses, use UP, for example, Oxford UP.

1. **Book with one or more authors.**

   Sample Parenthetical Citation

   Henley, Patricia. *The Hummingbird House.* Denver: MacMurray, 1999. Print.

   (Henley 135)

   Caper, Charles, and Lawrence T. Teamos. *How to Camp.* Philadelphia: Doubleday, 1986. Print.

   (Caper and Teamos 105)

   Setmire, Elisa. *Studies of Autism.* 3rd ed. Oxford: Oxford UP, 2007. Print.

   (Setmire 105–106)

   Nichols, James O., and Karen W. Nichols. *The Departmental Guide and Record Book for Student Outcomes and Assessment and Institutional Effectiveness.* New York: Agathon, 2000. Print.

   (Nichols and Nichols 65)

   Nazario, Luis A., Deborah D. Borchers, and William F. Lewis. *Bridges to Better Writing.* 2ⁿᵈ ed. Boston: Cengage, 2012. Print.

   (Nazario, Borchers, and Lewis 317)

   Gilman, Sandor, et al. *Hysteria Beyond Freud.* Berkeley: U of California P, 1993. Print.

   (Gilman et al. 370)

2. **Book with no author named.**

   Freedom: A Profile in Courage. New York: Macmillan, 2003. Print.

   (*Freedom* 370)

3. **Book with an editor.**

   Chavez, Crystal, ed. *Tales of Women Entrepreneurs.* New York: Bedford/ St. Martin's, 2007. Print.

   (Chavez 205)

   (Use abbreviations "ed." for "editor" and "eds." for "editors.")

4. **Section from an anthology (a work by many authors or different works by the same author).**

   Levy, Steven. "iPOD Nation." *Mirror on America.* Ed. Joan T. Mims, New York: Bedford/St. Martins, 2007. 346–59. Print.

   (Levy 349)

Examine the works cited page that follows based on the preceding nine books.

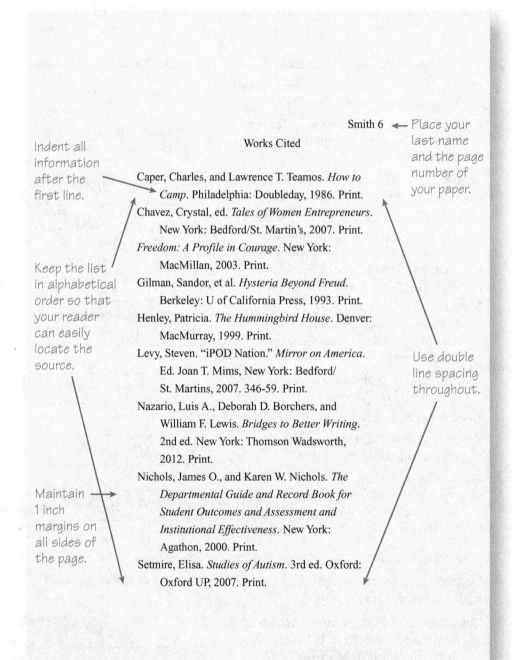

Smith 6 ← Place your
last name
and the page
number of
your paper.

Works Cited

Indent all
information
after the
first line.

Caper, Charles, and Lawrence T. Teamos. *How to Camp*. Philadelphia: Doubleday, 1986. Print.

Chavez, Crystal, ed. *Tales of Women Entrepreneurs*. New York: Bedford/St. Martin's, 2007. Print.

Freedom: A Profile in Courage. New York: MacMillan, 2003. Print.

Keep the list
in alphabetical
order so that
your reader
can easily
locate the
source.

Gilman, Sandor, et al. *Hysteria Beyond Freud*. Berkeley: U of California Press, 1993. Print.

Henley, Patricia. *The Hummingbird House*. Denver: MacMurray, 1999. Print.

Levy, Steven. "iPOD Nation." *Mirror on America*. Ed. Joan T. Mims, New York: Bedford/ St. Martins, 2007. 346-59. Print.

Use double
line spacing
throughout.

Nazario, Luis A., Deborah D. Borchers, and William F. Lewis. *Bridges to Better Writing*. 2nd ed. New York: Thomson Wadsworth, 2012. Print.

Nichols, James O., and Karen W. Nichols. *The Departmental Guide and Record Book for Student Outcomes and Assessment and Institutional Effectiveness*. New York: Agathon, 2000. Print.

Maintain
1 inch
margins on
all sides of
the page.

Setmire, Elisa. *Studies of Autism*. 3rd ed. Oxford: Oxford UP, 2007. Print.

PRACTICE 13-7

Write the following books in correct MLA format as they would appear on a works cited list. Number each source the order in which each source would appear on a works cited page.

1. A book published by Texas Tech University Press with the title *Children of the Dust: An Okie Family Story*, written in 2006 by Betty Grant Henshaw and published in Lubbock, Texas.

    Works cited entry # : _____

    _____

    _____

2. A book titled *House of Tears*, published in Guilford, Connecticut, by Lyons Press in 2005 and edited by Dr. John Hughes, a professor at St. George's School in Vancouver, Canada.

    Works cited entry # : _____

    _____

3. A book by Keith Thomas, a lecturer at Oxford University, titled *Religion and the Decline of Magic*, published in New York in 1999 by Oxford University Press.

    Works cited entry # : _____

    _____

4. A short story titled "Paul's Case" by Willa Cather in an anthology titled *Literature: An Introduction to Reading and Writing* by Edgar V. Roberts and Henry E. Jacobs. The anthology was published in 2004 by Prentice Hall in Upper Saddle River, New Jersey, and the story appears on pages 164–176.

    Works cited entry # : _____

    _____

    _____

    _____

5. An essay in *The Best American Essays 2005*, edited by Susan Orlean; the title of the essay is "Old Faithful" by David Sedaris on pages 195–202. The publisher of the book is Houghton Mifflin Company of Boston.

    Works cited entry # : _____

    _____

    _____

Documenting Periodicals from Print and Online Sources

Periodicals—newspapers, magazines, and journals—can provide current and reliable information if you choose them correctly. The following diagram summarizes the most common types of sources you are most likely to use and document.

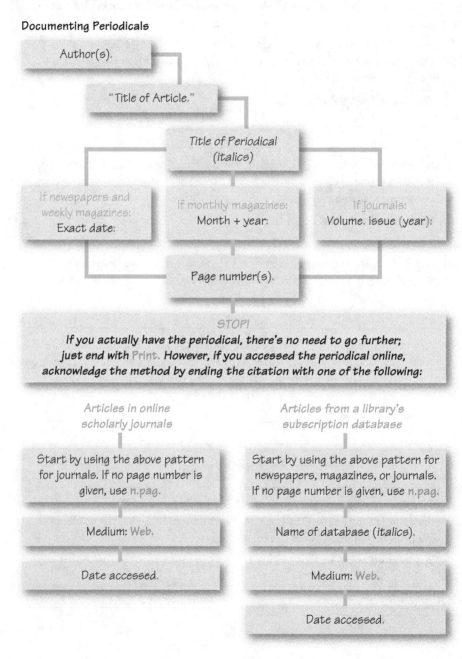

Documenting Periodicals

Author(s).

"Title of Article."

Title of Periodical (italics)

If newspapers and weekly magazines: Exact date:

If monthly magazines: Month + year:

If journals: Volume. issue (year):

Page number(s).

STOP!
If you actually have the periodical, there's no need to go further; just end with Print. However, if you accessed the periodical online, acknowledge the method by ending the citation with one of the following:

Articles in online scholarly journals

Articles from a library's subscription database

Start by using the above pattern for journals. If no page number is given, use n.pag.

Start by using the above pattern for newspapers, magazines, or journals. If no page number is given, use n.pag.

Medium: Web.

Name of database (italics).

Date accessed.

Medium: Web.

Date accessed.

When documenting periodicals, be sure to follow these guidelines.

1. Use a colon after the date to indicate the page numbers (Sept. 2007: 45–36.). Articles accessed online often do not have page numbers. In such cases, use "n. pag." for no page number.

2. Use quotation marks to indicate titles of articles. However, use italics for titles of periodicals (newspapers, magazines, and journals), names of websites, and names of databases.

3. Abbreviate all months except May, June, and July.

4. If the online article is provided as a PDF file, which is an actual copy of the article as it was published, you should use the page numbers provided. If a subscription database service, such as Gale, gives you a choice between PDF and HTML (a text file with no page numbers), choose the PDF file so that you can refer the reader to the exact location of the information in your parenthetical citations.

5. The range of page numbers in the examples that follow shows information appearing on consecutive pages. However, if the article does not continue on consecutive pages but jumps to another section of the periodical, let the reader know by giving the starting page and a plus sign (25 Aug. 2006: 17+.).

6. For titles of articles, be sure to capitalize the first letter of the main words (adjectives, adverbs, verbs, nouns, pronouns) even if your source doesn't. Don't capitalize the first letters of *a, an, the* (referred to as articles); prepositions; or coordinate conjunctions (*for, and, nor, but, or, yet, so*) unless any of these words start or end the title.

As you review the following examples, go back to the preceding diagram to see how they fit.

UNDERSTANDING
Sources

1. **Article from a weekly magazine.**

   Carter, Lana. "Educators Advocate Early Intervention." *Newsweek* 23 June 2007: 36–45. Print.

   Sample Parenthetical Citation

   (Carter 38)

2. **Article from a monthly magazine.**

   Engle, Michael, and Donna Fitzsimmons. "Gender Violence in Schools." *Psychology Issues* Feb. 2006: 15–23. Print.

   (Engle and Fitzsimmons 20)

3. **Article from a journal.**

   Provide volume and issue numbers for all journals.

   Kingrey, Gail, et al. "Spinal Injuries." *New England Journal of Medicine* 13.6 (2006): 413–35. Print.

   (Kingrey et al. 423)

4. **Article from a daily newspaper.**
   a. **Lettered sections.** Some newspapers divide their sections by letters.

   Witters, Lani, and Rose Henri Santiago. "Public Schools in Fairfield under Fire." *The Chieftain* [Pueblo] 8 Feb. 2006: A2. Print.

   (Witters and Santiago A2)

   Note: If the city of publication is not in the title, include the city (do not italicize) in brackets at the end of the title.

   b. **Numbered sections.** Some newspapers mark their sections by numbers.

   Alfonso, Nick. "DNA Evidence under Question." *New York Times* 31 Nov. 2007, sec. 1: 6. Print.

   (Alfonso 6)

   c. **Newspaper editorial.** Cite newspaper editorials as you would any newspaper article. Just insert the word *Editorial* after the title of the article.

   "Let's Send a Message." Editorial. *Denver Post* 23 Nov. 2007: A14. Print.

   ("Let's Send" A14)

5. **Article with no author named.**

   "Bilingual Education under Scrutiny: A Progress Report." *The Times* 19 Apr. 2007: 25–32. Print.

   ("Bilingual Education" 27).

6. **Two or more articles by the same author.** Don't repeat the name of the same author. First, alphabetize the same authors by the next unit: the title of the article or book. After the first source, use three hyphens followed by a period to indicate "same as above."

   Morales, Juan. "All Facts about Carbohydrates." *Food & Nutrition* 12 June 2009: 29–32. Print.

   (Morales, "All Facts" 32)

   ___. "Diet Fads and Insanity." *Food & Nutrition* 21 Mar. 2009: 7–9. Print.

   (Morales, "Diet Fads" 8)

7. **Article accessed through a library subscription database service.** Your college library or your public library may provide databases that you can access from your home computer. Through such services as Gale, EBSCOhost, Infotrac, Proquest, or JSTOR, thousands of periodicals are at your disposal. Documenting such sources is simple; first follow the rules for documenting periodicals, as explained and illustrated earlier, and then tag on the service information: name of the database + the medium + the date you accessed the document.

McKinnon, Sara. "Juvenile Overhaul a
Gamble." *New Statesman* 13 Oct. 2006:
7–12. *Academic Search Premier.* Web.
12 Nov. 2010.

(McKinnon 7)

8. **Article in an online scholarly journal.** Follow the pattern for print journals
up to the date and add medium (Web) + date accessed.

Abrams, Laura S. "Listening to Juvenile
Offenders: Can Residential Treatment
Prevent Recidivism?" *Child and Adolescent Social Work Journal* 23.1 (2006):
n.pag. Web. 23 Apr. 2010.

(Abrams)

Name of author(s).

"Title of Article."

Name of newspaper/magazine (italics).

Sponsor of website. If none given, use N.p.,

Update. If there is no date, use n.d.

Medium consulted: Web.

Date accessed. (Day + month + year)

9. **Article in an online magazine or newspaper.** For articles retrieved from an
online magazine or newspaper, follow this pattern: name of the author + title
of article within quotation marks + name of magazine or newspaper, italicized +
the sponsor of the website (or N. p. if no sponsor is given) + the date of
publication (or n.d. if no date is given) + the Medium (Web) + the date you
accessed the source.

Edwards, David, Nelda Wade, and Cindy
Graham. "Reading, Writing, and Revo-
lution: A Look at the Artist." *New York
Times.* New York Times, 9 Oct. 2005.
Web. 27 Oct. 2010.

(Edwards, Wade, and
Graham)

UNDERSTANDING
Sources

PRACTICE 13-8

Write each of the following periodicals in correct MLA format as it would appear on a works cited page. Choose only the information necessary for MLA works cited entries. Also, apply the rules for the correct use of capitalization, periods, commas, colons, parentheses, and quotation marks.

1. Print Source: A monthly magazine article with the title "She Uses Honey, and Pepper, to Get Job Done" by Duane Garrett and Jean Fish-Davis, published in *American Theater* in March 2006 in volume 241, issue 52, on pages 13–21.

   Works cited entry:

   _____

   _____

2. Print Source: In the Annals of Science section of *The New Yorker*, a magazine article titled "The Denialists: The Dangerous Attacks on the Consensus about H.I.V. and AIDS," published on March 12, 2007, and written by Michael Specter. It appears on pages 32–38.

   Works cited entry:

   _____

   _____

3. Online Source: A newspaper article titled "Internet Bullying," written by Denise Borrero and Dina Cerrano. The article, published on July 30, 2008, appears in section B, page 3 of the *San Juan Star*. This article was accessed by the student on January 21, 2010 through *Newspaper Source*, a database.

   Works cited entry:

   _____

   _____

4. Print Source: In the *New York Times*, a newspaper article called "Hard Look at Mission That Ended in Inferno for 3 Women" written by Michael Moss. It appears on page 14 in section 2, dated December 20, 2005.

   Works cited entry:

   _____

   _____

5. Online Source: An article in *Time*, accessed online, published on December 15, 2010, by Sean Gregory, with the title "Congress Tells Commercials to Quiet Down." The article was accessed on December 20, 2010, and the publisher/sponsor is Time, Inc.

Works cited entry:

_____

_____

6. Online Source: A newspaper article dated July 11, 2007, from _The Washington Times_, page C1, titled "Wrestling with Steroids." The article was accessed on December 2, 2010 through the library database _Regional Business News_.

Works cited entry:

_____

_____

Documenting Internet Sources

In the preceding section, you cited periodicals from online magazines and newspapers. Documenting Internet sources follows a similar pattern: author. + "Title of article." or _title of book, play, or poem (italics)._ + _name of website (italics)._ + sponsor (N.p. if none given), copyright date (n.d. if none given). + medium-Web. + date accessed.

Author(s).

"Title of article."

Name of website (italics).

Sponsor of website.
If none given, use N.p.,

Copyright date.
If none given, use n.d.

Medium: Web.

Date accessed.
(Day + month + year)

a. **Entire website.**

National Crime Prevention Council. N. p., 2006. Web. 15 Oct. 2010.

b. **Article within a website.**

"Racial Profiling: Old and New." *American Civil Liberties Union.* ACLU, 2007. Web. 23 July 2010.

c. **Online books, plays, or long poems.**

Bronte, Emily. *Wuthering Heights. Literature.org.* Knowledge Matters, Ltd., 2006. Web. 15 May 2011.

Sample Parenthetical Citation

(*National*)

("Racial Profiling")

(Bronte)

2. **Online government document.** When documenting government documents, start by indicating the type of government document:

Federal government   =   United States

State government   =   Florida, California, Ohio, and so on

City government   =   Denver, Houston, Portland, and so on

Then name the specific government organization that supplied the information, followed by the title of the document.

United States. Department of Commerce. Census Bureau. *Income, Poverty, and Health Insurance Coverage in the United States: 2005.* U.S. Dept. of Commerce, Aug. 2010 Web. 13 Oct. 2010.

(United States)

Documenting Other Sources

The following types of sources will be common and useful in your courses.

1. **Interview.**

Milkowski, Melinda. Personal interview. 6 Oct. 2007.

(Milkowski)

2. **CD-ROM.** Document a CD-ROM the same way you would a book. Simply add the medium, *CD-ROM*, at the end.

"Holocaust." *Encarta.* Seattle: Microsoft, 2004. CD-ROM.

("Holocaust")

PRACTICE 13-9

Write the following online sources in correct MLA format as they would appear on a works cited page. Use only the information required. Then write the correct parenthetical citation enclosed in parentheses.

1. A short article retrieved from *CNN.com*, titled "Lack of Proper Rest Poses Health, Education Risks." It was published on September 29, 2000, accessed by the student on April 6, 2010, and sponsored by Cable News Network

   Works cited entry:

   _____

   _____

2. An interview with Esther Huckleberry, director of the Planned Parenthood Center in Paterson, New Jersey, conducted on February 16, 2007.

   Works cited entry:

   _____

   _____

3. A CD-ROM written by Sophia Maldonado, titled Exotic Cuisine, published in Boston in 2003 by Nutritional Living, Inc.

   Works cited entry:

   _____

   _____

4. A short article from the *MayoClinic.com* website, which is sponsored by Mayo Foundation for Medical Education and Research, under the Teen's Health section, titled "Teen Sleep: Why Is Your Teen So Tired?" The article was published on August 8, 2005, and accessed by the student on April 6, 2010.

   Works cited entry:

   _____

   _____

5. An online document titled "What We Need to Know about Drugs," written by Jay Francis Wright and Kay McKnight. This article comes from the website *Drug Infonet.com* and has no known sponsor. The copyright date is unknown. The article was accessed on July 23, 2010.

   Works cited entry:

   _____

   _____

Writing Your Research Paper

"Knowledge is of two kinds. We know a subject ourselves, or

we know where we can find information on it."

— *Samuel Johnson*

YOUR GOALS

Understanding the Value of Research

1. Understand the importance of research.
2. Use research to tap into a wider academic world.

Writing Your Research Paper

1. Use prewriting techniques appropriate to your topic.
2. Choose a topic for your research paper.
3. Plan your research paper.
4. Use the library and the Internet to gather information.
5. Evaluate the reliability of your sources.
6. Create a working bibliography, and write notes as a way to gather and manage information from sources.
7. Prepare a formal outline.
8. Incorporate in-text citations into your draft.
9. Format your draft according to an approved standard.
10. Proofread for common grammar errors.

Access grammar exercises for this section in your English CourseMate, available through CengageBrain.com.

As a student, you may dread the idea of doing research. You envision yourself spending hours in a quiet library or online at home looking for sources and trying to figure out "where this whole thing is going." Yet at some point, we all need to learn how to research topics of interest and importance to us. The ability to conduct research independently is at the heart of what it means to be an educated person.

Professionally, you may have to investigate the marketability of a product; research consumer opinions; talk to different people to assess the benefits of relocating a business; investigate how customers, clients, or employees will react to certain changes or a new policy; or assess the morale in your workplace.

Research is part of everyday life. When you need to go shopping, you take an inventory of what you have and note what you need. When you're trying to decide what movie to see, you might go to a website to find out what the critics are saying; and if still not totally convinced, you ask someone who has seen the movie and whose opinion you trust.

Whether you're trying to figure out a medical condition, learning how to make good investments, determining the causes of a certain behavior in a relative or yourself, or simply checking a TV guide, you're conducting research. This chapter lessens much of the confusion and anxiety surrounding research, shows you how to manage your information, and puts you in control of the research process.

Let's Warm Up!

Reflect on your experiences researching information in school, for a job, or for personal interest. What activities and challenges do you associate with researching? Make a list of your research activities and challenges, and then compare it with a classmate's list. How can you deal with some of the challenges of researching a topic?

Tetra Image/Jupiter images

Understanding the Value of Research

The word *research* comes from Old French *recherché*—to seek out or search again. As you take on a topic or question to research, you are seeking out information on your topic. The major value of research is that it allows you to learn the truth about something—at least as far as experts in the field know it. For example, if you want to make up your mind about the existence of global warming, then you read a variety of studies by environmental scientists. You try to read enough studies so that you feel comfortable coming to your conclusion about global warming.

Another value of research is that it sharpens your critical thinking skills. You simply cannot accept all information as equally valid and relevant. Instead, you must constantly read with skepticism: Is this study large enough to warrant such a conclusion? Does this writer have the authority to make this claim? Does this researcher cite sufficient sources to verify the information? Is this information relevant to the focus of my research?

Finally, research is the vehicle for transporting you, the student, into a much wider academic world than the one you have access to physically. Through research, you are able to access the best and brightest of minds and add your voice and experience to the many experts and scholars who have written on the topic you choose.

In this chapter, we follow one student's research process as an extended example to illustrate each specific stage of the research process. Joshua, an education major, is a part-time student. He's married, has one child, and holds a part-time job. Therefore, being organized and wasting the least amount of time are crucial to him.

Writing Your Research Paper

To ease you through the research process, we have broken it into six main stages.

These stages take you from finding a topic to completing the final draft of your research paper. If you follow the stages diligently, by the end of this chapter, you should complete your research paper.

Prewriting and Planning

One pleasure of research is being able to learn new information from experts in the field and not just rely on your experiences and observations. The challenges are organizing your research, finding the information you are looking for, and incorporating it smoothly into your writing style. However, with solid and careful planning, you can make this project a satisfying and manageable one. Just keep in mind that you must break each stage into steps and allot sufficient time to accomplish each one.

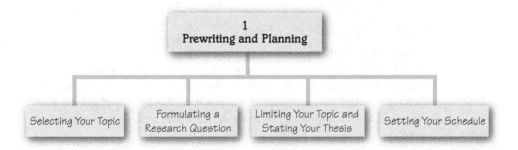

Selecting Your Topic

Remember that a key point in research is making sure that the topic you choose fits the assignment for the specific course. Your instructor may assign a topic or give you a choice from several topics. You may also be given general guidelines: For a history paper you may be asked to write about some aspect of the Civil War; for an art history class, you may be assigned a Renaissance painter whose style and influence you must explain; or for a biology class, you may have to describe how a specific organ of the human body functions. Just be sure that you read your instructor's guidelines for the assignment several times and ask specific questions to ensure that you understand the task:

- Can you choose your own topic?
- Does the topic have to be approved by your instructor?
- What documentation style is required: MLA, APA, or another style?
- What are the minimum and maximum lengths of the paper?
- Should you write your paper to a specific audience?
- What types of sources are permissible: electronic or print sources; interviews or other primary sources; or charts, tables, graphs, or other illustrations?

WRITING
Your Research Paper

- What types of sources are not permissible: wikis, blogs, or discussion list postings?
- Will you be able to get your instructor's input on a draft or parts of your paper before you hand it in for a grade?

Brainstorming for a Topic

If your instructor has not assigned a topic, start thinking of the many topics that interest you. Think about your major, the many issues and conflicts in your community, or interesting discussions you have had on topics in other courses. You might start your search for a topic by listing your areas of interest, applying one or more prewriting techniques, and then asking questions to identify a subject so that you can then narrow the subject down to a topic. You have practiced many ways to brainstorm for topics in earlier chapters, so apply those prewriting techniques that you feel have resulted in the most useful ideas and information.

Formulating a Research Question

After you have a tentative topic of interest, start asking questions about the topic to guide your research and to lead you to a practical thesis. A useful list of questions with which to start is the traditional *who, what, when, where, why*, or *how* questions commonly posed by researchers and journalists. For example, if you choose a topic such as global warming, you might ask *what* evidence exists that global warming is actually occurring.

Before formulating your research questions, try doing some preliminary research. Initially, your research questions should be neither too broad nor too narrow. The number of sources you find during preliminary research helps you determine whether your question is too broad. For instance, if you find so many sources that you're not sure how to even begin a more focused search, the topic of your question may be too broad. In contrast, a topic that is too narrow may be too difficult to research in the time you're given because sources may be scarce or more difficult to locate. However, a question that's sufficiently narrowed may lead to an interesting in-depth discussion.

Practice formulating possible research questions by doing the following activity.

Collaborative Critical Thinking

In small groups, for each of the following topics, put a check mark by the research question that you consider more interesting and relevant for an academic paper. Share your answers with other groups and be prepared to justify your group's choice.

1. Solar power

    _____ a. How much does it cost to build a solar home?

    _____ b. Should homeowners who live in solar homes receive tax credits?

2. American families and Chinese adoptions

_____ a. How many Chinese orphans are adopted by Americans?

_____ b. What are the advantages and disadvantages for Americans adopting Chinese babies?

3. CEO salaries

_____ a. Why do CEOs of major American companies earn huge salaries even when their companies are losing money?

_____ b. Who are the highest paid CEOs in the United States?

Joshua decides to retrieve sources from a subscription database service that helps him locate recently published sources that have a high degree of legitimacy. He can always go to the Internet later, when his knowledge of his topic has grown from other research, and he can more easily weed out the useless hits. At the end of this initial plunge into the world of research, Joshua has arrived at a tentative topic:

> Computers in education, and the ways the so-called "digital divide" is mirrored and propagated in our public school system

Joshua raises the following research questions:

1. What is the status of computerized learning in public schools nationally? In the state?
2. Is there a digital divide in our public schools, and can I find source material to support my answer?
3. If there is such a divide, how are students at each level affected by it?
4. What are some causes of technology gaps in schools?
5. How can those causes be attacked meaningfully?
6. What are schools doing to solve their technology problems?

Choose one topic, conduct preliminary research as necessary, revise your topic if necessary, and write research questions that you may have to consider when you develop your paper. If you find that your first choice of topic is not working out, jump to your second choice. During this stage, everything is tentative. You have plenty of time to focus your topic and, if you choose, to change your topic.

WRITING   **14-1**

After your preliminary research, write down your topic. Then write as many research questions as you feel you need to answer to fully develop your topic.

Tentative topic: _____

Research questions

1. _____
2. _____
3. _____
4. _____

Limiting Your Topic and Stating Your Thesis

At this point, your topic needs to take on a more narrowed focus and a sense of purpose, which leads you to your thesis. As Joshua continues in his research, he begins to ask questions about the purpose of his paper.

1. Will I explain the digital divide, its origins, and its causes?
2. Will I explore why it took hold so strongly in my community?
3. Will I focus on measures to improve the situation?
4. Will I argue that educational leaders should find ways to reduce the influence that income disparity has on public education?

During this step of prewriting and planning his research, Joshua begins to save the more useful articles in his computer so that he can easily find them later. He also prints out sources he feels help him limit and focus his topic. Now he is ready to write a tentative thesis.

Pueblo's digital divide has created a serious problem for the public schools.

Joshua's research questions helped focus his topic, giving his paper some direction. Your own thesis statement results naturally from your questions, providing your paper with a specific and straightforward claim.

WRITING 14-2

Look over your questions, conduct additional research, or review the sources you encountered during your initial research. Then formulate a tentative thesis statement for your topic, and write it here.

Tentative thesis: _____

_____

WRITING 14-3

Test your thesis within the writing context by answering the following questions.

You the Writer

1. Why is this topic important to you? Why does it interest you? _____

_____

_____

2. On a scale of 1–10, how strongly do you feel about your topic? _____

3. What assumptions or opinions about the topic do you already have?

_____

_____

4. What is your attitude or opinion about this topic? _____

_____

5. How much do you already know about this topic? _____

_____

6. What do you and your reader have in common? _____

_____

Your Reader

1. What audience (person or group) would benefit most from your writing? _____

_____

2. What would your reader gain from your essay? _____

_____

3. What previous knowledge does the audience have of your topic? _____

_____

4. What information does your audience need? _____

_____

5. What is your purpose? _____

_____

6. What effect do you want your essay to have on your audience? _____

_____

Your Writing Situation

1. Is this topic related to another class, a particular project, a personal interest, a strongly held belief, or something else? Explain. _____

_____

2. What format, requirements, or constraints must you observe? _____

_____

The Content

1. What kind of sources do you need to consult? _____

_____

2. What information do you need first? _____

_____

3. What kind of source is likely to supply it? _____

_____

4. Review your answers and reflect on your writing context. At this point, what strategies can help make your essay effective: illustration, process, classification/division, cause/effect, comparison/contrast, definition? _____

_____

5. What other information do you need to provide, for example, statistics, case studies, or historical background? _____

_____

Based on your responses here, make any changes to your thesis that you feel are appropriate at this time.

Setting Your Schedule

Divide the task up into weeks, and give yourself deadlines. For example, the following schedule might work for you:

Week 1

- Decide on a topic.
- Find five to seven sources with useful information.
- Read the sources, and highlight useful information.
- Take notes in your own words to avoid unintentional plagiarism.

Warning: Be sure that you have enough information for your topic because you don't want to change topics close to the deadline for the paper and thus run out of time to complete the project.

Week 2

- Write a tentative outline of the paper.
- Insert your notes into the sections of the paper where they fit.
- Look for holes or areas where more information is needed.
- Find more sources to fill gaps in the outline.

Warning: Don't become so involved in accumulating sources and finding new information that you get behind in reading your sources, taking notes, and deciding on the subtopics of the paper.

Week 3

- Type up a tentative Works Cited page.
- Start writing the first draft of the paper, inserting the research (and parenthetical citations) as you go.

Warning: Do not put research in the first draft of the paper without correctly crediting the specific source right away. If you try to go back later and remember where your information came from, you may credit the wrong source or forget to credit some information, thus committing plagiarism.

Week 4

- Revise the first draft, omitting information that is irrelevant or extraneous and adding any new and useful information.
- Put the paper aside for at least a day, and then edit the draft for grammar, punctuation, and transitions.
- Polish your Works Cited list.

Warning: Proofreading is essential to catching basic and distracting errors. You are checking not just for grammar and punctuation but also for correct documentation.

> **Computer Tip!**
> Use an electronic calendar, such as MS Outlook or one provided online, and enter all assignments and dues dates. Set the calendar to send you e-mail reminders.

WRITING
Your Research Paper

WRITING 14-4

Plan your schedule, and make a commitment to stick to it. A research paper is not something you can put together overnight.

Stage and Step of Research Process	Date Due	Date Completed
1. Prewriting and planning	_____	_____
a. Selecting your topic	_____	_____
b. Formulating a research question	_____	_____
c. Limiting your topic and stating your thesis	_____	_____
d. Setting your schedule	_____	_____
2. Researching your topic	_____	_____
a. Using the library	_____	_____
b. Using databases	_____	_____
c. Using the Internet	_____	_____
d. Evaluating the reliability of your sources	_____	_____
e. Identifying subtopics	_____	_____
3. Managing your information	_____	_____
a. Writing a preliminary bibliography	_____	_____
b. Writing electronic notes	_____	_____
4. Drafting and revising your paper	_____	_____
a. Preparing your outline	_____	_____
b. Writing your first draft	_____	_____
c. Revising and proofreading your draft	_____	_____
5. Formatting your final paper	_____	_____
a. Formatting your final outline	_____	_____
b. Formatting your final draft	_____	_____
c. Formatting your final bibliography	_____	_____
6. Reflecting	_____	_____

Researching Your Topic

You are ready to locate sources that can offer a broad understanding of your topic. During this stage of research, you make a conscientious, careful, thorough attempt to find the most current and informative sources that exist.

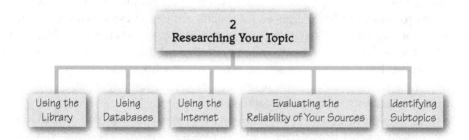

Using the Library

You may wonder why you should bother going to the library when you can go online and find an array of information. Libraries are places where researchers can peruse resources physically. Sometimes new ideas are best stimulated by being surrounded by print sources, which can suggest topics and areas of interest that you might not find online.

Probably one of the best reasons for visiting a library is to take advantage of the vast knowledge and research skills of a professional reference librarian or media specialist, who can guide you to many useful and relevant sources. In addition, if your library doesn't have a promising source, the librarian can order the source from another library through interlibrary loan. Receiving the source may take time, so it's important that you visit the library early in your research process.

You may "visit" your college library online as well. Through the library's website, you can access the databases that the library subscribes to and check what books and journals the library carries through the library catalog and electronic indexes and databases. Through your library catalog, you can locate books, articles in periodicals, and government documents in a short time. You can search for a simple title or author, but if you don't have this information, you can always search by subject.

It's almost impossible for a library to store the thousands of available magazines, journals, and newspapers. Therefore, indexes such as The Reader's Guide to Periodicals, Expanded Academic, and CINAHL provide bibliographical information by author, title, and/or subject so that you can find the article. Although some indexes are available in print form, many are available on CD-ROM or computer databases. Don't hesitate to consult your librarian, who can guide you through the indexes and through the many databases available to obtain the article you're seeking.

Using Databases

Indexes are databases that reference articles; they don't offer the articles themselves. Such databases are known as *bibliographical databases*. However, some full-text retrieval services, such as the Electric Library, FirstSearch, EBSCOhost, and Ingenta, offer bibliographical information, abstracts, and full-text articles.

Subscription services, such as Gale, EBSCOhost, InfoTrac, and ProQuest, offer access to thousands of articles about specific topics. These articles have been "refereed," or evaluated for reliability and credibility by experts before publication. Thus, they are better sources than you can typically find just by surfing the Internet for information. In most cases, by simply going to your library's home page and following the links to electronic resources, you can find these subscription services, which give you access to their many databases.

As you continue to develop your research skills, you will continue to discover the types of sources that provide the evidence and support that you need to develop your research paper. With all these sources at your disposal, think twice before telling your instructor that you're unable to locate information on your topic.

Using the Internet

Researching has become simpler in some ways than it used to be with the ease of logging on to the computer and accessing databases or "Googling" a topic. However, the massive amounts of information online can overwhelm you or divert you from your research as you become distracted by e-mail, Facebook, chat rooms, or downloaded music.

Google is just one popular search engine. There are millions of pages on the Internet; no one engine can search the entire web. Use other search engines such as Yahoo!, MSN Search, or Ask.com to broaden your search.

As you gain experience using the Internet to conduct research, you will become more proficient and more skillful in narrowing your search to find exactly what you want.

Evaluating the Reliability of Your Sources

You must be critical as a researcher to ensure that the information you use for your papers is worthwhile, accurate, and credible. Anyone can post information to the Internet that may not be true or accurate and make it look as if it is. For example, *Wikipedia*, the online encyclopedia, allows anyone to add entries or edit them. If your instructor approves the use of wikis, you should cross-check all information with other information sources.

Be especially wary of dot-com sites. Such sites are commercial; thus, one of their goals is to make money. Dot-gov and dot-edu sites have more credibility; however, you still have to be skeptical. For example, a student at a university can put up a personal website, have a dot-edu address, and supply information that is inaccurate.

Criteria for Evaluating Your Sources

Use the following criteria, adapted from "Evaluating Information Found on the Internet," by Elizabeth E. Kirk, to determine the reliability of the sources you find on the Internet:

1. **Authorship.** Most often, you are not familiar with the author of your information. However, it's important that you determine whether the author is one you and your reader can trust. Start by asking the following questions:
   - Who wrote this article, and what are their credentials?
   - If the website is related to a particular field, is the writer trained and certified in that field?
   - If the website provides information on a controversial issue, does the author or organization have a political affiliation or a noticeable bias on the topic?

2. **Currency.** How up-to-date is this information? Check the dates of the facts cited, as well as the last update of the article. If you are writing about global warming, what would be the farthest back in history you would go to cite studies about whether or not it is a reality?

3. **Publisher or sponsor.** Study the website carefully to determine who published or sponsored the site. Is it a political organization, a university or college, a nationally known company, an individual, a government agency, a retail store, or an organization trying to free political prisoners? Look at the site's home page to find out what the organization's goals are and how it plans to achieve these goals.

4. **Audience.** For whom is the website designed? Whom would it attract or appeal to? If you are doing a paper on global warming and find a website designed by Mrs. Smith's fifth-grade class in Helena, Montana, you might decide that the level of research and writing is too basic for your purposes. If the website is sponsored by a group that advocates peaceful demonstrations to protest the proliferation of SUVs, you might be skeptical as well.

5. **Relevancy.** Essential to your research is determining whether or not the information that you've found relates to your topic and thesis. It may be intriguing and you may want to spend time reading it to understand the scope of information on the topic, but it may not fit the focus of your paper. Ask the following questions to test relevancy:
   - Does this information fit under one of your subtopics?
   - Does this information relate to your overall purpose or thesis?
   - Can you integrate this information into your paper, or does it just seem dropped in?
   - Does this information fit what your reader needs to know about your topic?

6. **Accuracy of information.** Ask the following questions to determine the quality of the information:
   - Do other sources you've read corroborate what this source claims?
   - Does this source cite some of the most comprehensive studies on the topic?

- Does any information contradict what you've read in other sources?
- Does the source provide references to verify its information?

7. **Style and format.** When you're reading a professional piece of writing, you have some expectations of the writer's writing and research skills. Ask the following questions:
    - How well is the article written? Does it contain grammatical errors, missing words or phrases, misspellings, punctuation errors, or obvious errors of fact?
    - What kind of support does the writer offer? Does the writer cite well-respected authorities and provide references so that the reader can verify information?
    - What is the tone of the article? Does it contain inflammatory language? Does it try to sell the reader something? Does it ignore other points of view? Does it commit logical fallacies?

Elizabeth E. Kirk, "Evaluating Information Found on the Internet." Adapted from the Johns Hopkins University, The Sheridan Libraries website: http://www.library.jhu.edu/researchhelp/general/evaluating/. Reprinted by permission of the Johns Hopkins University.

Identifying Subtopics

Before you take off on your research, you need to determine the limits or scope of your research. You can easily become sidetracked and spend hours reading information you may not even need. To maintain your focus on the thesis you have identified, start by specifying the subtopics you need to research to explain or prove your thesis. Can you identify specific causes and effects? What comparisons can you draw? Would your topic benefit from statistics? Where in your paper would you insert these statistics?

Joshua ended his first stage of the research process with the following tentative thesis:

Pueblo's digital divide has created a serious problem for the public schools.

Before Joshua continues his research, he must identify important subtopics to explore. He decides to focus on explaining the problem by researching its causes and effects. He identifies the following subtopics:

A. Causes
  1. Hardware deficiencies
  2. Lack of software
  3. Lack of teacher awareness
  4. Lack of expertise
  5. Lack of training

B. Effects
  1. Students don't understand the full potential of computers.
  2. Students don't develop necessary skills.
  3. Graduates have trouble getting jobs.
  4. Community will be affected.

These subtopics need to be more focused, but providing this focus is the purpose of research. For now, Joshua has a plan, as you soon will.

WRITING 14-5

Develop your plan for getting your sources. Start by dividing the idea in your thesis statement into subtopics. Write the subtopics you plan to research in the spaces that follow.

Thesis: _____

_____

Subtopics to research

1. _____

2. _____

3. _____

4. _____

5. _____

Review the subtopics you have identified, and make sure that these subtopics indeed explain or prove your thesis statement. If not, revise the subtopics that aren't relevant, or refocus your thesis.

Managing Your Information

When you start your preliminary search for materials on your topic, you may become overwhelmed by the amount of information you find. The goal of this stage of the research process is to organize, manage, and think critically about your information. Not being organized makes your research frustrating, and you lose valuable time.

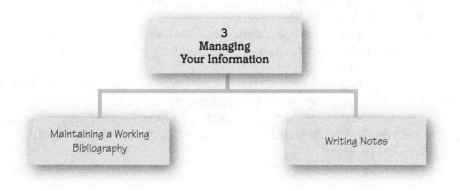

Maintaining a Working Bibliography

Maintaining a working bibliography provides a helpful record of all books, periodicals, databases, and websites that you might consider using later. It serves the following purposes:

1. Keeps you organized
2. Helps you record all information needed to locate the source should you decide to use it when you're ready to write your paper
3. Provides the information you need to prepare your final bibliography—your Works Cited list

At this stage of the research process, you are still discovering and gathering information that supports your thesis, so it is likely that you will record more sources than you ultimately use in your final draft. When you start drafting your paper, you will most likely omit sources, as well as do additional research to get additional sources. All you need to do then is delete the sources you didn't use from your working bibliography and add any new sources. By constantly updating your working bibliography, you're on your way toward your final Works Cited list, which becomes the last page of your research paper.

Examine Joshua's preliminary bibliography. It should immediately be clear to you that he has entirely too many sources for a four- to six-page research paper. At this point, Joshua is still reviewing his sources and is not sure which ones are best for his paper. Also notice that Joshua uses MLA style to document his sources; check with your instructor before you start developing your working bibliography.

> Check your **Computer** library or the **Tip!** Internet for free citation-management software. You'll save time, but you still need to check the citations for accuracy.

Working Bibliography

"Are Teachers Using Computers for Instruction?" *Journal of School Health* Feb. 2001: 83–84. *ProQuest*. Web. 20 Mar. 2010.

Becker, Henry Jay. "Who's Wired and Who's Not: Children's Access to and Use of Computer Technology." *The Future of Children* 10.2 (2000): 44–75. *ProQuest*. Web. 18 Jan. 2010.

Chideya, Farai. "Bridging the Digital Divide in the Classroom." *NPR News & Notes* 3 Jan. 2007. *Newspaper Source*. Web. 16 Feb. 2010.

Clements, Douglas H., and Julie Sarama. "The Role of Technology in Early Childhood Learning." *Teaching Children Mathematics* Feb. 2002: 340–43. *ProQuest*. Web. 13 Mar. 2010.

Debenham, Jerry, and Gerald R. Smith. "Computers, Schools, and Families: A Radical Vision for Public Education." *The Journal* 24 (2009): 58. *Academic Search Premier*. Web. 16 Feb. 2010.

"Digital Divide Basics Fact Sheet." *Digital Divide Network*. N.p., 2002. Web. 18 Mar. 2010.

Gill, Keith. Personal interview. 16 Apr. 2010.

Lewis, Anne C. "Kids and Computers." *The Education Digest* Apr. 2008: 67–69. *ProQuest*. Web. 13 Mar. 2010.

Monroe, Barbara Jean. *Crossing the Digital Divide: Race, Writing, and Technology in the Classroom*. New York: Teachers College Press, 2004. Print.

Nielsen, Clark. Personal interview. 20 Apr. 2010.

Simkins, Michael. "Dealing with the Donation Dump." *Technology & Learning* Sept. 2008: 52. *Academic Search Premier*. Web. 13 Mar. 2010.

"What Is the Digital Divide?" *Power Up*. N.p., 2002. 14 Mar. 2010.

WRITING 14-6

Develop your working bibliography for the sources you obtained when you did Writing 14-5. Refer to Chapter 13 for explanation and examples of MLA documentation.

Writing Notes

From this point on, any additional research is based on the subtopics you've settled on. These subtopics may eventually become the main sections of your paper. Your goal here is to find valid information to support each of the major points of your topic. Open a word processing file. Assign a page to each of your subtopics by writing the subtopic as a heading to the page. As you find interesting and relevant facts in your sources, write them down under the appropriate heading.

Use the following six ways to write your notes: quotation, paraphrase, summary, outline, personal, and combination. We use Joshua's sources to illustrate each type of note.

Quotation Notes

Differentiating your words from your sources' words is crucial. Use quotation marks to make this distinction; otherwise, you have committed plagiarism even though you cite your source.

Quotation Note

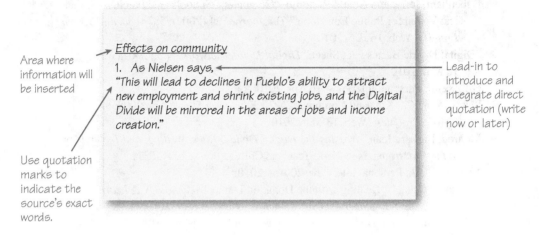

Area where information will be inserted

Use quotation marks to indicate the source's exact words.

Effects on community

1. As Nielsen says,
"This will lead to declines in Pueblo's ability to attract new employment and shrink existing jobs, and the Digital Divide will be mirrored in the areas of jobs and income creation."

Lead-in to introduce and integrate direct quotation (write now or later)

Paraphrase Notes

A paraphrase is simply a restatement of the writer's ideas. When you paraphrase information, you use your own sentence structures, wording, and style. Most information you get from sources will be paraphrased. In fact, every sentence and idea you write down should be in your own words and writing style unless it is directly quoted. If a reader doesn't see quotation marks, the reader assumes that the information is a paraphrase—your own phrasing and style. If this assumption is not correct, you may have committed plagiarism.

Bridging Knowledge

See Chapter 13 for information on paraphrasing and quoting information.

Paraphrase Note

Area where information will be inserted

Cause section – teacher training

1. However, a national survey involving more than 4,000 teachers showed that only 22% of science teachers, 12% of social studies teachers, and 13% of math teachers used software related to their subject matter, and even then, only occasionally. The same study showed that children still lacked access in core classes to computer assisted instruction that encourages imaginative thinking; most children interested in getting to use really exciting and educational software had to take a separate computer class (Becker 51-52).

Paraphrase should be your own words, sentence structures, and style.

Summary Notes

A summary captures the gist of an author's main idea. It is your condensed version of the main point or points of several paragraphs, an entire essay, a chapter in a book, or the complete book. Because a summary is your analysis and conclusions of a larger text, the wording must be entirely yours.

Summary Note

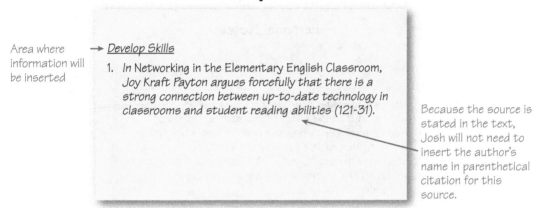

Area where information will be inserted

Develop Skills

1. In *Networking in the Elementary English Classroom*, Joy Kraft Payton argues forcefully that there is a strong connection between up-to-date technology in classrooms and student reading abilities (121-31).

Because the source is stated in the text, Josh will not need to insert the author's name in parenthetical citation for this source.

Outline Notes

Similar to an outline, this type of note lists a series of points made by your source. When you draft your paper, you can then choose to present the information using bullets or numbers, or you can discuss the points in the form of a paragraph. Get your instructor's approval should you decide to use bullets or numbers.

Outline Note

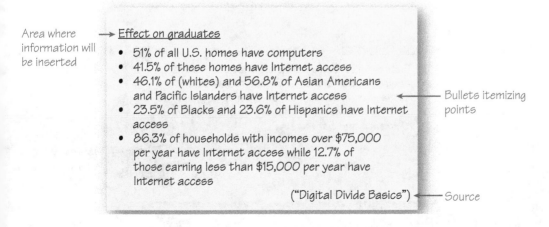

Area where information will be inserted

Effect on graduates

• 51% of all U.S. homes have computers
• 41.5% of these homes have Internet access
• 46.1% of (whites) and 56.8% of Asian Americans and Pacific Islanders have Internet access
• 23.5% of Blacks and 23.6% of Hispanics have Internet access
• 86.3% of households with incomes over $75,000 per year have Internet access while 12.7% of those earning less than $15,000 per year have Internet access

Bullets itemizing points

("Digital Divide Basics")

Source

WRITING
Your Research Paper

Personal Notes

As you review your sources, you develop your own ideas about the topic. Write them down immediately. Write the word *personal* to indicate that this is your thinking, indicate the area of your paper where you plan to insert your idea or comment, and then write your comment. You don't need to worry about plagiarism here because you are the author of this idea, nor do you need to cite it in your paper.

Personal Note

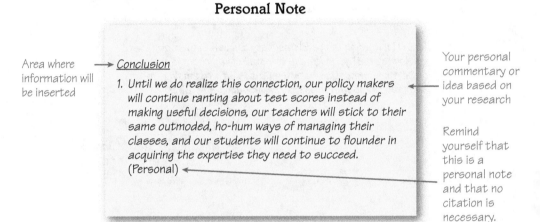

Area where information will be inserted → *Conclusion*

1. *Until we do realize this connection, our policy makers will continue ranting about test scores instead of making useful decisions, our teachers will stick to their same outmoded, ho-hum ways of managing their classes, and our students will continue to flounder in acquiring the expertise they need to succeed.* (Personal)

Your personal commentary or idea based on your research

Remind yourself that this is a personal note and that no citation is necessary.

Combination Notes

You're allowed to combine any of the preceding types of notes. However, for obvious reasons, you shouldn't combine a personal idea with information from a source that you must cite.

Combination Note

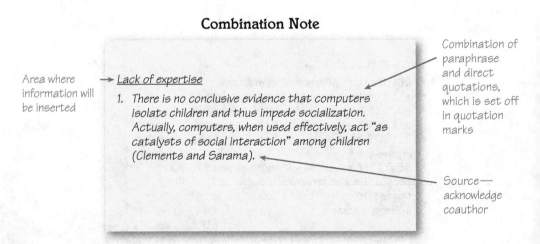

Area where information will be inserted → *Lack of expertise*

1. *There is no conclusive evidence that computers isolate children and thus impede socialization. Actually, computers, when used effectively, act "as catalysts of social interaction" among children* (Clements and Sarama).

Combination of paraphrase and direct quotations, which is set off in quotation marks

Source— acknowledge coauthor

WRITING 14-7

Read your sources carefully, and start writing notes. Follow these guidelines:

1. Do not place all notes from several subtopics on one page. Instead, dedicate one page (or more) to each category. Don't combine subtopics in any one page.
2. Make sure you give the source of the information. This notation is how you credit your source in your paper. Remember: Not citing your source constitutes plagiarism.
3. Be sure to place quotation marks around any phrases or sentences you copy directly from your source regardless of how many. The quotation marks remind you that these are not your words and that if you use this source, you should paraphrase the information, integrate it into your text as a direct quotation, or use a combination of paraphrase and direct quotation.
4. If you feel that your paraphrase is too close to the original, highlight it, and return later and try again.
5. Number each piece of information you insert into that subtopic. Whether the information is from the same source or from a different source, you want to remind yourself that each is a separate bit of information. You don't want to make the mistake of blending together information that may not be completely related to a specific point you are making. During the drafting stage, going back to your source and trying to unravel this confusion can cost you precious time.
6. The number of notes per source depends on the amount of information you consider useful for your paper. One source can have one note; another can easily have over a dozen. Just make sure that the information you choose to use explains one of the subtopics you have identified, which in turn supports the thesis. If this is so, you're on your way to a unified research paper.

Drafting and Revising Your Paper

Drafting the research paper is essentially a three-step process. You begin by ensuring that your outline is well organized and detailed enough to serve as the basis for your first draft. Then, using your outline and notes, you create your first draft as quickly and efficiently as possible. Next, you spend considerable time going through your draft, adding to and reorganizing your information and sources, as well as proofreading for grammar and style problems.

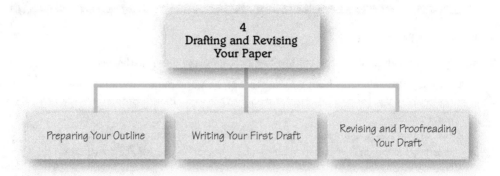

Preparing Your Preliminary Outline

In any research project, you want to work from an outline. You may believe that your writing process is more efficient without an outline; however, for research papers, you should make the formal outline a required part of your process because you have a lot of material to manage. Not only do you have all the source material you collected, but your own ideas have also been taking shape since the project began.

Formal outlines use a standard and common set of visual conventions:

- Write your last name and the page number in the upper-right corner of your outline. The page numbers should be in lowercase Roman numerals, for example, *i, ii, iii, iv, v.* Your actual paper should be in Arabic numbers: *1, 2, 3, 4,* and so on.

- Represent higher-level, or more general, ideas to the left of lower-level ideas:

  I. (most general idea)
     A. (less general idea)

- Represent the highest level of ideas with Roman numerals (I.), the next highest with capital letters (A.), the next with Arabic numerals (1.), and the next with lowercase letters (a.). Examine the different levels to see how the position of each level indicates how the information is related to each level:

  I. (most general idea)
     A. (less general idea—supports idea I)
        1. (supports idea A)
        2. (supports idea A)
           a. (supports idea 2)
           b. (supports idea 2)
              (1) (supports idea b)
              (2) (supports idea b)
        3. (supports idea A)
     B. (supports idea I)

- As a reminder to yourself and your reader (sometimes you include an outline with your research paper for evaluation), place your thesis at the beginning of the outline following the title.

Joshua is ready to type his preliminary formal outline. As he types out the outline, he checks his notes, making sure the outline contains a reference to each source. By doing this, he later knows where to insert each source into the draft. He can eliminate these references from the outline after he's written his draft and is ready to revise the outline. Here is Joshua's preliminary outline.

Outline

Thesis: It is unfair to our youth, as well as to the community at large, to let the technology gap continue to grow. Only by understanding it in detail can we begin to solve it.

I. Introduction
   A. Highlight benefits of computer technology to various types of people
      1. Seniors have new form of enrichment
      2. Families use computers for entertainment and other purposes
   B. Introduce disparities of access to computers
      1. 51% own computers, and 41% have access to the Internet ("Digital")
      2. This gap is the digital divide ("What")
      3. Lack of access is related to income levels
   C. Focus on education, and narrow the topic to Pueblo
      1. Poorer districts suffer from lack of access
      2. Although Pueblo is technically an urban setting, it shares the lack of technology with poorer rural areas (Nielsen)
   D. Give thesis and three-part map
II. Causes of the problem
   A. Explore hardware deficiencies
      1. Deficiencies involve many types of hardware: computers, monitors, mouse devices, printers, and so on
      2. Lacking steady funding, schools apply for grants, which are hit or miss (Nielsen)
         a. Relying on grants causes even greater disparities among schools
         b. Minnequa Elementary received the G-Tech grant; test scores went up
      3. Schools try donation programs, such as S.E.E.D.S.
         a. Explain how they work ("Background")
         b. Policies prevent schools from repairing donated items (Gill)
   B. Explain lack of software
      1. Even when schools gain hardware through grants and donations, they have trouble securing licenses for more than a few computers (Nielsen)
      2. Pricing of software licenses can make purchases expensive

---

    C. Describe lack of teacher awareness, expertise, and training
        1. Curriculum and room design are key features of effective electronic teaching (Clements and Sarama), but few teachers use computers (Becker)
        2. Pueblo teachers seem to lack interest in computerized learning (Nielsen)

III. Effects of the problem
    A. Today's students can operate computers well enough, but they don't know how to use them to their fullest potential
        1. Research
        2. Communication with experts
        3. Math and science programs
    B. Graduates will have trouble getting good jobs and succeeding in college ("What")

IV. Conclusion
    A. It is unfair to continue as we have
    B. The technology gap is widening; Pueblo is falling behind

WRITING 14-8

Start preparing your preliminary outline using Joshua's outline as a model. Don't forget to number and indent correctly the levels you use. Try to use three to four levels for some of your subtopics.

  II.

    A.

      1.

        a.

          (1)

            (a)

Writing Your First Draft

    If you have not completed the stages in this chapter, the best advice we can give you is to stop now, go back, and do them. If you begin drafting without completing these tasks, you are destined for a confusing and inefficient process.

    Before drafting your paper, move your sources (books, articles, printouts of web sources, and so on) to another area where you won't be tempted to look at them as you draft. Unless you feel comfortable switching from one document to another, print a copy of your outline and your notes (quotation, paraphrase, summary, outline, personal, and combination). Keep these documents in front of you for easy reference although you will be pulling the information from your electronic notes file.

Follow the outline you've created as you draft your paper. When you reach a point in the draft where you need to incorporate source material, take that source material directly from your notes file. Paste the information into your paper. If it is a quotation, make sure you are quoting properly; if it is a paraphrase, make sure the information is accurate and the wording and style your own.

After you have discussed a subtopic and applied your research, proceed to the next outline subtopic, and continue drafting. If you find that you are stuck in a particular section, just move to another section, but keep your notes organized as you switch between sections. Keep in mind that this draft is only your first draft. It won't be perfect the first time, nor should you expect it to be.

Writing Your Introduction

In theory, the introduction of a research paper is no different from any other type of introduction you've learned to write. You still must interest the reader in your topic, establish your credibility as a writer, and state your thesis. However, most research papers, in keeping with their serious purpose, adopt an objective and informational tone from the start. Therefore, you probably want to avoid lead-in techniques that are too informal or humorous to play a part in the serious purpose of research. (This is not to say a research paper can *never* be informal or humorous, but it doesn't happen often.)

Instead, keep in mind the two most common purposes of researched writing: to *explain* a topic thoroughly so that the reader understands it in a new way or to *persuade* the reader to adopt a point of view on an issue of importance. Notice that research writing is not its own mode like the others you've learned this semester. All you are doing in this assignment is adding research into the process of developing an explanation or an argument.

WRITING 14-9

Begin drafting your introduction. Don't forget that you can always come back to it and revise it at any time, as many times as you wish. As you create the draft, consider the following issues:

1. Your introduction should be engaging and make your reader want to read more.
2. Your introduction should indicate the serious and objective purpose of your paper, not only in your choice of language but also in the use of source material early in the paper.
3. The introduction of a research paper is commonly used to give background information (again, based on source material) as a way of getting the reader into the topic.

4. Your introduction does not have to confine itself to one paragraph; you probably want to use more. However, make sure the introduction has its own unity and coherence leading naturally to the thesis.

5. Your thesis should clearly indicate the focus of your paper. If it is an explanation, which aspects of the topic do you discuss? If it is an argument, what kind of claim are you making and what is your position?

Share your introduction with others. Let them tell you what they enjoy most or least about your introduction. Ask them what they think about the organization of the introduction. Use their comments as a basis for revision.

Writing Your Body Paragraphs

Examine one body paragraph from Joshua's first draft.

> The first cause is that many schools do not have sufficient hardware to accommodate the number of students. The hardware includes monitors, printers, speakers, mouse devices, and the computer itself. The school districts lack the funds needed to purchase new computer equipment; so instead, they apply for grants given to schools by various computer corporations and organizations, including companies such as Dell and Microsoft. Unfortunately, these grants are only given to a select few schools each year (Nielsen). Essentially, these grants greatly benefit those schools they are given to, but they also increase the inequality among schools because they are not given to every school. Nielsen gives a good example involving three elementary schools within District 60: Minnequa, Columbian, and Bessemer elementary schools. He reports that Minnequa recently received a G-Tech grant that gave the school new state-of-the-art equipment for the classrooms. Minnequa was one of only a handful of lucky schools picked to receive the grant, and Bessemer and Columbian were not among the schools chosen. As a result, Minnequa's state assessment scores were much higher than either of the other two schools. The higher scores may not have been entirely due to the new computer equipment, but the computers are believed to have played a part in the higher scoring, according to Nielsen.

In his first body paragraph, Joshua is off to a good start. He moves quickly to show how technology grants awarded to a small number of schools actually increase the digital divide within school districts. His point makes sense; that is, we can easily see how it might be true. But does he prove that it is true? Joshua needs to beef up the evidence and the conclusions he draws from it to thoroughly convince his reader.

WRITING 14-10

Start creating your first draft. Your goal is to fully and completely support your thesis. Follow these guidelines.

1. Try to adhere to your outline. As you draft, however, make any changes to the outline that you feel help your essay.
2. As you encounter the places in your text where you need to use source material, go ahead and make the effort to enter the quotation or paraphrase correctly. Do *not* type borrowed material into your draft without citing it. You are likely to lose track of it and could be guilty of plagiarism in the final product.
3. Make sure your sources are varied in terms of their number and type.
4. Add transitions to keep your ideas flowing smoothly and to guide your audience through your information. Focus especially on signal phrases to introduce borrowed material smoothly.
5. Try to avoid going back to your printed sources as you draft your paper. This only slows you down and takes you backward in the writing process.
6. If you come across a point that needs support or stronger evidence, make a note that you need to conduct additional research to support that point. But keep drafting.

Writing Your Conclusion

Remember that your conclusion is not a paragraph you can dash off simply by repeating some of the major ideas you've just stated in the paper. You need to devote time and attention to showing the reader the importance of the topic and emphasizing the major point you want to leave the reader with. Even though his paper is an explanation, Joshua hopes to stimulate his reader into thinking about what to do to help solve the problem.

WRITING 14-11

Write a conclusion for your research paper using the skills you have already learned. We repeat some previous advice here:

1. Reiterate the importance and significance of your topic. You can use one of the following techniques to help you do this:
   a. If you choose to summarize your key points, don't just repeat the same points mechanically. You can be sure that your reader hasn't forgotten them. Instead, show how these points are vital evidence in proving your thesis.
   b. Consider using an emotional appeal. But be careful not to overdo it.
   c. Pose a question. Leave your reader pondering the question.

    d. Emphasize the urgency of the issue by making a call for action.

    e. Build on or refer to a scenario, example, description, or anecdote that may have appeared in your introduction. This approach not only gives cohesiveness to your essay but also lets the reader know that you have accomplished your goal.

2. Read your introduction and then your conclusion to make sure that there's a smooth connection between them.

Revising and Proofreading Your Draft

Start the revising stage with this question: "Have I accomplished my goal?" Review your first draft, circling the strengths and underlining the weaknesses as you perceive them. How can you build on your strengths? How should you address the weaknesses? How do you feel about what you have written? With these questions in mind, start revising the content, as well as the integration of sources, in your paper. As you go through your paper, integrate all that you've learned about proofreading to correct errors of grammar and style.

WRITING 14-12

Start your revision. Don't leave any part of your essay untouched. Take a couple of days, if you have them, to read your paper several times, as follows:

1. Read your essay through one time, looking for problems in the organization of your major ideas (usually found in your thesis, topic sentences, and conclusion).

2. Read your essay through again looking for problems with supporting ideas (found in your body paragraphs).

3. Read your essay a third time looking for ways to improve its coherence. Make sure you offer enough transitions, including signal phrases to introduce sources, to help guide your reader.

4. Go through your essay again looking for problems with the use of sources. Make sure your in-text citations lead the reader to the right entry on the Works Cited page.

5. Read your essay one more time looking for ways to improve the style: the use of diction, modifying phrases, different types of sentences, active versus passive voice, and so on.

    The next section should help you address some of the more confusing problems with sources.

| PROBLEM | SOLUTION |

RESEARCH

Some of my sources don't seem to add much to my paper.

1. Are your sources relatively recent? If you are writing about a "hot" contemporary issue, you should be relying on sources published quite recently, perhaps within the past six months to a year.

2. Do your sources come primarily from the Internet? Your reader is automatically suspicious of most Internet sources except for government or professional association websites. Make sure you are avoiding general Internet sources.

3. Are your interview sources believable? If you can't find a reliable "expert" to interview, don't use an interview in your paper.

4. Do you rely on multiple sources throughout your paper? If your reader sees the same source repeatedly, that reader will begin to question the thoroughness of your research.

RESEARCH

I just don't know if I'm using my sources correctly especially when it comes to paraphrasing and quoting.

1. Have you properly understood your sources in their original context? It never hurts to go back and read a source just to make sure you've captured the author's intended meaning correctly.

2. Do you use your sources appropriately to support a point you are trying to make? Use source material in supporting paragraphs to provide the evidence you need to back up your points.

3. Do your quotations need to be quotations, or would they work better as paraphrases? Remember to use quotation sparingly and only when the phrasing is memorable or unique.

4. Are you overusing research material by inserting source after source (whether paraphrased or quoted) with none of your own thinking and writing included? Remember, a research paper is composed of your own reasoning supported by an appropriate mixture of primary and secondary evidence.

INCORPORATING SOURCES

I don't know if my signal phrases and in-text citations are doing the job they are supposed to do.

1. Do you vary your signal phrases as appropriate throughout the paper? Try to avoid repeating the same signal phrase in the same location (for example, using "According to" at the beginning of every citation).

2. Do you move from source to source, without including your thoughts and ideas about the topic? If so, your essay can sound like a compilation of other people's work, not your own.

WRITING
Your Research Paper

Collaborative Critical Thinking

Asking Your Peers

After you have completed the writing process and have a polished final draft, exchange papers with a classmate for peer review. Use the following questions to guide your review of your peer's paper.

1. Who is the writer? Who is the peer reviewer?

2. Go to the essay and underline the thesis statement. Is the thesis clear? Does the introduction lead to the thesis?

3. Where does the writer give background information on the topic? Is the information clear and relevant?

4. What additional background information do you feel the writer should supply?

5. How does the writer support his or her view of the topic (examples, statistics, facts, testimony, and so on)?

6. Is there any weak, unclear, or confusing information? Explain. (Circle any points that are illogical, confusing, or ambiguous.)

7. Evaluate the writer's presentation of the topic. Is it credible? Does it respect the audience? Is it too opinionated? How does the writer come through (negatively or positively)? Explain your view.

8. Does the writer support the topic with sufficient and relevant research materials (such as examples, statistics, facts, or expert testimony)? Where could the writer strengthen his or her case by adding a reference?

9. Are there any problems in documentation of sources? Explain. (Examine in-text citations and the Works Cited or References page.)

10. List some strengths and weaknesses of the paper.

Formatting Your Final Paper

Welcome to the last stage of the research process. The final goal of this stage is for you to present all parts of your paper—outline, final draft, and bibliography—to your instructor. Your instructor may also want your notes, first draft, and copies of all your sources. Examine how Joshua prepared his paper. Start with his outline.

Formatting Your Final Outline

If you recall, Joshua's preliminary outline was rather detailed. Noting lots of details and the sources that support his points helped him draft his paper. In revising his outline, he's moving from his needs as the writer to the needs of the reader. The final outline is concise.

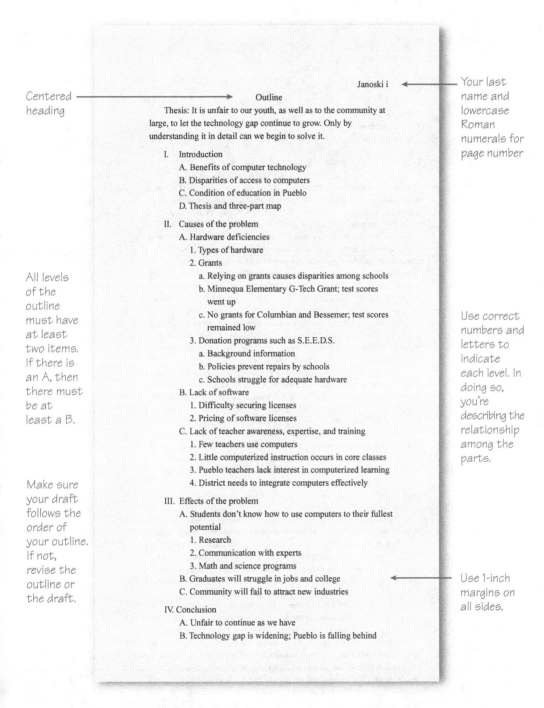

Janoski i

Centered heading →

Outline

Thesis: It is unfair to our youth, as well as to the community at large, to let the technology gap continue to grow. Only by understanding it in detail can we begin to solve it.

I. Introduction
    A. Benefits of computer technology
    B. Disparities of access to computers
    C. Condition of education in Pueblo
    D. Thesis and three-part map

II. Causes of the problem
    A. Hardware deficiencies
        1. Types of hardware
        2. Grants
            a. Relying on grants causes disparities among schools
            b. Minnequa Elementary G-Tech Grant; test scores went up
            c. No grants for Columbian and Bessemer; test scores remained low
        3. Donation programs such as S.E.E.D.S.
            a. Background information
            b. Policies prevent repairs by schools
            c. Schools struggle for adequate hardware
    B. Lack of software
        1. Difficulty securing licenses
        2. Pricing of software licenses
    C. Lack of teacher awareness, expertise, and training
        1. Few teachers use computers
        2. Little computerized instruction occurs in core classes
        3. Pueblo teachers lack interest in computerized learning
        4. District needs to integrate computers effectively

III. Effects of the problem
    A. Students don't know how to use computers to their fullest potential
        1. Research
        2. Communication with experts
        3. Math and science programs
    B. Graduates will struggle in jobs and college
    C. Community will fail to attract new industries

IV. Conclusion
    A. Unfair to continue as we have
    B. Technology gap is widening; Pueblo is falling behind

→ Your last name and lowercase Roman numerals for page number

All levels of the outline must have at least two items. If there is an A, then there must be at least a B.

Use correct numbers and letters to indicate each level. In doing so, you're describing the relationship among the parts.

Make sure your draft follows the order of your outline. If not, revise the outline or the draft.

Use 1-inch margins on all sides.

Formatting Your Final Draft

Just like the outline, your final draft should be presented in the format required by your instructor. Examine Joshua's final draft. Pay close attention to the features pointed out.

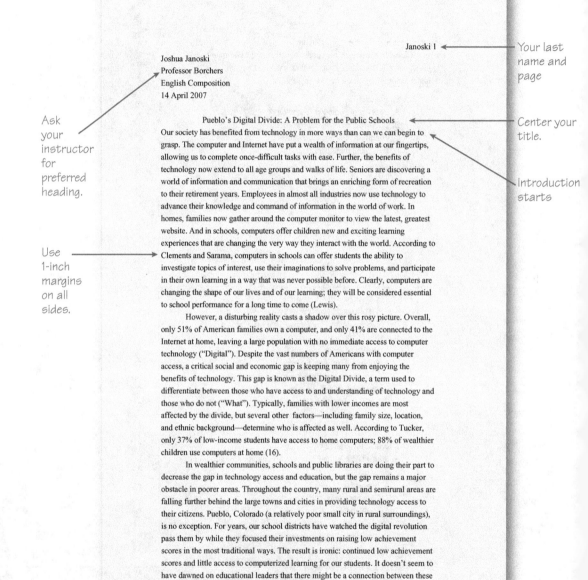

Janoski 1

Joshua Janoski
Professor Borchers
English Composition
14 April 2007

Pueblo's Digital Divide: A Problem for the Public Schools

Our society has benefited from technology in more ways than can we can begin to
grasp. The computer and Internet have put a wealth of information at our fingertips,
allowing us to complete once-difficult tasks with ease. Further, the benefits of
technology now extend to all age groups and walks of life. Seniors are discovering a
world of information and communication that brings an enriching form of recreation
to their retirement years. Employees in almost all industries now use technology to
advance their knowledge and command of information in the world of work. In
homes, families now gather around the computer monitor to view the latest, greatest
website. And in schools, computers offer children new and exciting learning
experiences that are changing the very way they interact with the world. According to
Clements and Sarama, computers in schools can offer students the ability to
investigate topics of interest, use their imaginations to solve problems, and participate
in their own learning in a way that was never possible before. Clearly, computers are
changing the shape of our lives and of our learning; they will be considered essential
to school performance for a long time to come (Lewis).

However, a disturbing reality casts a shadow over this rosy picture. Overall,
only 51% of American families own a computer, and only 41% are connected to the
Internet at home, leaving a large population with no immediate access to computer
technology ("Digital"). Despite the vast numbers of Americans with computer
access, a critical social and economic gap is keeping many from enjoying the
benefits of technology. This gap is known as the Digital Divide, a term used to
differentiate between those who have access to and understanding of technology and
those who do not ("What"). Typically, families with lower incomes are most
affected by the divide, but several other factors—including family size, location,
and ethnic background—determine who is affected as well. According to Tucker,
only 37% of low-income students have access to home computers; 88% of wealthier
children use computers at home (16).

In wealthier communities, schools and public libraries are doing their part to
decrease the gap in technology access and education, but the gap remains a major
obstacle in poorer areas. Throughout the country, many rural and semirural areas are
falling further behind the large towns and cities in providing technology access to
their citizens. Pueblo, Colorado (a relatively poor small city in rural surroundings),
is no exception. For years, our school districts have watched the digital revolution
pass them by while they focused their investments on raising low achievement
scores in the most traditional ways. The result is ironic: continued low achievement
scores and little access to computerized learning for our students. It doesn't seem to
have dawned on educational leaders that there might be a connection between these
two conditions. It is unfair to our youth, as well as to our community, to let this gap
continue to grow, but only by understanding it in detail can we begin to solve it.

Clark Nielsen, who leads an organization called "Wired to the World,"
devotes much of his time to improving technological access within Pueblo's
schools. According to Nielsen, the inadequacy of technology within Districts 60

Your last name and page

Ask your instructor for preferred heading.

Center your title.

Introduction starts

Use 1-inch margins on all sides.

Thesis

Janoski 2

and 70 can be broken into three parts:

    1) Lack of adequate computer hardware in the schools

    2) Lack of the most up-to-date software applications

    3) Lack of teachers who are properly trained to use computers to their full potential.

Consider each of these problems separately.

    The first cause is that many schools do not have sufficient hardware to accommodate the number of students. The needed hardware includes monitors, printers, speakers, mouse devices, and the computers themselves. Of course, the deeper cause is that the districts lack the money or the will to apply available funds to technology; instead, their strategy is to apply for technology grants from various corporations and organizations, including companies such as Dell and Microsoft. Unfortunately, these grants are awarded only to a select few schools each year, according to Nielsen. While these grants provide some benefit to a few schools, they have the paradoxical effect of widening the technology inequities within the districts. Nielsen gives a good example involving three elementary schools within District 60: Minnequa, Columbian, and Bessemer elementary schools. He reports that Minnequa recently received a G-Tech grant that gave the school new state-of-the-art equipment for some classrooms. Bessemer and Columbian were not among the schools chosen for the grant. When Minnequa later reported higher state assessment scores than the other two schools, much credit was given to the grant-supported infusion of computer technology directly into the classroom. It wasn't just the other two schools but also their students who lost out in this imbalance of resources. Shanklin reports on another aspect of the hardware problem; she describes an elementary school in Florida 10 years ago was a "technology showcase" but that has been unable to fund needed upgrades to its computers. It now is far behind other schools in the state, writes Shanklin.

    Clearly, technology investment is a long-term process requiring a long-term commitment. What options are available to schools that don't win the luck of the draw in the game of technology grants? The answer, unfortunately, is other "patchwork" solutions. For example, one source of computer technology for public schools is a highly laudable program begun by Congressman Scott McInnis in 1996 called "Sharing Electronic Equipment District and Statewide," or S.E.E.D.S. ("Background"). The program receives computers from businesses and organizations that have upgraded their systems and no longer need their old equipment. S.E.E.D.S. refurbishes these systems and distributes them to schools and nonprofit organizations that need them. This is a great way for schools with small budgets to get computers for their classrooms; however, S.E.E.D.S. can never provide a comprehensive answer. According to Keith Gill, S.E.E.D.S. coordinator at Pueblo Community College, the program is limited by district policies that prevent allocating funds to maintain computers donated by the S.E.E.D.S. program. Instead, thedistricts insist that donors of used equipment maintain that equipment after it is donated to the schools. Technology recycling programs have a big enough task collecting, refurbishing, and delivering computers without having the added cost and burden of maintaining the systems they donate, so they often refuse to provide the added maintenance. The result is that many of our schools are left in limbo: they don't receive grants, and they have no way of supporting used, donated technology. The digital divide only deepens.

Map of cause section

Cause section

Janoski 3

Obtaining the necessary hardware is only part of the problem, however, according to Frank Mortensen, computer engineer and parent of a District 60 elementary student. Schools that manage to jump over the hardware hurdle are faced with another problem: acquiring the appropriate software. Columbian Elementary offers a prime example of this problem. Columbian has some computer hardware but hardly any of the right software to go along with it. As a result, says Mortensen, students are not able to use the equipment to its full potential. Software licenses cost money, and a separate license is required for each computer using a particular brand of software. For example, 20 computers running the Microsoft Windows operating system require 20 licenses to operate legally. For schools trying to run multiple computers, these costs can easily outrun a technology budget, especially because encyclopedias, magazine subscriptions, and other educational software (much of it not to be found in any hardcopy form) are needed to stock a fully functional computerized learning network.

Schools lucky enough to gain grants for hardware and software, meager as those grants often prove to be, must then ensure their teachers, especially teachers of core subjects, can effectively operate the technology and incorporate it into their lesson plans. According to Clements and Sarama, two key components of electronic learning are the way teachers design their curriculum and the layout of their classrooms, and these elements of the teaching situation require significant training before teachers of core subjects can integrate them effectively into their students' daily instruction. However, a national survey involving more than 4,000 teachers in 1998 showed that only 22% of science teachers, 12% of social studies teachers, and 13% of math teachers used software related to their subject matter, and even then, only occasionally. The same study showed that children still lacked access in core classes to computer- assisted instruction that encourages imaginative thinking; most children interested in using exciting and educational software had to take a separate computer class (Becker 51-52).

Although we lack similar data for Pueblo's schools, Mortensen reports that many teachers have no idea of the true power of digitized learning and prefer not to be bothered with "just another initiative of the administration." Somehow, even in cases where we've been able to integrate technology into the classroom, teachers allow their use only for the most basic functions: typing papers, performing routine and uninstructed internet searches, and playing games that come installed on the computers. We could have all the technology in the world, but it will never benefit student learning unless teachers are encouraged to employ it effectively and the districts can train them to do so.

In one sense, the causes are easy enough to understand: it all boils down to money and commitment. But what about the effects? The Digital Divide is increasingly impacting today's generation of students, who may be computer savvy in elementary ways—they know more about operating a computer and fixing its problems than their teachers—but who don't know how to use computers to do research, communicate appropriately with experts in various fields, operate mathematical and scientific software, or present complex concepts to others using combinations of the written word and effective graphics. Without a proper understanding of technology, students will have a hard time obtaining quality jobs in the future and will be deprived of the quality education that all American citizens require to achieve success ("What").

Effect section

Janoski 4

A lack of motivation among high school graduates to enter higher levels of academics will emerge because almost every college and university now incorporates computer technology into classrooms and lesson plans. In a National Public Radio interview, technology expert Mario Armstrong tells of visiting poor classrooms throughout America and discovering that even in the poorest the existence of technology is a sign to children that "somebody cares" about their education (Chideya). Pueblo's schools are sending the wrong message to students; we should surround them with the tools they need to succeed, but we continue our policies of deprivation.

In addition to the effects on our youth, the Digital Divide will affect our ⟵———— Conclusion
community as a whole. Even some rural schools are now seeing the need to invest in technology and have begun doing so at a faster rate than Pueblo School Districts 60 and 70. If our local districts don't keep pace with technology, our city will maintain its "rural" educational status despite its urban setting and population. As Nielsen says, "This will lead to declines in Pueblo's ability to attract new employment and shrink existing jobs, and the Digital Divide will be mirrored in the areas of jobs and income creation."

It is simply not fair to deprive our youth of educational and employment opportunities that students in other districts are now taking full advantage of because of the foresight of their educational policy makers. We must begin to narrow the gap that is widening faster as the digital revolution picks up speed and momentum. We are falling behind not only in terms of technology but also in terms of student learning, yet nobody seems to realize the connection between the two. The book by Joy Kraft Payton, Networking in the Elementary English Classroom, argues forcefully that there is a strong connection between up-to-date technology in classrooms and student reading abilities. Until we realize this connection, our policy makers will continue to rant about test scores instead of making useful decisions, our teachers will stick to their same outmoded, ho-hum ways of managing their classes, and our students will continue to flounder in acquiring the expertise they need to succeed. The true tragedy will hit later, when our graduates fail to pursue higher education or seek high-paying jobs simply because they are standing on the wrong side of today's Great Divide.

Formatting Your Final Bibliography

You end your research paper with your Works Cited page if you're using MLA or your References page if you're using APA. Examine Joshua's final Works Cited page. Again, pay close attention to the features labeled.

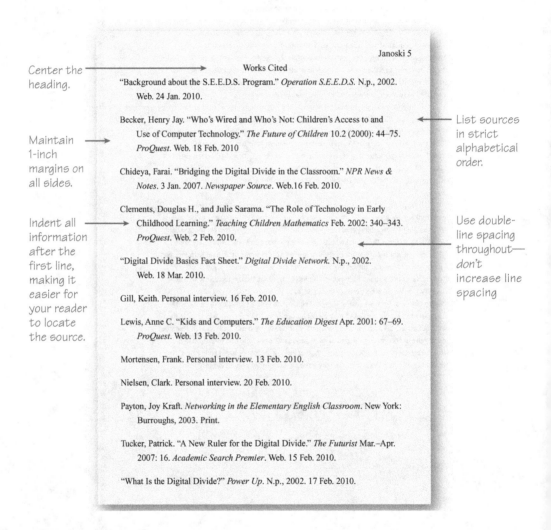

Center the heading.

Maintain 1-inch margins on all sides.

Indent all information after the first line, making it easier for your reader to locate the source.

List sources in strict alphabetical order.

Use double-line spacing throughout— don't increase line spacing

Janoski 5

Works Cited

"Background about the S.E.E.D.S. Program." *Operation S.E.E.D.S.* N.p., 2002. Web. 24 Jan. 2010.

Becker, Henry Jay. "Who's Wired and Who's Not: Children's Access to and Use of Computer Technology." *The Future of Children* 10.2 (2000): 44–75. *ProQuest.* Web. 18 Feb. 2010

Chideya, Farai. "Bridging the Digital Divide in the Classroom." *NPR News & Notes.* 3 Jan. 2007. *Newspaper Source.* Web. 16 Feb. 2010.

Clements, Douglas H., and Julie Sarama. "The Role of Technology in Early Childhood Learning." *Teaching Children Mathematics* Feb. 2002: 340–343. *ProQuest.* Web. 2 Feb. 2010.

"Digital Divide Basics Fact Sheet." *Digital Divide Network.* N.p., 2002. Web. 18 Mar. 2010.

Gill, Keith. Personal interview. 16 Feb. 2010.

Lewis, Anne C. "Kids and Computers." *The Education Digest* Apr. 2001: 67–69. *ProQuest.* Web. 13 Feb. 2010.

Mortensen, Frank. Personal interview. 13 Feb. 2010.

Nielsen, Clark. Personal interview. 20 Feb. 2010.

Payton, Joy Kraft. *Networking in the Elementary English Classroom.* New York: Burroughs, 2003. Print.

Tucker, Patrick. "A New Ruler for the Digital Divide." *The Futurist* Mar.–Apr. 2007: 16. *Academic Search Premier.* Web. 15 Feb. 2010.

"What Is the Digital Divide?" *Power Up.* N.p., 2002. 17 Feb. 2010.

Reflecting

Any time you complete a research project, spend some time reflecting on how the process went. Research is such a massive undertaking that you are not equally capable in all aspects of it the first time around. Each time you take on a new project, try to improve in your areas of weakness.

WRITING 14-13

Self-Reflection

Before you hand in your paper, write one–two paragraphs in which you reflect on your research process. Referring to specific parts of the research process, include your feelings on the following questions:

1. What do you feel you did best?
2. What part of the process was most challenging to you?
3. In which stages do you feel you need the most practice?
4. How can you address your challenges or weaknesses and improve the quality of future research papers?

After you have completed this self-reflection, carefully review your instructor's comments. Write down your instructor's comments about your use of sources; then write a short response to each one, either acknowledging or questioning its validity. If you don't understand a comment, make sure to visit with your instructor for clarification. How might you use research outside of this English course?

- **College:** _____
- **Your profession:** _____
- **Everyday life:** _____